MW01502559

AUTOMATING YOUR FINANCIAL PORTFOLIO

an investor's guide
to personal computers

AUTOMATING YOUR FINANCIAL PORTFOLIO
an investor's guide to personal computers

donald r. woodwell

DOW JONES–IRWIN
Homewood, Illinois 60430

This book was produced by Tribeca Communications, Inc. of
New York, N.Y. and publication of this work was arranged by
that company.

This publication is designed to provide accurate and
authoritative information in regard to the subject matter
covered. It is sold with the understanding that the
publisher is not engaged in rendering legal, accounting, or
other professional service. If legal advice or other expert
assistance is required, the services of a competent
professional person should be sought.

*From a Declaration of Principles jointly adopted by a Committee
of the American Bar Association and a Committee of Publishers.*

ISBN 0-87094-399-5

Library of Congress Catalog Card No. 82–73637

Printed in the United States of America

3 4 5 6 7 8 9 0 MP 0 9 8 7 6 5 4 3

This book is dedicated to Doris, Donna, and Doug whose help and patience contributed to its completion.

Preface

Riding the investment roller coaster the past few years hasn't been easy. Favorite investment vehicles have not reacted in the ways we traditionally expect them to. Bonds, once a safe haven for widows and orphans, have become as volatile as common stocks, which have gone in and out of favor with investment analysts and brokers as fast as actors change costumes.

During the past 15 years the Dow Jones Industrial Average has actually plunged more than 70 percent if measured in inflation-adjusted dollars. Precious metals have gyrated wildly, with gold peaking at $850 per ounce and then falling to less than $300 per ounce in a little over two years. The bottom fell out of the residential real estate market as prime interest rates of over 20 percent all but dried up mortgage money. Commercial property also has been in the doldrums. Tangibles have lost their appeal as inflation hedges, too. In the meantime, new investment vehicles have come and gone. The phenomenal success of money market funds is testimony that many investors were scared stiff and looked to these funds as secure investments for their dollars.

Even "tax shelters" no longer provide the protection from taxes that they once did. The 1981 and 1982 tax law revisions have changed things even more, but some new investment opportunities have resulted from the changes. That means that the average investor needs to rethink his or her plans and reshape an investment program and portfolio to take advantage of the new tax laws.

The financial planning community has added new people to cope with the demand for its services in these uncertain times, and some investors have turned to investment education courses to help them better understand their choices. Others are using personal computers to cope with uncertainty. For them, inexpensive microcomputer technology is the new weapon in their investment arsenal.

This book is about ways that you, too, can use personal computers to your investing advantage. Using a computer to gather stock or company data; to screen stocks, bonds, or real estate for buy opportunities; to manage an investor portfolio; or to take advantage of smart insurance, pension, and estate planning is not difficult. You don't have to be a computer technician or programmer, nor do you have to hire one. Instead, prepackaged programs (computer instructions) for all of these investment tasks are readily available. They are relatively inexpensive (the price range is from $50 to $1,500), and most of them are easy to use. Their big advantages are that they take much of the tedium out of manual computations and data analysis, and they make record-keeping much simpler and more organized. Consequently, investment selection is made more precise with better chances for profit, and managing your portfolio becomes less of a chore.

In this book you will read about the ways the computer can help in such diverse tasks as setting quantitative investment goals; controlling personal finances; gathering data with your computer from an information service; selecting portfolios in stocks and bonds, real estate, commodities, and tangibles; and planning for retirement. Maximizing aftertax profits with computer techniques is also explored, as are ways to automate the evaluation of your portfolio's performance.

Each chapter is divided into roughly two parts. The first part is a description of the fundamentals of portfolio planning, personal finance, or specific investment vehicles. The last part describes one or more programs to manage these fundamentals.

The programs discussed in the chapter are off-the-shelf merchandise that can be quickly learned and put to use. All you have to add is data. The programs have been chosen for discussion primarily because they have been on the market for a while and have been proven in use. This does not mean they're the best ones for your particular style of investing, and other choices are available. It's your job to pick the programs best suited to your needs.

In most cases I don't state prices for specific products because the prices change too frequently. Personal computer programs are updated to improve their usefulness and reliability, as often as once a year in some cases. The prices change, too, usually upward. The higher price brings with it more uses, though, and consequently greater justification for a program's purchase.

Computer equipment should be selected after you choose the programs you want to use. Computer components do not by themselves help you plan, select, and manage investment portfolios. Only the programs do this. Don't think you have to rush out and buy a computer to make use of this book. Read the book thoroughly, think about what you need, and shop selectively for the combination of affordable components (hardware) and programs (software) that will do the job you want.

Personal computers can help serious individual investors and professional advisors, brokers, and managers. This book will give investors and speculators alike a greater familiarity with the power of the computer as an aid to profitability in an age of constant economic changes. Taking the plunge into computers now will be important to your financial well-being in the future. A computer could be the best investment you ever make.

Don Woodwell

Contents

Personal Computers and Investor Profits

As investors we need to weigh reams of financial data to make the best possible investing decisions. In pursuit of this we read economic forecasts and the financial statements of specific companies. We pay attention to our broker's recommendations. We listen to financial and political news stories and wonder how they may affect our investments. Out of this welter of information we try to make some order, to establish a coherent direction, and to apply all of this to our investing decisions—in short, to make profitable the use of our time and money.

Making good decisions, however, takes time. And given the speed with which markets move these days, time is in short supply. By the time many investors have assessed all the pertinent market data and are ready to invest, their buying opportunity has often come and gone.

To deal with this critical problem of timing we need a "mental lever." Electronic technology has given us that tool: the computer. Personal computers multiply our mental strengths, and, in investing, computers contribute to greater efficiency and higher productivity—contributions that can be measured not only in terms of more free time but in fatter profits, as well.

UNCERTAIN ECONOMICS AND MARKETS

Some investors have parlayed a few lucky hunches into considerable fortunes. But such spectacularly lucky calls are all too rare. To make money in any market—be it in stocks, bonds, or real estate—a lot of hard work and careful analysis are required. The personal computer can make the discipline of that work easier, and it can provide invaluable assistance in organizing and structuring your investment program. In today's volatile and complex markets it is that combination of organization and in-depth analysis—a logical decision process—that pays the biggest dividends year in and year out.

THE LOGICAL DECISION PROCESS IN ILLOGICAL TIMES

The purpose of the logical decision process (LDP) is to provide a structure people can use to conceive, plan, and execute an investment program that will net them good profits in uncertain markets. The key to the LDP is the personal computer.

The LDP is a partnership between you and your computer, which becomes the most important tool in your investing activities. As a mental level it multiplies your brain power by relieving you of menial and repetitive tasks, such as hand calculations and record-keeping. This gives you more time to examine, analyze, and sift market data.

Professional traders review vast amounts of data every day, and frequently the flood of information is so great that they have to spend many hours putting the data in order. That often leaves little time to adequately evaluate it. Thus the next day's trading decisions may be less well informed than the broker would like.

Personal computers, however, can take over the trend analysis and plotting tasks, providing a valuable mental and time lever for professionals and amateurs alike. We can all be more productive analyzing trends instead of plotting them. This improves the quality of our buy/sell decisions and allows us to be in the market more often because we can evaluate more data faster. The logical decision process is a perfect blending of man and machine.

THE COMPUTER AS A LOGICAL AID

No matter in what you invest there's probably some computer program or method available to aid you. For example, if stocks are your strength, you can choose from among more than a dozen different programs or systems. These range from record-keeping to complex technical analysis programs. All are designed to help you reduce your risks and enhance your profits. These programs also make it very easy for you to measure your portfolio's success through periodic automated updates of your portfolio's worth.

Computers can also help you get a handle on your personal finances. Checkbook balancing is a popular application for personal computers, including everything from entering transactions into the computer to tallying them on a running basis and reconciling them at month's end. Keeping track of your checking account, however, does not require a $2,000 personal computer. A $500 computer or perhaps even a simple hand-held calculator could prove adequate to the task. As your personal financial management needs grow beyond such basics as checkbook tallying to more complex things like net worth calculations, comparative annual analysis, and tax record-keeping, your need for ever-more sophisticated electronic aids grows, too.

The personal financial management programs currently on the market allow you to quickly generate statements on your current net worth, graph your monthly or yearly expenditures to analyze your spending trends, and keep a running record of taxable capital gains. You can also program your computer for speedy retrieval of key data for assessing spending patterns. With that data you can, for instance, quickly show your spouse how many charges he or she has run up in the last few months at that favorite store. Your spouse may not agree, but the fact that a $100 computer program can perform all of these complex tasks is nothing short of phenomenal.

THE INVESTMENT PROCESS

Is your investment strategy "hit or miss"? Do you consider any other tips than your broker's recommendations? How effective is your investment advisory service? More important—do you have a plan?

Talking about investment planning either makes people yawn or become glassy-eyed. Nevertheless it is an essential part of the investing process. The purpose of planning is to establish financial objectives so that you will have something against which to measure your investing performance. For example, you may wish to double your net worth in the next five years. If you are worth $150,000 now you are aiming for the $300,000 level in five years. That means average increases of 20 percent per year. On a graph that is a nice straight line. In actuality you may attain the 20 percent growth rate in only one of the five years. Other years may be less than or greater than 20 percent. A sample net worth increase curve (see Exhibit 1–1) illustrates the impact of compounding your returns on investments. It shows, too, that relatively modest early gains can be readily translated into big gains in later years.

Once you have set your targets you need to select the investment

Exhibit 1-1. Typical Investment Objectives

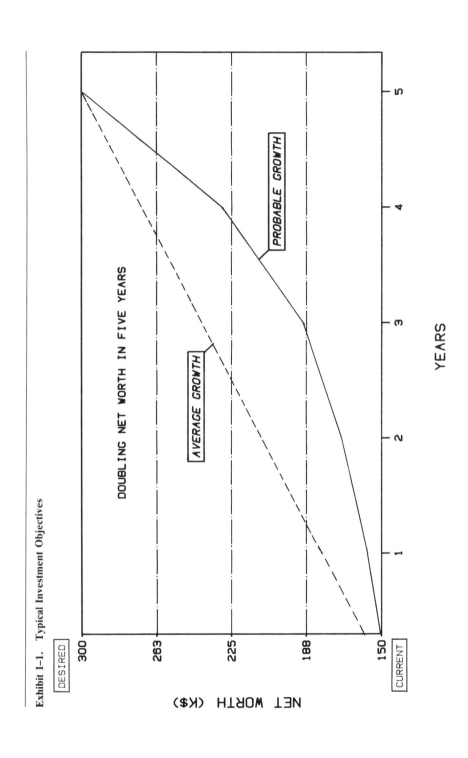

medium that you expect will have a growth curve that most closely matches your needs. Alternatively, you may choose several investment media that have return on investment curves whose sum equals your planned growth; this is a diversified approach in which several different investments are chosen to spread risk, such as stocks/bonds, commodities, tangibles, and real estate. Managing your portfolio's year-to-year gains can be made easier with a personal computer.

COMPUTER-MANAGED RISK

Filtering out all uncertainties is impossible unless you have absolute control over an event. Yes, you can be sure of your steak dinner tonight if you are willing to cook it, but no, you will never be sure of what horse will finish first, or what stock will outperform all the others. The challenge every investor faces is how to minimize uncertainty, or risk, in an event.

Since a computer is basically a mathematical tool for solving complex problems quickly, and since uncertainty and randomness are mathematically definable, it follows that computers can help you reduce your investing risks. The computer accomplishes this invaluable task in two ways. First, it lays before you a clear mathematical description of the risks associated with specific investments. Thus you are alerted to the sort of results you might expect before you count your money. And second, by plotting historic price trends the computer allows you to carefully time your market entry to catch rising waves early.

To perform these functions computers make use of mathematical models. These models are loaded into a computer via prepackaged programs and are used to statistically track performance and allow you to project expected returns. The objective is simple: to reduce the risk in a highly risky investment and to give you a much better chance to cash in on an investment's potential.

FOLLOWING THE MARKET

The tracking and evaluation of any type of investment is a mathematical operation. Not surprisingly, the more-volatile investment vehicles like commodities and options require more complex mathematical tools to discern patterns in their price movements. Less-volatile investments may be tracked with simpler techniques. For example, tracking 10 blue-chip stocks isn't terribly difficult. It can be done manually. Because these stocks change relatively slowly, you can react in time to make a trading decision that will be timely enough to net you a profit. If, however, you are following a dozen or more issues scattered in several different industries, each reacting differently to the latest trend in inflation or interest rates, then you will need much more than a pencil and paper. A personal computer may be the answer.

Ideally, you should be able to calculate the value of your entire portfolio to find out what it is worth on the market at this very minute just by typing a simple command into your computer. Most experienced investors set prices at which they will either sell or buy additional shares. It should be possible, therefore, to record those levels in your computer's memory banks and have it alert you, much like an alarm clock would, when it is time for action.

This ideal case can be a reality—now! Several stock, bond, options, and commodity tracking programs currently offer just such features. The benefits are obvious. They include:

Freedom from tedious record-keeping.

Easier and more accurate portfolio updating.

Early warning of approaching critical decision points.

Potentially more timely and profitable trading decisions.

KNOW YOURSELF . . . AND YOUR COMPUTER

As important as quantitative decisions are to investing success, one factor can't be reduced to a computer solution: your personality. What kind of investments do you feel comfortable with? Is planning an estate or pension your forte? Do you see bonds as more profitable and possibly more enjoyable? What are your personal objectives? How much risk is too much? What is your spouse's opinion? Is your job secure? Is your house secure? What are the ages of your children? How much can you afford to invest—or to lose?

All these factors should be reflected in your financial objectives. If you have not yet defined them it should be your first priority, just as it is the first priority of this book. Frankly, there is no point in using a computer to automate your portfolio if you don't know what to expect from your investments.

Like anything else, however, there may be one exception to that rule. With personal computers that exception is record-keeping. For as little as $500 you can buy a small personal computer to run simple personal finance programs to balance your checkbook and to keep computer records of your checks, credit card transactions, and major purchases. These records can be very useful at tax time. Your tax returns can be more effectively supported by good records, particularly when you itemize personal and business deductions. You may be able to pay for your computer in one year by filing more detailed deductions, which may possibly increase your refund. Of course, once you have the computer there are many other home financial applications, such as mortgage and loan analyses, budgeting, and net worth reporting that you may also find worthwhile.

DO I NEED A COMPUTER?

"What you have just described does not require an expensive computer," you say. "Why, I can do that with my manual methods."

Of course you can. But how many stocks can you evaluate simultaneously? Are you limited to low-volatility issues because you cannot quickly respond to rapidly changing market conditions? Are your decisions data up to date? How much time does it take to reprice your portfolio, analyze the changes, and make a decision to trade?

You should ask yourself, "Is it worth my time to do all this work and only get a 5 percent return on my investment?" Maybe it would be faster and easier to take your broker's blanket recommendations. After all, the law of averages says you should be profitable at least some of the time.

Now you have come full circle, back to letting chance and uncertainty control your profitability because you don't believe a computer has the potential to significantly enhance your investing profits and productivity.

Many people develop a syndrome called "computer avoidance." The symptoms are:

You know you need a computer to aid your investing, but computers scare you.

You should be learning about them, but can't find the time.

You need more answers, but don't even know the questions or whom to ask.

You are afraid that what you decide to do may turn out to be wrong because you don't know what is right.

You feel that without a computer your investing program may never be really profitable.

LOGICAL DECISIONS AND INVESTING

Once you make the decision to include a computer in your investing program your next concern should be making the best use of it. Computer-aided investing covers a broad range of investing avenues. As we discussed earlier, a good place to start is with your personal financial management. Controlling your finances is as important as putting gas in your car before a trip. Without money as fuel you cannot start an investment trip. Managing and fine-tuning your personal finances can and should be done even if you have no immediate plans to invest anything.

There are so many advantages to computer-aided personal financial planning that it alone can justify the purchase of a computer system. Not only that, you are so familiar with your personal financial needs for day-to-day living that it is an excellent beginning for an investment program. Starting with the basics of personal finance enables you to implement the logical decision process more quickly and effectively than if you plunged directly into a stock evaluation program. Further, during the time you are setting up your personal financial books you can begin planning ways to meet your investment objectives with your computer. By taking one step at a time you create a logical decision process by which your computer helps you make money. It doesn't become a money machine. Instead it helps change your way of thinking about finances. Cobwebs begin disappearing and clear, logical thought replaces them.

A STRATEGY FOR SUCCESS

You can use your computer to help you meet and conquer any number of financial or investing challenges. These include personal financial management, profit planning, and stock and bond trading. Your choice depends on your specific interests. An interest that all of us ultimately share, for example, is planning for retirement. There are many computer programs that can help there, too. Through your computer, you can keep close track of your individual retirement account (IRA), coordinate your insurance and pension plans, and so forth.

Tax planning is another central element in your investment process. Understanding the tax consequences of your financial successes and failures is of the utmost importance, making coordination with your total program essential. Pencil and paper methods are traditional, but a point may be reached where you just don't have enough time to analyze complex tax issues. A better tool is needed. Your personal computer is that tool. Each application for which you use your computer becomes part of the "structure," and the structure then provides the common thread throughout your total investment program.

A SCHEDULE FOR AUTOMATING
YOUR PORTFOLIO

Automating your financial portfolio obviously takes time. How much time is largely a function of the complexity of the tasks you set for your computer to solve. A computer-aided personal financial management system can be set up in three to four months. Commodities trading analysis may take 6 to 12 weeks if you understand the market, or 6 to 12 months if you are a novice. At the outset of the automation process you can expect to invest both money and time in setting up your system. Those original investments, however, will soon seem small when compared to the dividends of time and money your automated system will pay out year after year.

Since your automated system can last a lifetime there is no need to hurry. Go slowly at first. Take the time to carefully set your priorities on the tasks or applications you want your computer to tackle, and allow two to three months between each. Start out with the three that are most important to you, and later assess the results. Are you satisfied? If not, go back and fix whatever problems you have. Learn more about the programs. Are there functions you are not using? Will using them produce better results? Once you have analyzed your computerized financial system you are ready to move on to the next set of applications. Repeat the first cycle. Do this until you have completely automated your financial portfolio, and don't be surprised if it takes two to three years.

Orderly applications growth also helps you plan your computer purchases. Don't buy the biggest computer initially. Start at the minimum level needed to implement your first two or three applications, and then add hardware and software components as needed to meet the challenges of your applications.

Be aware, too, that Uncle Sam may have a happy surprise for you. If you qualify, current tax laws let you depreciate a sizeable amount of your computer and computer software purchases in the first year. That deduction goes a long way toward putting the computer within the financial reach of most investors.

A MEANS TO AN END

In my early discussions with personal computer salespeople, we always seemed to end up discussing the relative merits of different hardware components, such as which processing units have more memory, which printer has the best price/performance ratio, and how much data the diskette can hold, like a capacity of 160,000 or 320,000 characters (160K or 320K). Quite frankly, I don't care about these technical discussions, and neither should you. The primary objective is to get measurable results from the computer, and you can measure the results quite easily by the income produced by your efforts. The program vendor will specify which computer is needed to run the program. This is the type you should buy. Remember, the dog is the program, the tail is the computer. Be sure the correct one is doing the wagging.

The point is this: a computer is a means to an end—an electronic tool that investors can use profitably. If you understand market dynamics and finances, you can certainly handle personal computers.

WHERE DO I BEGIN?

. . . at the most useful place—the beginning. The next chapter's focus is a computer buying guide for you. We will cover in detail how a computer works and what hardware components are needed. Along with the hardware considerations, we will review software buying criteria, and I will give you tips on where to buy good investor programs.

Personal Computer Buying Guide

You don't have to understand how personal computers work to use them effectively as an aid to investing and money management. The most important thing to understand is your financial objectives and how you want to accomplish them with the computer. Once that is done, you can move onto the next step—acquainting yourself with the basic components of computers and with the types of computers and accessories that are currently on the market. Just keep in mind that buying a computer is like any other large purchase—it pays to know exactly what you are getting for your money.

WHAT PERSONAL COMPUTERS ARE MADE OF

Computers are not difficult to understand. Consider the familiar typewriter as an example. It is a mechanical device that has no intelligence. What you key into the machine is precisely what you see typed on the paper. Input is the same as output, only in a different form. We can, however, turn that typewriter into a computer by adding just a few pieces of special electronic equipment.

Some typewriters have an electronic memory inserted between the interaction of the keyboard and the paper. This allows you to keep the information you keyed—as long as you don't turn off the power. In some cases you can even alter the output of the data stored in this memory through the keyboard. The typewriter is not smart enough to make output changes on any other basis. For that, more intelligence is needed. By adding to the typewriter's electronic memory storage capacity a set of rules for altering this input data, a quantum leap is made in increasing the machine's intelligence. Data can now be altered according to the rules that you specify instead of making you key in instructions for each change.

This type of electronic programming, with both input data and rules, is the essence of a computer's memory. The rules are called instructions, and a set of instructions makes up a program. The memory is called random access memory (RAM). Add additional circuitry to give the RAM the capability for logical decision making and you have the "processor."

The primary components (hardware) of a computer are its input (keyboard), processor (RAM and logic circuits), and output (type). Most computers today use a video display unit (VDU) similar to a TV screen for their output. Typed or hardcopy output can be obtained by hooking a printer to the computer. These devices are generally sold as optional rather than standard equipment.

The RAM in most personal computers ranges from a capacity of 16,000 to 256,000 characters (16K to 256K) of data. The amount of RAM that you need depends on the kind of programs you expect to use. For example, the Apple Dow Jones Portfolio Evaluator program put together by Apple Computer, Inc., requires a 32K random access memory, which is the minimum size on the Apple II processor that can run the Portfolio Evaluator. Other programs from other sources likewise require varying amounts of computer memory.

Your choice of memory capacity depends on the largest program you currently expect to run. At the start, buy only the minimum amount you'll need. Don't worry about being stuck with insufficient capacity. If you decide later to run larger programs to keep computer records of three or four portfolios, a personal financial database, and annual tax records, you can usually add capacity to the computer's RAM.

STORING RECORDS

Personal computers use one of two devices to store records: magnetic tapes or disks. These convenient, compact devices long ago replaced the cumbersome stacks of punched cards that earlier generations of computers relied upon.

Magnetic tape is stored on cassettes. A small tapeplayer is attached to the computer to read data from the tape into the computer, or vice versa. If you have loaded the program you are using into the computer from the tape, you then enter the specific information required by your program through the keyboard. For example, you may be entering check transactions. When you are done, you will want to permanently store this data. At that point, your program will ask you if you are finished. By depressing a specific key you automatically transfer the data from computer memory (RAM) to tape storage. When the computer is turned off, the data are permanently recorded on the tape. If data were left in the computer's memory they would be erased the instant you turned off your computer.

The crucial drawback to tapes is that data are stored sequentially on it the way storage is made on a video or audio cassette. This is all right if you do all your data manipulation in the computer memory. But if you need to sort or search your records, tape processing can become very cumbersome. For example, if you need to go through your records and pull out all the checks you have written to your child's orthodontist to back up an insurance claim, tape processing would necessitate searching one by one through your check transactions until all orthodontist payments had been found—a very time-consuming operation. If you had stored your records on a disk, however, the search process would be much faster.

When searching records for a number of items, time becomes important. Therefore, if you need to frequently search through or sort data, you are better off using a disk storage system. But if you think you will not be doing much of this kind of data processing and want to stick to a relatively inexpensive medium, then tape should be your choice. Tapes provide a simple and relatively inexpensive way to permanently store data, but what they don't provide is the kind of flexibility required by more demanding programs, such as portfolio evaluators and others. These programs depend on a facility for quick and easy sorting of data—the flexibility that only disks can offer.

On disks, data can be sorted and inquiries can be quickly completed. Disks offer the additional advantage of being exceptionally easy to handle and store. Unfortunately, disks are also a much more expensive proposition than tapes. A typical cassette tape drive costs less than $100, as opposed to $650 for a typical disk drive. The magnetic diskettes themselves cost about $40 for a box of 10, as opposed to $30 for 10 tape cassettes.

Most of the popular personal computers can handle up to four of the typical thin, "floppy" disk drives. A single diskette holds an average of 140,000 characters of data, and some newer diskettes hold as much as 320,000. Thus, with four disk drives attached to your computer you can have from 560,000 to 1,280,000 characters of data available for inquiry, report writing, or processing. (In practice, only about 80 percent of the total diskette capacity is actually available, due to space requirements for the computer's operating system.) Realistically, amateur investors rarely need more than two disk drives at one time. Brokers may need more if they want their entire client database available all the time. But if they divide their client records and only work on one set at a time, then obviously less disk space is required. Some investor programs require as many as three drives—one for the program, one for the permanent records, and one to be used for "scratch pad" work files.

An alternate disk system for personal computers is the "hard" disks. Hard disks are rigid spinning disks similar to phonograph records and hold significantly more data than the floppy disks we have been talking about. Usually, their storage capacity ranges from 3 to 10 million characters per disk drive. They are often nonremovable, which means you need an auxiliary diskette or tape system to back up the transactions stored on the hard disk. Most investors won't need a hard disk since they don't have enough records to justify the investment, but small businesses with large customer or inventory files could benefit from the huge storage capacity offered by hard disks.

Whether your system uses tape or disks you should know a few terms. When you are searching for data, the program reads the data *record* stored on the tape or disk. A name and address is a record, and so is the data you maintain on a particular stock. The current market price within the stock record is a data *field*. A complete portfolio containing a whole set of stock records is a *file*, and is analogous to an office file cabinet. Instead of being arranged and used by hand, a computer has the capability to *process* its files according to the rules (computer *instructions*) contained within the given application programs.

KEEPING YOUR RECORDS SAFE

Once data are transferred to either tape or disk they are permanently stored. The computer itself, however, only stores data or programs when the power is on. Any data in its memory are lost the instant power is put off. This could occur by someone kicking out the plug or by some electrical disturbance, such as an electrical storm.

To insure against data loss you can do two things. First, install a monitor that can absorb minor power line fluctuations. Some of the simpler units (costing about $75) plug directly into your outlet and your computer is then plugged into them. You can also buy units with multiple sockets to plug in several pieces of computer equipment. These electrical devices are a good investment if you want to protect your expensive computer electronics from power surges or spikes that can wreak havoc with the computer memory and disk drives. Similarly, buildup of static electricity can be a nuisance, too, but you can use antistatic sprays or floor mats to minimize or eliminate it.

Second, you can minimize the risk of data loss by frequent transference of your data onto tape or disk. If you are entering 50 checks, for example, stop halfway through and send the first 25 transactions onto the computer's auxiliary storage device. Then go on and complete the entry of the remaining 25 checks.

You shouldn't get the idea that personal computers are finicky. My experience has been quite the contrary. They are extremely reliable and relatively indifferent to their environment. Your financial data, however, are very important, and you will want to take every possible step to insure their safety. A combination of common sense with a few simple precautions and procedures will help in preventing computer problems due to the environment.

PRINTING AND GRAPHING

If you want to keep data on paper, include an optional printer in your equipment package. These machines are easily attached to your computer via an attachment board and cable. There is a wide variety of printers available. They range from the low-cost wire matrix "thermal" printers to the expensive "letter-quality" printers used mainly for word-processing applications. The matrix printers are quite sufficient for the needs of the average investor and cost from $400 to $800.

Computer graphics add another dimension to investment tracking and evaluation and can be added to your computer at a modest cost. (Some printers have graphics "chips" that give the printers the capacity to produce graphic images. These chips are in the $100 to $150 range.) Graphics, particularly statistical plots, are usually associated with technical analysis. But graphics can also be a useful tool in analyzing a range of financial data. You may, for instance, in totaling your year's expenses, find that you are way over your budget. By going back and plotting your expenditures month by month you can easily locate the month or months when you jumped your budget tracks. To further clarify the source of your problem, you can then plot the individual elements of expense and determine which of these may be contributing to your budget variances. More ambitious investors may also use graphics to plot such things as a multiple regression trend line of stock prices.

Whatever the application, the "pictures" of computer graphics can help the investor evaluate trends and patterns. If you understand the possible causes of the abnormal patterns, then you can quickly look at the elements contributing to the pattern and make adjustments to correct the abnormalities. Graphics are an important analytical aid and should not be overlooked when selecting your computer equipment. If you aren't sure that the equipment you want to buy will support graphics—many don't—ask the salesperson. You may not need this capability initially, but it is an option worth keeping open. If the basic support is not there, it can't be added in the future. By planning for graphics now, you may save money down the road.

COMPUTERS AND TELEPHONES

The last attachment you may want to consider is a communications line, which will allow you to connect a telephone to your computer. A phone call to Dow Jones News/Retrieval® service plugs vast amounts of financial data directly into your computer. A "modem," an electronic device that converts computer signals into phone signals and vice versa, needs to be attached between your telephone line and computer. The communication line attachment and modem cost about $450, and, you may also need a communications program in your computer to allow the computer to converse with the database. There is a variety of programs available specifically for communicating with Dow Jones News/Retrieval®; also, Videotex is available from Radio Shack for communication with the CompuServe information utility. Other general purpose programs allow access to other databases, so your choice of programs will depend largely on the financial database you wish to use and the other type of communications facilities you need. Electronic mail—the sending of "letters" from one computer to another across standard telephone lines—can be easily done using some general purpose programs.

LEARNING ABOUT SOFTWARE

In shopping for software, what's important to remember is to start with the basics that can be applied to an investing area you fully understand; later you can move on to a more complex application. Several avenues are worth pursuing in sizing up software—namely, the hardware vendors, independent software companies, and user groups.

The hardware vendor usually maintains what is called "an application library," which is usually stocked with a variety of his own software and with contributions from outside sources. A consideration to keep in mind is program reliability. Unfortunately, a lot of software is for sale that doesn't work as advertised. Choose only thoroughly tested, user-proven programs. Ask the store or vendor for user references and contact them to assess the software's reliability before buying.

The independent software companies produce some of the best programs on the market. The reason is quite simple: their business depends upon it. Well-established software companies frequently specialize in investor software, and you should contact these specialists for good alternatives to the standard program packages offered by your hardware vendor. An investor like yourself may well end up selecting several programs from software houses as your investment sophistication increases. Excellent stock evaluation programs have been written by several large and small independents. The underlying design for each program will reflect a different style or technique for managing a stock, commodity, or real estate portfolio. The techniques are often peculiar to the designers, who usually have some kind of market experience. The software product is tailored around their trading knowledge. You can benefit from a designer's investment philosophy, particularly if it has been successful and it parallels your own.

When selecting investor software, you must ask yourself several questions:

Do you understand the investment philosophy used?

Do you understand the particular investment market you are trying to analyze?

What indicators does the program provide, and how can you use them to trade more effectively?

What is the cost of the software—and of the hardware needed to run it?

Are these costs within your budget? If not, what alternatives do you have?

Are the program's investment objectives consistent with your own?

Personal computer user groups or clubs often have listings of member-contributed software. These programs usually don't have the same rigorous testing behind them as do vendor-supplied programs. Nevertheless, you may find a few specialized financial or investing programs that would be worthwhile supplements to your primary programs.

PROGRAMS: CHOOSING YOUR SOFTWARE

The cost of application software will become a significant part of your total computer costs. The price of usability and reliability comes high, as you might expect. A good strategy for keeping your software costs down would be to mix the vendor's programs with programs supplied by your user club. The latter are often free to members. As your experience grows, you should be able to establish an optimum mix between the two. At the outset, though, you should expect to pay from $100 to $300 for your initial program library.

As you begin shopping around for investor software, you may find that more than one source has programs you might find useful. This can present a problem. Programs that run on one type of computer usually do not run on other types. The reason is that different makes of computers often use different languages and control programs. Most personal computers use a language called "Basic." There are, however, several variants of Basic. Applesoft[1] Basic, for instance (and for an example, see the mortgage analysis at the end of the chapter), is different from TRS-80[2] Basic. Although the differences are not great, programs written in one Basic will not run on the other manufacturer's equipment. The differences often exist because the manufacturer wants you to use as many of its computer's particular hardware features as possible. Since each brand of computer is different, it follows that each's Basic language is unique.

A second source of problems limiting the adaptability of programs is the control program used by each computer. Control programs provide a linkage between the hardware and the software application programs. When you ask the computer to read a stock record from your disk, the control program actually controls the reading and passes the data to the application program, which in turn displays it for you. These are built-in supervisory programs that manage the computer's resources and allow the application programs to operate efficiently. Thus, you have two potential levels of programming. The first is at the language level and the second is at the control program level.

Since there is little you as a user can do to overcome the incompatibility problem, what you need to do is select the brand of computer that will be most useful to you; that is, the computer that will accept the largest number of the programs you plan to use. Begin by selecting several programs you believe will give you the results you want and compare these programs feature by feature. When you have narrowed your choices to two or three, list the computers required to run them. If one computer appears more frequently than others for your first choice of application programs, then choose that one. Once you do this, then select your alternate choice of the remaining programs which run on that computer. Exhibit 2–1 illustrates this selection procedure.

Assume for the moment that you want to use your computer to aid you in your personal financial management and real estate analysis, and to give you access to a financial database via Videotex. Looking at the chart, your choices in each of these applications include: Apple II+, IBM Personal Computer[3], and TRS-80. The Apple II+ would appear to be your first choice overall, except that it doesn't have a program to support access to a financial database via Videotex. What do you do now? You have two choices. You could go to your second choice on the first two applications and to first choice on the third, which is the TRS-80 microcomputer, or you could select the Apple II+ and settle for database

---

[1] Apple and Applesoft are trademarks of Apple Computer Inc.

[2] TRS-80 is a trademark of the Radio Shack division of Tandy Corporation.

[3] Personal Computer is a trademark of the IBM Corporation.

Exhibit 2–1. Selecting Programs

Application	Your Choice	Apple II+	TRS-80	IBM PC	ATARI	Hewlett-Packard
Personal finance	1	X				
	2		X			
	3				X	
Stock evaluation	1	X				
	2			X		
	3		X			
	4					
Bond analysis	1	X				
	2					
Planning aids	1	X		X		
	2		X		X	X
	3		X			
Real estate analysis	1			X		
	2	X				
Graphics	1					X
	2			X		
	3	X				
Communication with a database	1 (Videotex)		X			
	2 (DJN/R)	X		X		

access via DJN/R. Upon further investigation, however, you will find that Radio Shack offers a Videotex program for the Apple II+ computer. With it you can safely select your first choice in both the personal finance and real estate application programs—the Apple II+. You should include in your selection chart whatever applications you need, and if necessary, the entire range of personal computers available. Based on the application plan you will develop in Chapter 3, the above selection process should be quite simple for you.

Finally, look ahead to future investor applications. Will the computer you select now be able to support your next set of applications? If you aren't sure, then return to the selection chart and include your future application needs in your selection criteria. You may find that your computer choice has changed.

DO-IT-YOURSELF PROGRAMS

There is enough good investor software on the market today to keep you busy for at least one to two years without having to write your own programs. This means you should be able to increase your investing productivity without having to spend your own time and money to develop new programs. But the time may come when you will want to tackle the process of designing, writing, testing, and documenting your own programs. Although you don't need to become a programmer to use a computer for investment management, you might want to supplement your prepackaged programs with ones you have designed to suit your own specific needs. For example, you may want to buy a house or piece of real estate, and need to evaluate mortgage rates and monthly costs. Since you don't make these kinds of calculations often, you might prefer to program them yourself in a simple, straightforward fashion instead of buying an expensive program package. An example of a simple program for mortgage analysis is to be found at the end of this chapter. You'll be pleasantly surprised at the number of factors it can handle for you.

Successful programming is both an art and a science. Some very talented people make poor programmers, but excellent programmers might not know a stock option from a mutual fund. To be successful at both skills you need to learn a programming language. Assuming you already have a computer or access to one, your obvious choices among languages are the ones that are compatible with your computer. These could be Basic, Pascal, Fortran, Cobol, or Assembler, among others. As we have already mentioned, the most common is Basic, and it is probably a good place for the novice programmer to begin.

There are excellent books, classroom-type instruction at computer stores, and computer-assisted instruction courses that can help you learn to program your computer. In addition, most computers come equipped with tutorial aids in the form of user manuals.

When you start your programming exercise, keep it simple. Complexity can come later. Good sources for basic financial formulas are the instruction booklets provided with many pocket calculators, surprising as that may sound. You can emulate the steps shown in these booklets with a few lines of Basic programming code. The advantage of programming these calculations instead of doing them individually on a calculator is speed. A mortgage analysis, for example, may call for a series of iterations using different interest rates, time periods, or downpayments. I have found that entering the variable data and then running the program a number of times is quite fast compared to using a calculator and computing each and every result separately.

A COMPLETE HARDWARE SYSTEM

Now it is time to start assembling your equipment package. Let's assume that you want to do the following three things:

Manage your personal finances.
Analyze real estate investments.
Have access to a financial database.

The programs you choose to perform these functions or applications will require a 48K processor, one disk drive, and a communications line. Two optional components you will also want are a video display and a printer. Your package would then look like this:

1.	Keyboard/processor (48K)	$1,500
2.	Disk drive/controller	$1,175
3.	Communication attachment	$150
4.	Modem	$300
5.	Printer attachment	$125
6.	Printer	$675
7.	Video display	$275
	TOTAL	$4,200

Depending upon the vendor, the cost of this system could be higher or lower. Mail-order discounts are often available at savings up to 35 percent, but buying your computer through a mail-order source can be tricky. If you know precisely what you need, and don't want the guidance of the salesperson at your local computer store, then you may be well advised to buy through a mail-order firm. Remember, however, that by buying from a local source you establish a relationship that can provide you with advice and guidance long after your original hardware purchase.

As a novice user of a personal computer, you will undoubtedly profit from advice on how to get the most from your machine and a good computer store can give you that. Choose a local store that has an excellent reputation for treating personal computers as business machines and their customers as business people. In my case that choice cost me about $400—the difference between what my local store charged me and what I would have paid using a mail-order firm. It has been worth it, however. I have needed help since the sale, and at one point I even needed access to the store's printers for output from my word processor before I'd acquired my own printer. The help was gladly given.

Write a request for proposal (RFP) to your local store or vendor. State your software needs and priorities, and your budgeted range for both hardware and software. Request a description of services and an itemized list of their costs. Most dealers will offer a wide range of services, including maintenance, programming, and computer education. You may want to ask them what makes their store unique and why you should do business with them. The response you get from this RFP should tell you not only what the particular vendor has to offer in equipment and services but, just as important, should indicate the degree of interest the store has in your business. If its response is clearly laid out, and if it answers your questions, then and only then should you consider evaluating its offerings. If its response is unsatisfactory, it may be, too.

AFTER-SALE SERVICE

Another important consideration is where you will get service if your system malfunctions. Although personal computers are quite reliable, they can and do go awry, so getting them back in working order in the shortest possible time and at a reasonable price may not always be easy. There are repair shops in or near most metropolitan areas that may either be associated with the store where you bought your system or be independent. If you have a choice of two or more service centers, get recommendations either from your dealer or from a local computer user group. You should expect repair work to cost about $40 to $50 per hour for labor, and one to two days to get your computer in and out of the shop. If you live in an area where there are no service centers, you will probably need to send your equipment to a center in another location. Hardware manufacturers often support large, centralized service operations in several locations around the United States and the rest of the world.

Of all the computer's hardware, the electronic components are least likely to fail. These include the keyboard/processor, attachment cards, and modem. Mechanical devices, such as disk drive and printer, may require more frequent servicing or adjustment, but routine maintenance is easy to do yourself. Special head-cleaning diskettes are available to help keep your disk drive clean. Your printer may also need cleaning periodically, along with an occasional ribbon change. In general, though, your printer should require no more servicing than a typical electric typewriter.

ASK SOMEONE WHO OWNS ONE

Finally, before making your hardware selection, talk to users of different makes of computer. Find out what they like and dislike about their components. An excellent source for user recommendations is a local or national use group. These groups usually focus on one brand of computer, such as Apple, Radio Shack, or IBM. Your computer store can give you the contacts in the user groups. Call or write them and ask whatever questions haven't been well answered elsewhere.

FINANCING YOUR PACKAGE

Once you have selected your personal computer equipment package and software, and have a firm price, discuss financing alternatives with your supplier. Some stores may allow a 10 percent discount on purchases of a complete package, but be sure to ask for it. Once you have a good idea of your costs, check with your bank or credit union for the most favorable financing terms. If you don't want to commit yourself to a large cash outlay, explore the possibilities of leasing a computer. Some stores as well as third parties will lease computers.

Current tax laws make it easier to afford a computer because a personal computer purchased as an investment aid may be tax deductible. The Economic Recovery Tax Act of 1981 allows individuals to depreciate a computer under an accelerated cost recovery system. The depreciation schedule set forth is: first year, 15 percent; second year, 22 percent; third through fifth year, 21 percent. You may also choose to take a 10 percent investment tax credit (ITC) and depreciate on the above schedule. If you lease your computer package, your leasing arrangements may be considered as either a true lease or as a time purchase for tax purposes. You can take an ITC provided the lessor agrees to pass it through to you. Whatever the case, you should discuss your computer purchase with your tax advisor. In any case, you will undoubtedly find that the real cost of the computer is far less than it appears to be on the surface.

As a sophisticated investor, you will of course want to predict your expected return on investment before you buy a computer. Begin by estimating how much you expect to improve your annual cash flow, increase capital gains and dividends, and avoid expenses through better cash management. Other personal ROI criteria can be similarly compared and included with the financial evaluation. Your evaluation should contain three major elements: the purchase or lease costs of the hardware, software, and services; the tax effects of the purchase or lease; and the financial return on the investment. You will probably find your return to be quite favorable in a relatively short time—perhaps within as little as 24 to 36 months.

Magazines like *Personal Computing, Creative Computing,* and *Popular Computing* are written for the personal computer user and usually provide nontechnical descriptions of how to get the most from your computer. Other magazines, such as *BYTE,* are more technical but may have some pertinent articles to help you understand personal computers. User groups also have publications, many of which are excellent. Often they focus on specific brands of computers, providing detailed information about individual makes. Computer vendors and stores can also supply excellent pamphlets, magazines, and books. Spend whatever time is necessary to understand the variety of hardware and software available. Read thoroughly and, if you don't understand, don't be afraid to ask questions. After all, only a small percentage of the total population understands personal computers, and, even to professional data processing people, personal computing is a comparatively new and unfamiliar ball game.

NEXT UP

In the next chapter, we describe in detail how to plan for profits by computer. You should approach this topic as if you were a business person setting up the company books. This will be your first application of the computer's logical decision process. Once you master this application, you should be in a much better position to plan your broad investing strategy. There are two reasons for this: one, you should have a better understanding of your personal finances, and two, the computer will have become a familiar and valued aid.

APPENDIX

Mortgage Analysis Program

This program was written in Applesoft Basic and runs on an Apple II+ computer. (It can be easily converted to run on other computers using the Basic language.) Its purpose is to quickly compute a range of home prices—given certain mortgage amounts, interest rates, time periods, and other factors. It prints to the computer's display screen.

```
100 REM INPUT SECTION
105 HOME
105 INPUT "GROSS INCOME?";I
120 INPUT "LIMIT OF MONTHLY PAYMENTS?";L
130 INPUT "TAX/INSURANCE %?";A
140 INPUT "DOWNPAYMENT %?";B
150 INPUT "MORTGAGE TERM IN YEARS?";T
160 INPUT "MORTGAGE INTEREST RATE?";R

165 REM PROCESSING SECTION
168 REM CALCULATE LOAN PAYMENTS (P)
170 P = I * L
175 REM CALCULATE TOTAL MONTHLY PAYMENTS (Q)
180 Q = P/(1+A)
185 REM CALCULATE TOTAL MONTHS (N)
190 N = T * 12
195 REM CALCULATE MONTHLY INTEREST RATE (J)
200 J = R/12
205 REM CALCULATE MORTGAGE REQUIRED (M)
210 M = Q * (1-((1+J)^-N))/J
215 REM CALCULATE HOUSE COST (H)
220 H = M/(1-B)
225 REM CALCULATE DOWNPAYMENT (D)
230 D = H - M

233 REM OUTPUT SECTION
235 PRINT:PRINT "OUTPUT FACTORS"
240 PRINT "MONTHLY LOAN PAYMENTS";P
250 PRINT "TOTAL MONTHLY PAYMENTS";Q
260 PRINT "DOWNPAYMENT";D
270 PRINT "MORTGAGE";M
280 PRINT "HOUSE COST";H
290 PRINT:PRINT
300 END
```

NOTE: Statements 120, 130, 140, and 160 require decimal input (O.XX).

Resource List

Computer System	Resource
Atari 400, 800, 1200XL	Atari Personal Computer Division 1265 Borregas Road Dept. C Sunnyvale, CA 94096
Apple II+, IIe, III	Apple Computer Inc. 10260 Bandley Drive Cupertino, CA 95014
Personal Computer	IBM Corporation Personal Computer Dept. P.O. Box 1328 Boca Raton, FL 33432
Vic 20, 64, PET Super Pet, CBM	Commodore Business Machines Personal Systems Division P.O. Box 500 Conshohocken, PA 19428
H-89	Heath Company Dept. 334-914 Benton Harbor, MI 49022
Xerox 820	Xerox Corporation Xerox Square Rochester, NY 14644
Horizon	North Star Computers, Inc. 14440 Catalina Street San Leandro, CA 94577
TRS-80 Model I, II, III, 16	Radio Shack Dept. 83-A-423 1300 One Tandy Center Fort Worth, TX 76102
Personal Computing Option	Digital Equipment Corp. Terminals Product Group 2 Mt. Royal Avenue UPI-5 Marlboro, MA 01752
HP-86	Hewlett-Packard Co. 1820 Embarcadero Rd. Palo Alto, CA 94303
ACE 1000, 1200	Franklin Computer Corp. 7030 Colonial Highway Pennsauken, NJ 08109

Computer System	*Resource*
PC-8000	NEC Home Electronics (USA) Personal Computer Division 1401 Estes Avenue Elk Grove Village, IL 60007
NECIS	NEC Information Systems, Inc. 5 Militia Drive Lexington, MA 02173
ZX81	Sinclair Research Ltd. 2 Sinclair Plaza Nashua, NH 03061
TI-99/4A Home Computer	Texas Instruments Inc. P.O. Box 53 Lubbock, TX 79408
Empire Series	Tarbell Electronics 950 Dovlen Place Suite B Carson, CA 90746
Microengine	Western Digital Corp. 2445 McCabe Way Irvine, CA 92714
Superbrain	Intertec Data Systems 2300 Broad River Road Columbia, SC 29210

Planning for Profits

No matter what you invest in, you must take the time to carefully plan your strategy. You have too much money riding on the outcome of your investment decisions to act on impulse. But where should you begin the planning process? Certainly we all invest with one purpose—to make money. But how much would you like to make, and over what length of time? These are the crucial questions. Fortunately, they can be answered in objective and quantitative terms—the kind of terms that computers process beautifully. It is up to you to set your goals, but once you have done that, your computer can provide invaluable assistance in helping you meet them.

Your personal computer can serve you in two ways, first by helping you build a model of your objectives, and second by clarifying exactly what you can commit in the way of available financial resources.

Setting objectives is easy, but meeting them is not. They're a lot like New Year's resolutions: easy to make, hard to keep. A simple objective might be to make a lot of money; another would be to have a comfortable lifestyle. Neither of these objectives is quantified, however, and cannot therefore be supported by computer planning. Restating them in quantitative terms would look like this:

Case 1:

A. To make an average salary of $100,000 per year for 10 years ($1 million).

B. To make $50,000 per year for 20 years ($1 million).

Case 2:

A. To get salary increases equal to or greater than 5 percent above the average rate of inflation.

In the first case, a $1 million objective is to be met in both A and B, the difference being the length of time you have allotted yourself to meet your goal. In Case 2, you can add 5 percent to the expected inflation rate to know what your annual salary increases must average. The next step is to build a model. This is easy once you have reduced your broad objectives to mathematical terms. On accompanying Exhibits 3–1 and 3–2, Cases 1 and 2 are plotted on a graph. Admittedly, they are simple representations of these objectives.

In Case 1, the $1 million is not an increase in net worth but merely the total of salary received. Income doesn't build wealth unless you manage it properly. For example, it may cost you 95 percent of your annual salary to live the kind of lifestyle you desire; on an income of $50,000 per year you might spend $47,500 on living expenses and taxes. A $2,500 surplus remains to build your wealth. If you can invest that $2,500 at an annual before-tax yield of 14 percent over a 20-year period, it increases to over a quarter of a million dollars—quite an achievement! The challenge, of course, is to maintain the 14 percent annual return in today's market, where uncertainties cause wide swings in the rates of return on virtually all types of investments. It is these market and interest rate risks that a personal computer can help minimize.

In Case 2, the goal is to have salary increases outpace the rate of inflation by 5 percent a year. As inflation varies from year to year, so does the growth of your income. Exhibit 3–2 is a simplified representation of this. Unfortunately, the performance of wages in the real world is not as neat and predictable as this chart would suggest. For instance, most people find that the higher the rate of inflation, the more difficult it becomes to keep their raises running 5 percent ahead of it. Exhibit 3–3, which illustrates this common pattern, presents a more realistic picture than the previous chart, but it also clearly shows some of the pitfalls on the road to your goals. If you reach a limit on the rate at which your salary increases in high inflation periods, how will you sustain your lifestyle? Astute management of your investment program can supplement a lowered rate of income growth during hyper-inflationary times. Your investment income can help you bridge those temporary gaps, allowing you to maintain your lifestyle and still provide added funds for future investments.

Exhibit 3-1. Salary Objectives—Case 1

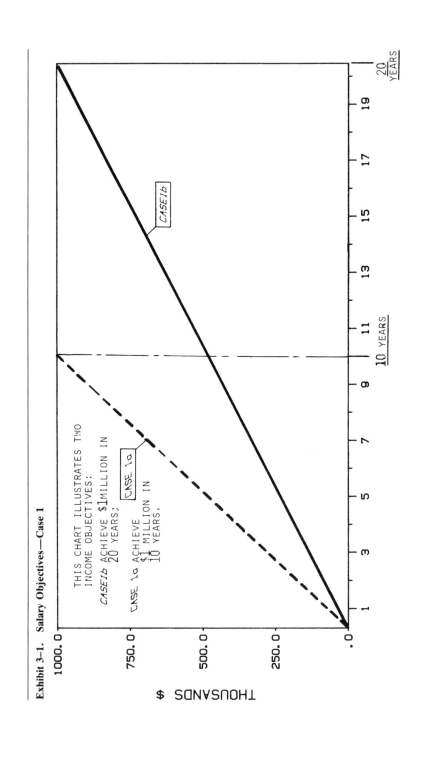

THIS CHART ILLUSTRATES TWO
INCOME OBJECTIVES:

CASE1b ACHIEVE $1MILLION IN
20 YEARS;

CASE 1a ACHIEVE
$1 MILLION IN
10 YEARS.

CASE 1a

CASE1b

10 YEARS

10 YEARS

20 YEARS

Exhibit 3–2. Salary Objectives—Case 2

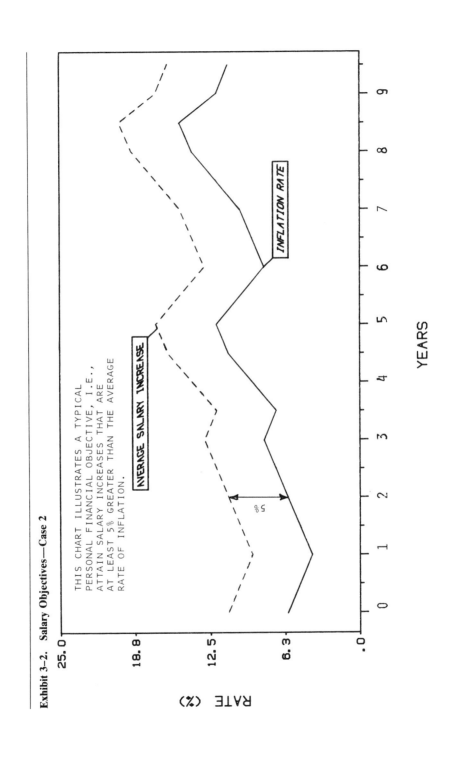

THIS CHART ILLUSTRATES A TYPICAL
PERSONAL FINANCIAL OBJECTIVE, I.E.,
ATTAIN SALARY INCREASES THAT ARE
AT LEAST 5% GREATER THAN THE AVERAGE
RATE OF INFLATION.

AVERAGE SALARY INCREASE

INFLATION RATE

5 %

RATE (%)

25.0

18.8

12.5

6.3

.0

0   1   2   3   4   5   6   7   8   9

YEARS

Exhibit 3-3. Salary Objectives—and Inflation

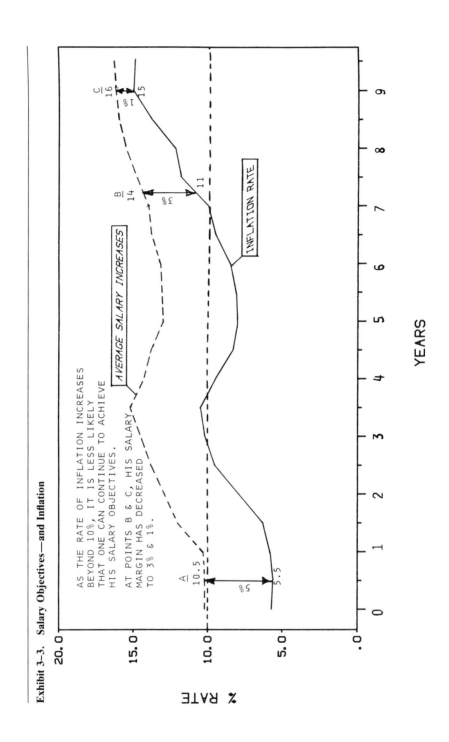

In both cases a personal computer can aid in achieving your objectives. As a starter, write down your financial goals, assign numerical values to them, and plot them over a realistic time frame. Having this plan in front of you as we progress through the book will be useful for reference.

ELEMENTS OF THE PLAN

A true measure of any company or individual's finances is the difference between assets and liabilities. In business, this is called owners' or shareholders' equity. For individuals it is referred to as net worth. Most businesses have some type of computer or computer service to aid them in managing their assets and liabilities. Your personal financial well-being is no less important. Now is an excellent time to automate your financial portfolio—no matter what your investments. Individuals stand to benefit from computer management of their assets and liabilities no less than businesses do.

Within your overall objectives there are subelements of income and expense to be coordinated. The simplest way to ensure that you meet your goal is to maximize income and minimize expenses. Your discretionary income is the difference between the two. Obviously, the greater the positive difference, the more disposable income you have left for investing. Maximizing the difference can be accomplished by either increasing income or decreasing expenses.

For many people, increasing income is difficult, particularly for salaried persons or wage earners. Commissioned salespeople, of course, can try to work harder, close more sales, and earn more commissions. Large numbers of people have also begun looking at investing as a way of increasing income. Rather than risk anything, some people do nothing. What should *you* do? Most people don't understand economics or finances, and would rather not ask themselves such questions.

Are personal computers able to help? Certainly, if you are willing to spend the time to learn how to use the computer and to learn something about investing fundamentals. Getting a computer to help you invest more successfully implies that you are serious about using it to increase your income through a carefully planned and managed system.

Planning is of critical importance in reducing that one expense all of us would like to do without—taxes. Few elements in our financial lives have more of an impact on our bottom line.

Taxes are deducted from income every payday. If taxes were less, your net income would be more. You can plan to minimize your taxes now. Tax avoidance is legal—tax evasion is not. If you shopped for a home recently, you know that mortgage rates are brutally high. On the plus side, though, those high interest rates make a fine tax deduction. But what happens to your cash flow while you are waiting to receive your tax refund? Mortgage payments restrict your cash supply by significantly increasing your monthly expenses since you make payments on your mortgage 12 times a year but only get your tax refund once a year. How can you compensate? One way is by increasing your tax allowances, thereby decreasing your monthly withholding. IRS Form W-4 gives you specific instructions for doing this.

Are you planning your computer purchase this year? If so, how will you deduct it to maximize your tax benefit? What were your itemized deductions last year? Do you expect them to increase this year? Are you considering a trust fund for your children's education or a gift to minors? Will you receive an inheritance this year or be involved in a corporate move? All these items need to be considered in your tax planning. By judiciously considering the impact of each tax element, you can make allowances and reduce your monthly tax bite.

RISK ASSESSMENT

As you begin choosing different investment media, you must understand the risks associated with each. Table 3–1 shows the risks commonly associated with different kinds of investments.

Table 3–1. Investment Risks

Investment Vehicle	Risk Level	Risk Type	Objective
Savings account	Low	Interest rate	Safety
Money market funds	Low	Interest rate	Principal protection
Common stocks	Medium to high	Interest rate, financial	Income, capital gains
Preferred stocks	Low to medium	Interest rate	Income
Corporate bonds	Medium to high	Interest rate	Income
Municipal bonds	Low to medium	Interest rate	Tax-free income
Real estate	Medium to high	Market, financial, interest rate	Income, capital gains, tax advantages
Mutual funds	Low to medium	Market, financial	Income, capital gains
Stock options	High	Market, financial	Capital gains
Commodities	High	Political, market, interest rate	Capital gains
Tangibles	Medium to high	Market, political	Capital gains, diversity

From the preceding table, it is obvious that commodities and options trading are not for widows and pensioners. For others, speculation may be a fine way to gain highly leveraged returns. The choice of investment media depends upon the risk you are willing to accept.

MATCHING INVESTMENTS TO YOUR GOALS

Once you select a set of objectives and feel comfortable with the risk, you should determine which investments best meet your goals. There are several ways to do this. If common stocks and money market funds are your tentative choices, begin by looking at each category and setting criteria for their specific selection.

For example, stock screens can be set up in several ways. A simple way would be to build a balanced portfolio of 20 percent speculative, 30 percent income-producing, and 50 percent high-growth stocks. Sample stock screens are shown in Exhibits 3–4, 3–5, and 3–6.

Exhibit 3–4. Growth Stock Screen

A. Procedures:

    1. List all stocks on exchanges or in other markets that have reported a 20 percent increase in earnings over the same quarter last year.
    2. From these, select the stocks having at least a 10 percent earnings growth for the past three years.
    3. Choose those that have a steady increase (5 to 10 percent) in the past three quarters.
    4. Choose those that are in a basic uptrend.
    5. Buy the remainder and calculate the annual return.

B. Data required—earnings history:

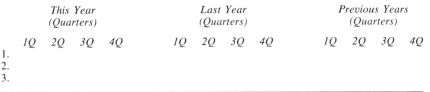

	This Year (Quarters)				*Last Year (Quarters)*				*Previous Years (Quarters)*			
	1Q	*2Q*	*3Q*	*4Q*	*1Q*	*2Q*	*3Q*	*4Q*	*1Q*	*2Q*	*3Q*	*4Q*
1.												
2.												
3.												

Courtesy of Northington Limited

Combine the computed annual returns to ensure that they exceed your 15 percent objective.

Each set of stock screens is considered a submodel. Your submodels allow you to choose the best portfolio by combining them into one large model. With your computer you can evaluate the effect of each submodel on your overall portfolio. In this way you can build several "dream portfolios" and track them before actually investing any money in individual

Exhibit 3–5. Income Stock Screen

A. Procedures:

1. Choose stocks that are in cyclically good industries for the current economy.
2. Choose ones whose dividends are covered by adequate earnings per share.
3. Select a stock with a yield more than the industry average or whatever yield seems appropriate at the time.
4. Eliminate those stocks which haven't paid a dividend every quarter for the past 20 years.
5. Look for stocks that have increased their dividends more than 5 percent in each of the last five years.
6. Eliminate those with price earnings ratios of more than 10.
7. Buy the remainder and calculate the annual returns.

B. Data required—dividends history:

	Dividends Consecutive		*Avg. Annual Incr.*						*Current Yield*
Selection	*Quarters*	*CY*	*−1*	*−2*	*−3*	*−4*	*−5*	*P-E*	*(percent)*
1.									
2.									
3.									

Courtesy of Northington Limited

Exhibit 3–6. Speculative Stock Screen

A. Procedures:

1. Choose stocks in cyclically good industries for the economy.
2. Look for volatility—choose stocks whose high price for each year should be twice the low price in that year for each of the last three years.
3. Choose stocks that are trading within 10 percent of the current year's low price.
4. Eliminate all stocks with a P-E ratio of more than 20.
5. Look for stocks with thin floats and high short interest.
6. Consider buying the remaining stocks provided the markets are not near a high point.
7. After your final selection is made, calculate the annual returns.

B. Data required—price history:

	Price									
	CY		*−1*		*−2*		*P-E*	*Thin*	*High Short*	
Selection	*High*	*Low*	*High*	*Low*	*High*	*Low*	*(<20)*	*Float*	*Interest*	*Peak*
								Y/N	Y/N	Y/N
1.										
2.										
3.										

Courtesy of Northington Limited

stocks. This ability to test several hypothetical portfolios before committing your hard-earned money is the most important benefit your personal computer can give you; you risk nothing but time. (Later, we will look at this concept using a particular computer program.)

Another measure of the importance of planning is therefore the money you can save by working out bad decisions before you act on them. On the other hand, good decisions can make you money. After all, maximizing returns and minimizing risks is what good planning is all about.

Another element you may want to analyze is your money market fund's performance which is directly related to the level of interest rates. How many years into the future do you want to project interest rates, and what generalized assumptions can you make about them?

Over the past several years the odds on successfully forecasting money market interest rates haven't been much better than gambling at Atlantic City or Las Vegas. For now, assume your money market fund will average 12 percent per year (or whatever figure you believe to be accurate). Spread the resulting interest payments over a period of three to five years. Do the same with your stocks and bonds, then add them all up. The bottom line is your expected investment growth rate over this period. How does this compare to your original financial objectives? If your ROI is too high, revise your expected returns downward.

Rebalancing the portfolio could also result in better coordination between goals and expected ROI. The choices of investments to meet your financial objectives are many and varied and the risks are different with each one. Some alternative routes besides stocks and bonds include options and commodities trading, real estate, and tangibles investing. To minimize the associated risks, you need to determine the best route for yourself. What follows is a discussion of programs that can help you make this determination.

PERSONAL COMPUTER AIDS

Several excellent programs are available that use an "electronic spreadsheet" technology. Imagine having an accountant's spreadsheet on your computer's display, an electronic worksheet that replaces paper, pencil, and calculator, and lets you define your investment objectives as mathematical rules at the intersection of the rows and columns on the worksheet. Some allow up to 15,000 data elements and others as few as 2,000. You can enter comparative data on, for example, stocks and bonds, and then run the model to determine which investment pays you the best total return. This capability enables you to play "What if" with different alternatives because the selection of the best investment is possible without risking any money. The example shown in Exhibit 3–7 is the result of the screening of several stocks to locate the undervalued ones.

Exhibit 3–7. Stock Screening Technique

```
COMPANY NAME    ABC COMPANY            !! =======
                                       !! IN THIS AREA, AND IN THE NEXT   !! WHENEVER YOU LOAD A FILE      !! "EVALUATION FORM"
(MMM) = MANDATORY INPUT                !! AREAS,YOU WILL SEE THIS FORMAT.  !! FROM DISK, (ONE THAT HAD     !!
LAST FULL YEAR OF DATA--    1981       !! PLACE 6 YRS. OF DATA IN COLUMNS. !! BEEN PREVIOUSLY SAVED), RE-  !! COPYRIGHT 1982 BY
DATE OF THIS FORM------- 4/23/82       !! $$$$ ACCURACY IS IMPORTANT $$$$ !! CALCULATE (!!!) THREE TIMES. !! INVESTOR'S SOFTWARE
DATA PUBLISHED ON (DATE)  2/5/82       !! ===========================================================================
DATA FROM (S&P) OR (V-L)    BOTH       !!        PRICE       EARN  BOOK   NET PROF (S&P)  SALES    DIV   PRE-TAX % EARN
(S&P) RATING------------     A-        !! YEAR   HIGH   LOW  PER   VALUE  MARGIN NET B4  (REV-    PER   PROF ON ON INV
(V-L) SAFETY RATING-----      3        !!                    SHARE       (V-L) TAXES  ENUES)    SHARE SALES % CAPITAL
(V-L) TIMELINESS RATING-      4        !! ===========================================================================
(V-L) 5 YR EPS PROJ----$   4.10        !! 1976   7.10  4.70  0.41  5.85   2.20   3.50  84.60    0.07  4.14   7.01
HIGH THIS YEAR---------$  26.63        !! 1977   9.80  5.30  0.73  6.46   3.20   6.70 105.70    0.13  6.34  11.30
LOW THIS YEAR----------$  15.13        !! 1978  16.20  8.00  1.37  7.70   4.20  12.70 156.00    0.17  8.14  17.79
PRESENT PRICE----------$  18.00        !! 1979  19.80 10.60  1.72  9.11   4.20  15.80 201.20    0.30  7.85  18.88
PRESENT DIV------------$   0.72        !! 1980  23.50 14.60  2.14 10.89   4.30  19.70 245.90    0.43  8.01  19.65
PRESENT P/E------------$   9.00        !! 1981  26.60 17.00  2.15 12.57   3.80  20.60 294.40    0.58  7.00  17.10
LATEST QUARTERLY EPS---$   0.45        !! ---------------------------------------------------------------------------
YR. AGO QUARTERLY EPS--$   0.50        !!          CONTINUE --->>> CONTINUE --->>> CONTINUE  RE-CALCULATE (!!!) 3 TIMES
RE-CALCULATE (!!!)-60 TO (I-11)        !! 6 YR AVG. WHERE APPLICABLE-->>>          3.65               6.91  15.29
===================================================================================================================
THE INFORMATION CONTAINED BELOW SHOWS THE COMPOUNDED RATE OF GROWTH FOR SALES, EARNINGS PER SHARE, AND DIVIDENDS, OVER THE MOST
RECENT 5 YEAR PERIOD.  (EXAMPLE: IF THERE IS A "TRUE" UNDER THE 13% COLUMN, BUT NOT UNDER THE 14% COLUMN, THE COMPOUNDED GROWTH
RATE OVER THE PAST 5 YEARS HAS BEEN AT LEAST 13%, BUT NOT AS HIGH AS 14%.
THE EPS ESTIMATE ROW INDICATES THE GROWTH OF THE PRESENT EPS --$   2.15 FOR THE YEAR--- 1986  AT THE VARIOUS COMPOUNDED RATES.
-------------------------------------------------------------------------------------------------------------------
5 YR. COMP. GROWTH RATE-   7%    8%    9%   10%   11%   12%   13%   14%   15%   20%   25%   30%   35%
SALES------------------  TRUE  TRUE  TRUE  TRUE  TRUE  TRUE  TRUE  TRUE  TRUE  TRUE  TRUE FALSE FALSE
EARNINGS PER SHARE------  TRUE  TRUE  TRUE  TRUE  TRUE  TRUE  TRUE  TRUE  TRUE  TRUE  TRUE  TRUE  TRUE
DIVIDENDS--------------   TRUE  TRUE  TRUE  TRUE  TRUE  TRUE  TRUE  TRUE  TRUE  TRUE  TRUE  TRUE  TRUE
1986 EPS ESTIMATE---      3.01  3.16  3.31  3.46  3.63  3.78  3.96  4.15  4.32  5.35  5.81  7.98  9.63
===================================================================================================================
THE FOLLOWING AREA RE-ARRANGES SOME OF THE INFORMATION FROM ABOVE INTO A FIVE   !! FORECASTING
YEAR FORMAT, AND ADDS A FEW CALCULATIONS FOR COMPARISON.                        !!
                                                                               !! AVG HIGH PE-  12.02 TIMES EST EPS-$  4.75
YEAR       PRICE        BOOK    EPS    PE RATIO  DIVIDEND   PCT  % HIGH !! EQUALS FORECAST HIGH PRICE--------$  57.15
         HIGH   LOW    VALUE            HIGH  LOW  PER SH  PAYOUT YIELD !!                                     =======
-------------------------------------------------------------------------------- !! AVG LOW PE TIMES ESTIMATED LOW EPS=$  14.62
   1977  9.80   5.30   6.46   0.73  13.42  7.26  0.13   17.81  2.45 !! AVG LOW PRICE OF LAST 5 YEARS------$  11.10
   1978 16.20   8.00   7.70   1.37  11.82  5.84  0.17   12.41  2.13 !! LOWEST PRICE OF LAST 3 YEARS------$  10.60
   1979 19.80  10.60   9.11   1.72  11.51  6.16  0.30   17.44  2.83 !! PRICE DIVIDEND WILL SUPPORT-------$  21.10
   1980 23.50  14.60  10.89   2.14  10.98  6.82  0.43   20.09  2.95 !!
   1981 26.60  17.00  12.57   2.15  12.37  7.91  0.58   26.98  3.41 !! AVERAGE = FORECAST LOW PRICE------$  14.35
-------------------------------------------------------------------------------- !!                                     =======
TOTALS          55.50             60.11 33.99         94.73  !! BUY-HOLD-SELL RANGES
AVERAGE         11.10             12.02  6.80         18.95  !!
-------PRESENT PE RATIO------- 9.00 AVERAGE PE RATIO------ 9.41-------- !!   14.35---TO---  28.62  BUY
============================================================================   !!   28.62---TO---  42.89  HOLD
BELOW: EVERY QUESTION LISTED IS AN IMPORTANT CONSIDERATION WHEN MAKING  BUY OR !!   42.89---TO---  57.15  CONSIDER SALE
       SELL DECISIONS.  YOU WILL RARELY HAVE ONLY TRUE RESPONSES.              !!
                                                                              !! BEST BUY WOULD BE LESS THAN ------$  21.49
THE MOST RECENT QUARTERLY EARNINGS ARE UP BY AT LEAST 10%--------------- FALSE !!--------------------------------------=======
GROWTH OF SALES AND EPS IS STEADILY HIGHER EACH YEAR-------------------- TRUE !! PRESENT YIELD -------------=   4.00 %
PRESENT PRICE OF THE STOCK IS IN THE BUY RANGE------------------------- TRUE !!                               =======
% PRE-TAX PROFIT ON SALES (GROWTH TREND IS UP)------------------------- TRUE !! AVG YIELD FOR NEXT 5 YRS---=   3.63 %
% EARNED ON INVESTED CAPITAL (GROWTH TREND IS UP)---------------------- TRUE !!                               =======
PROFIT MARGIN (GROWTH TREND IS UP)------------------------------------- TRUE !! UP-SIDE DOWN-SIDE RATIO----= 10.74 TO 1
GROWTH OF SALES HAS BEEN AT LEAST AS RAPID AS GROWTH OF EPS------------ FALSE !!                               =========
THE UP-SIDE DOWN-SIDE RATIO IS AT LEAST 3 TO 1 ------------------------ TRUE !! PRESENT PE RATIO IS   95.64 % OF AVERAGE PE
YEARLY RETURN (LOW--EPS+AVG YLD)   33.63% (HIGH--PRICE GROWTH+AVG YLD)-- 47.14%!!                               =========
TODAY'S PE RATIO IS LOWER THAN THE AVERAGE PE RATIO-------------------- TRUE !! IF YOU ALTER FIGURES, (!!!) THREE TIMES.
-------------------------------------------------------------------------------------------------------------------
NOTE: THIS MATERIAL INCORPORATES PRINCIPLES AND PROCEEDURES FROM THE NATIONAL ASSOCIATION OF INVESTMENT CLUB'S INVESTORS MANUAL,
1515 E. ELEVEN MILE ROAD, ROYAL OAK, MICHIGAN, 48068.  DUPLICATION OF THIS SOFTWARE IS PERMITTED FOR BACK-UP PURPOSES ONLY.
```

Courtesy of Investor's Software, Box N, Bradenton Beach, FL 33510

The original electronic spreadsheet was VisiCalc[1] from VisiCorp. It runs on most major computer brands and continues to be a bestseller. Exhibit 3–7 is the result of a VisiCalc analysis. There are also many other applications of VisiCalc to investment planning. Some brokers believe, for instance, that as a portfolio analysis tool VisiCalc helps them provide better client recommendations by segregating client assets within the electronic spreadsheet. That helps them analyze the many investments possible within a single portfolio. Weaknesses and errors stand out more clearly which means they can be more easily fixed.

ALTERNATE ROUTING TO RICHES

Over the last decade, real estate has become an extremely popular as well as a lucrative investment. If you are toying with the idea of buying real estate, keep in mind that there are a whole series of important calculations to be made first. If, for example, you are considering a multiple-unit apartment complex, you need to compute the income you will derive and the expenses you will incur, as well as taxes, maintenance costs, and potential for capital appreciation. Putting these factors together is complicated. Using a personal computer for planning your investment in this medium is immensely productive, and may be the only way to effectively evaluate the property.

VisiCalc is adaptable to this kind of computer-aided analysis, and recently its capacity has been greatly enhanced by the addition of the Visi-Calc Real Estate Templates from Apple Computer's contributed program library. The templates utilize built-in formulas and equations designed to speed up income property selection. They include income property investment, personal financial statement, amortization, mortgage loan analysis, and a comparative depreciation schedule.

The templates are a fine productivity aid for VisiCalc users who plan real estate purchases. They overcome some of the complexity in the use of VisiCalc by providing the formulas and recalculation commands needed for real estate applications. All you need to do is enter the data by moving the display window to the desired location (the intersection of the rows and columns), and then asking your computer to do the calculations.

As an example of how the templates work, assume you are interested in analyzing a mortgage loan. One of the templates analyzes up to five mortgages at once, calculating the number of years since acquisitions, the age of each mortgage at the time of the analysis, the principal balance at acquisition, monthly payments, and annual debt service. The mortgage loan templates also calculate such things as principal balance outstanding at the time of analysis, total principal paid off since acquisition, and the principal and interest paid over the last 12 months. The templates help

---

[1] VisiCalc is a trademark of Visicorp.

make VisiCalc easier to use for real estate investors. In time, more templates should be available to aid you in other investing media.

There are many other planning aids besides VisiCalc, and these other programs are available for most brands of computers. One particularly good program is Decision Support System/Finance (DSS/F) from Ferox Microsystems, which was patterned after a large computer timesharing system and contains many of that system's functions and flexibility. Its many financial functions, large model-handling capabilities, and built-in graphics capability make it attractive to investors and financial counselors alike.

The graphics capability of DSS/F adds a new dimension to your financial planning because the visual effect makes data interpretation faster and easier. Errors can be spotted and corrected more easily and your financial objectives can be summarized in color graphics with great visual impact. This makes it much easier to interpret the results of your planning, and the effect of these results on your objectives.

In addition, DSS/F gives you considerable flexibility in structuring your portfolio analysis methodology. Following logical steps in structuring your assets and sorting them by category quickly tells you how to arrange them for maximum benefit. Transferring assets between categories allows you to ask questions to develop an optimum asset configuration for any hypothetical prevailing market. The graphics capability enables you to see and compare the results of your hypothetical cases. Adjustments can be quickly made in your model and the new results displayed immediately. Once you have become conversant with this type of computer-aided analysis, the results in terms of increased productivity will be enormous.

Another interesting approach to portfolio planning is Portrate™ from Portware, Inc. It was designed specifically as an investment aid for options, cash management, and merger accounts, in contrast to electronic spreadsheets like VisiCalc and DSS/F, which are general purpose business planning tools. Portrate™ ranks portfolio holdings according to the investor's objectives. The quality index provides insight into how well a current portfolio meets the user's objectives. Deficiencies in the portfolio strategy can be quickly spotted, and so can clues to the appropriate changes. A redefinition of strategy is then possible. (See Exhibit 3–8.) There are other kinds of programs that run on the major computers, such as Apple II/III, IBM Personal Computer (IBM PC), Radio Shack's TRS-80 line, and CP/M²-based computers. They offer many time-saving advantages over manual methods, as well as an inexpensive way to plan for profits. Your choice of software is dependent on your planning needs, experience with modeling systems, and the type of computer you have or plan to buy.

---

² CP/M is a registered trademark of Digital Research, Inc.

Exhibit 3–8.   Portrate™

```
                                              DATE: 12/19/8
          CLIENT: SAMPLE PORTRATE 198

                                        PORTRATE   INVESTMENT
          PORTFOLIO PROFILE:            COMPUTES   TARGETS
          -------------------           --------   ---------

          1. PORTFOLIO VALUE         $    453566


          2. % CASH ($   165400)          36. 5%
             % FIXED INCOME ($   53750)   11. 9%
             % EQUITIES ($   234416)      51. 6%


          3. ANNUAL INCOME           $    51481


          4. PORTFOLIO YIELD              11. 4%


          5. PRICE/EARNINGS (EQUITIES)     6. 0


          6. RISK FACTOR (PORTFOLIO BETA)   . 5
                         (SECURITIES BETA)  . 8


          7. NO. OF INDUSTRIES             10


          8. LARGEST INDUSTRY HOLDING:  UTIL. -GAS/PIPL

                AS % OF SECURITIES VALUE   17. 1%


          9. NO. OF SECURITIES(EXCL. CASH)   15


          10. LARGEST SECURITY HOLDING IS   TENNECO

                AS % OF PORTFOLIO VALUE     10. 9%


          11. % OF EQUITY VALUE IN
              A- OR BETTER QUALITY          70. 5%


          12. % OF FIXED INCOME VALUE IN
              A OR BETTER QUALITY           47. 4%
```

Courtesy of Portware, Inc.

Exhibit 3–8 (*continued*)

PRICE/EARNINGS ANALYSIS

# SHARES OR BONDS	NAME	P/E	% WT
156	SFEIND	10. 0	6. 05
300	PACPW	9. 0	2. 67
1000	TENNECO	8. 0	21. 00
1000	DENNMFG	7. 0	7. 35
500	AT&T	6. 0	9. 59
1000	FLAPR	6. 0	5. 27
500	GTNONK	6. 0	8. 05
1000	PSVNM	5. 0	7. 62
500	ROBTSN	5. 0	8. 15
1561	KEYBANK	4. 0	8. 40
500	TRAVLRS	4. 0	7. 67
200	ROYLD	3. 0	8. 10

| EQUITIES P/E | | 6. 0 | |

SECURITIES DIVERSIFICATION

# SHARES OR BONDS	NAME	VALUE	% WT	CUM %
1000	TENNECO	49250	10. 85	10. 85
40	BCN8. 75	25500	5. 62	16. 48
500	AT&T	22500	4. 96	21. 44
1561	KEYBANK	19707	4. 34	25. 78
30	AVCO5. 5	19500	4. 29	30. 08
500	ROBTSN	19125	4. 21	34. 30
200	ROYLD	19000	4. 18	38. 49
500	GTNONK	18875	4. 16	42. 65
500	TRAVLRS	18000	3. 96	46. 62
1000	PSVNM	17875	3. 94	50. 56
1000	DENNMFG	17250	3. 80	54. 36
156	SFEIND	14196	3. 12	57. 49
1000	FLAPR	12375	2. 72	60. 22
1000	BOSE PR	8750	1. 92	62. 15
300	PACPW	6262	1. 38	63. 53
	CASH	165400	36. 46	100. 00

| PORTFOLIO TOTAL | | 453566 | | |

Exhibit 3–8 (*continued*)

RISK ANALYSIS

# SHARES OR BONDS	NAME	BETA	% WT
500	TRAVLRS	1. 20	3. 96
500	GTNONK	1. 10	4. 16
156	SFEIND	1. 05	3. 12
1000	DENNMFG	. 90	3. 80
1561	KEYBANK	. 90	4. 34
1000	TENNECO	. 90	10. 85
500	ROBTSN	. 85	4. 21
500	AT&T	. 70	4. 96
1000	FLAPR	. 70	2. 72
1000	PSVNM	. 70	3. 94
300	PACPW	. 65	1. 38
200	ROYLD	. 65	4. 18
1000	BOSE PR	. 60	1. 92
30	AVCO5. 5∕	. 50	4. 29
40	BCN8. 75	. 50	5. 62

SECURITIES RISK		. 80	
CASH		0. 00	36. 46
PORTFOLIO RISK		. 51	

QUALITY ANALYSIS

# SHARES	NAME	S&P QUALITY RATING	% WT
500	AT&T	A+	7. 80
1000	DENNMFG	A	5. 98
1000	FLAPR	B+	4. 29
500	GTNONK	A	6. 55
1561	KEYBANK	NR	6. 83
300	PACPW	A–	2. 17
1000	PSVNM	A–	6. 20
500	ROBTSN	B+	6. 63
200	ROYLD	A	6. 59
156	SFEIND	A	4. 92
1000	TENNECO	A	17. 09
500	TRAVLRS	NR	6. 24
1000	BOSE PR	BBB	3. 03
30	AVCO5. 5∕	B	6. 76
40	BCN8. 75	AA	8. 84

Exhibit 3–8 (*continued*)

QUALITY ANALYSIS SUMMARY

S&P QUALITY	NO	% WT	CUM WT
EQUITIES			
A+	1	9. 59	9. 59
A	5	50. 58	60. 17
A-	2	10. 29	70. 47
B+	2	13. 43	83. 91
NR	2	16. 08	100. 00
FIXED INCOME			
AA	1	47. 44	47. 44
BBB	1	16. 27	63. 72
B	1	36. 27	100. 00

INDUSTRY ANALYSIS

IND NAME	TOTAL VALUE	% WT	CUM % WT
UTIL. -GAS/	49250	17. 09	17. 09
TELECOMMUN	48000	16. 65	33. 74
UTIL. -ELEC	45262	15. 70	49. 45
PAPER	36125	12. 53	61. 99
BANKING	19707	6. 83	68. 83
AEROSPACE	19500	6. 76	75. 59
BUILDING	19125	6. 63	82. 23
OIL	19000	6. 59	88. 82
INSURANCE	18000	6. 24	95. 07
RR & EQPT	14196	4. 92	100. 00

INDUSTRY ANALYSIS - DETAIL

# SHARES OR BONDS	NAME	IND NAME
500	AT&T	TELECOMMUNIC
1000	DENNMFG	PAPER
1000	FLAPR	UTIL. -ELEC
500	GTNONK	PAPER
1561	KEYBANK	BANKING
300	PACPW	UTIL. -ELEC
1000	PSVNM	UTIL. -ELEC
500	ROBTSN	BUILDING
200	ROYLD	OIL
156	SFEIND	RR & EQPT
1000	TENNECO	UTIL. -GAS/PI
500	TRAVLRS	INSURANCE
1000	BOSE PR	UTIL. -ELEC
30	AVCO5. 5	AEROSPACE
40	BCN8. 75	TELECOMMUNIC

Exhibit 3–8 (*concluded*)

```
              YIELD ANALYSIS
# SHARES                            %
OR BONDS   NAME       INCOME   YIELD
------------------------------------------
      40   BCN8. 75     3500   13. 72
    1000   BOSE PR      1170   13. 37
    1000   FLAPR        1640   13. 25
    1000   PSVNM        2080   11. 63
     500   AT&T         2500   11. 11
     300   PACPW         612    9. 77
    1561   KEYBANK      1873    9. 50
      30   AVC05. 5     1650    8. 46
     500   TRAVLRS      1240    6. 88
     200   ROYLD        1300    6. 84
    1000   DENNMFG      1160    6. 72
     500   ROBTSN       1100    5. 75
    1000   TENNECO      2600    5. 27
     500   GTNONK        900    4. 76
     156   SFEIND        468    3. 29
           CASH        27687   16. 74
------------------------------------------
  PORTFOLIO TOTAL      51481   11. 35
```

```
MONTHLY INCOME FORECASTER/PLANNER

        MONTH      INCOME
--------------------------------------
         JAN        3553
         FEB        2827
         MAR        5701
         APR        5953
         MAY        2827
         JUN        4876
         JUL        3553
         AUG        2827
         SEP        5701
         OCT        5953
         NOV        2827
         DEC        4876
                  --------
        TOTAL      51481
```

Courtesy of Portware, Inc.

TAKING STOCK OF YOUR STATUS

As you become conversant with computer-aided investment planning, you will learn to quickly compare your investment performance with the goals you have set in your plan. (Measuring results is essential to long-range success.) Your plan tells you where you should be, and your profits or derived income tell you where you are. If the plan and profits are on divergent tracks, it is time to readjust your investment strategy. Your personal computer can be extremely useful here.

You may find that your mix of common stocks, bonds, and money market funds needs to be modified, and another series of hypothetical cases may need to be run. For example, if interest rates move higher, your stocks may not be performing well. Money funds, on the other hand, are probably increasing their yields. Real estate, particularly the income-producing type you may have chosen, will be doing well because more families will be renting than buying. After rerunning your model, you may decide to sell some stock and put the proceeds in a money fund. To do this, however, you are forced to sell your stock at a loss. What is the effect on your taxes? Use your tax-planner program to find out. The results of this analysis may show that you can take a deduction this tax year and next for a capital loss. Obviously, this can alter your tax profile for the current and next year.

An analysis like this may not appear so complex that it requires a computer. Certain simplifying assumptions were made for the sake of clarity, however. You can include more factors than have been considered here if you have a computer to aid you. A totally new and potentially more profitable course of action may be indicated. You won't know unless you build your own model and try it.

APPENDIX

A Fundamental Stock Screening Method

The material in Exhibit 3–7 is adapted from Ed Chiampi's description of stock selection based on fundamental company financial data.[3] Mr. Chiampi uses the VisiCalc electronic spreadsheet program to automate the stock selection techniques contained in the investor's manual of the National Association of Investment Clubs (NAIC, 1515 E. Eleven Mile Road, Royal Oak, MI 48068). Data input is supplied by the user and is gathered from libraries or brokers. The "library form" (Exhibit 3A–1) is supplied with the program and must be filled out with six year's data. It is then entered into the VisiCalc program via the computer's keyboard.

The resulting report (Exhibit 3–7) is neatly laid out, and gives the investor a lot

---

[3] Courtesy of Investor's Software, Box N, Bradenton Beach, FL 33510.

Exhibit 3A–1. (This data is input to a fundamental stock screening method)

```
LIBRARY FORM:  DATE-----------

COMPANY #1:                              COMPANY #2:

COMPANY NAME-----------------            COMPANY NAME-----------------
LAST FULL YR. OF DATA---------           LAST FULL YR. OF DATA---------
DATA PUBLISHED ON?-(DATE)-----           DATA PUBLISHED ON?-(DATE)-----
S&P OR V-L OR BOTH?-----------           S&P OR V-L OR BOTH?-----------
S&P RATING--------------------           S&P RATING--------------------
V-L SAFETY RATING-------------           V-L SAFETY RATING-------------
V-L TIMELINESS RATING---------           V-L TIMELINESS RATING---------
V-L 5 YEAR EPS PROJ.----------           V-L 5 YEAR--------------------
HIGH THIS YEAR----------------           HIGH THIS YEAR----------------
LOW THIS YEAR-----------------           LOW THIS YEAR-----------------
PRESENT PRICE-----------------           PRESENT PRICE-----------------
PRESENT DIVIDEND--------------           PRESENT DIVIDEND--------------
PRESENT PE--------------------           PRESENT PE--------------------
LATEST QTRLY. EPS-------------           LATEST QTRLY. EPS-------------
YR. AGO QTRLY. EPS------------           YR. AGO QTRLY. EPS-----------
```

INSERT THE LATEST 6 YEARS OF DATA IN THE FOLLOWING COLUMNS.

COMPANY #1:

YR	CE HIGH	LOW	EARN PER SHARE	BOOK VALUE	NET PROFIT MARGIN V-L	S&P NET BEFORE TAXES	SALES OR REVENUES	DIVIDENDS PER SHARE
19								
19								
19								
19								
19								
19								

COMPANY #2:

YR	PRICE HIGH	LOW	EARN PER SHARE	BOOK VALUE	NET PROFIT MARGIN V-L	S&P NET BEFORE TAXES	SALES OR REVENUES	DIVIDENDS PER SHARE
19								
19								
19								
19								
19								
19								

Courtesy of Investor's Software, Box N, Bradenton Beach, FL 33510 of data on which to make a comparative analysis. The following four factors are major considerations when selecting stocks based on fundamentals:

1. Look for constantly rising patterns of earnings:
   a. All investment projections are based on company earnings.
   b. The average annual growth of a stock over five years gives a good view of its potential.
2. Select companies that raise dividends 12 to 15 percent per year:
   a. Dividends should be paid a minimum of 60 consecutive quarters.
   b. Increasing dividends means that a company is in good financial shape.
3. Buy stocks only when the present price-earnings ratio (P-E) is lower than the average P-E over five years:
   a. Earnings reflect the quality of management decisions and the state of the economy.
   b. Price is an expression of all psychological pressures on the stock. When buying pressure is great, the price and P-E move up.
4. Evaluate the company's management performance and look for a constantly rising pattern of book value:
   a. The highest profit margin and net earnings before taxes are important.
   b. Pretax profit and return on invested capital help to assess management quality, too.

Bibliography

Perry, Robert L. "Crystal-Balling on Micros." *Computer Decisions,* October 1981, pp. 58–72, 162–74.
————. "Financial Modeling Software: Tools for the Overworked Manager." *Personal Computing,* June 1981, pp. 22–28, 70, 108.
"Planning Your Investment Portfolio." *Successful Investing and Money Management.* Toronto: Northington Limited, 1974.
"Common Stocks." *Successful Investing and Money Management.* Toronto: Northington Limited, 1974.

Resource List

Product	Resource	Computer
VisiCalc	VisiCorp 2895 Zanker Road San Jose, CA 95134	Apple II/III Atari 800 Hewlett-Packard TRS-80 Commodore CBM
Decision Support System/Finance	Ferox Microsystems 1701 Ft. Myer Drive Suite 601 Arlington, VA 22209	Apple II + /III IBM Personal Computer

Product	Resource	Computer
Calcstar	Micropro International Corp. 1299 Fourth Street San Rafael, CA 94901	CP/M-based
Profitplan and Microplan	Chang Laboratories Inc. 10228 North Stelling Road Cupertino, CA 95014	CP/M-based
Portrate	Portware 1234 Tucker Edina, MN 55436	Apple II +
Master Planner and Planner Calc	Comshare Target 1935 Cliff Valley Way Atlanta, GA 30329	CP/M-based
FIN PLAN	Hayden Publishing 50 Essex Street Rochelle Park, NJ 07662	TRS-80
Plan 80	Digital Marketing 2670 Cherry Lane Walnut Creek, CA 94596	CP/M-based
Multiplan	Microsoft Corp. 10700 Northrup Way Bellevue, WA 98004	Apple II+, IBM PC, CP/M-80-based, Xenix-based

Cash and Budget Management

Of all the potential uses of your computer, none is more important than cash and budget management. Your computer enables you to keep careful and constant track of your financial assets—an ability that is absolutely essential to successful investing and money management.

The software you choose for this application should meet four simple criteria. The software should be:

Simple.

Understandable.

Easy to use.

Believable.

Budgeting for everyday living is one thing; budgeting for investing is something else. The two are related, however, since both are based on the same source of income. Controlling your everyday expenses through the budget process is a prerequisite to having adequate resources left over for investing. The purpose of this chapter is to explain how a personal computer can help you plan to maximize the cash you have available for investing.

ASSESSING NET WORTH

Net worth should be the yardstick by which you measure your growing wealth. The components of net worth (assets and liabilities) are related to cash flow (income and expenses), as shown here in Exhibit 4–1.

Exhibit 4–1. Cash Flow Model (personal finances)

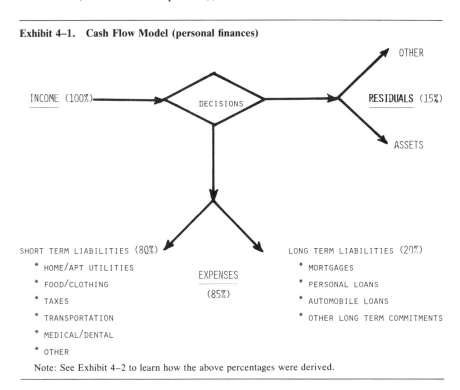

SHORT TERM LIABILITIES (80%)
* HOME/APT UTILITIES
* FOOD/CLOTHING
* TAXES
* TRANSPORTATION
* MEDICAL/DENTAL
* OTHER

EXPENSES
(85%)

LONG TERM LIABILITIES (20%)
* MORTGAGES
* PERSONAL LOANS
* AUTOMOBILE LOANS
* OTHER LONG TERM COMMITMENTS

INCOME (100%) DECISIONS OTHER RESIDUALS (15%) ASSETS

Note: See Exhibit 4–2 to learn how the above percentages were derived.

The obvious problem we face is how to sufficiently reduce expenses to allow cash inflows to stay well ahead of cash outflows and thus increase assets faster than liabilities. If you have no expenses, then your income exactly equals your accumulation of residual cash, and you have 100 percent efficiency. Unfortunately, all of us have expenses, and most of us live at levels of financial efficiency that are far closer to zero than to 100 percent. That does not mean, though, that we are all doomed to live at static levels of wealth. As we discussed earlier, cash flow efficiencies as low as 5 percent can yield handsome gains in net worth. Even at this low rate (assuming a $50,000 annual income), we chalked up investment gains of over a quarter million dollars over 20 years (assuming a 14 percent return on investment). Just imagine what you could do by improving your efficiency from 5 percent to 10 percent. At that rate we would have $5,000 remaining from a $50,000 annual salary instead of $2,500, and after 20 years at 14 percent would be worth well over a half million dollars. The bottom line is that simple expense planning via careful cash flow management can provide outstanding profit rewards.

A PERSONAL CASE STUDY

I tried many times to manually set up a system for analyzing my annual cash flow on paper only to find that it took hours of searching through old records, making up forms, penciling in numbers, and adding up all the columns. My final pencil and paper cash flow picture was actually pretty good, but the problem was finding a way to use it to manage my finances. It wasn't too difficult to update my numbers as I went along, but the recalculations were boring, and eventually I got further and further behind. When I bought my computer, however, I suddenly discovered I had the means to mechanize my cash flow sheet. The computer eliminated the tedious and tiresome work of searching through piles of old records and constantly recalculating my figures. It left me free to do the analysis and decision making.

Getting started wasn't difficult. The first step was to find a program to meet my needs that could be run on my computer. I found that several good products were available and finally chose a program that combined several desirable features—flexible transaction processing, a means of sorting out assets from liabilities by major accounts, and a capacity for net worth reporting and budgeting. I could even graph actual versus budgeted amounts, and search all my accounts for transactions applicable to budgeting or tax planning. This particular program was a newly refined and updated version of one that had been on the market for two years. That meant the manufacturer had included features that had been left out of the earlier version. The thing that really sold me, however, was that the program could be used for a small business as well as for personal finance.

One of the most pleasing parts of my purchase was the price: a program with all these features cost me less than $100.

PERSONAL COMPUTER AIDS

One of the first financial applications of the personal computer was in checkbook balancing. "Why in the world would someone spend so much money to balance a checkbook?" you may ask. The answer is simple. Hobbyists, who were the pioneers in personal computer use, bought computers for experimenting. Later they began to look for practical ways to apply the technology, and the necessary job of checkbook balancing seemed an easy application. In most cases, the hobbyists wrote their own programs since few prewritten ones existed.

Since those days there has been a tremendous evolution from the early programs to today's personal financial systems software. Although checkbook balancing programs are still available, many have been expanded to include a complete financial record keeping system. These pre-packaged financial programs run on most brands of personal computers. At the low end of the price spectrum you can buy one of several computers for about $500, connect it to your TV, add a tape cassette to load the program and store your data, and your total costs are less than $700. Creative Software's Household Financial Package, for instance, priced less than $50, was written for a small system, and has some excellent features. It can be used to do a fairly thorough accounting of family finances. It records, changes, and deletes expense and income items in 15 separate categories, and graphically displays monthly and yearly totals in any or all categories. It also provides a budgeting feature to help you come to grips with your spending, and has another feature that allows you to cull your annual expenses to locate tax deductible items. Creative Software also has supplemental programs to analyze car and loan costs.

If your interest in personal finance ranges to more complex functions, such as detailed analysis of income, expenses, and savings and credit card transactions, then Personal Finance Master from Spectrum Software may meet your needs. This program provides a "user-friendly" environment when analyzing your spending habits by computer. Programs that are user-friendly are those that employ several techniques to make the program easy to use. For example, display screen "menus" require only that you key in a number to select one of the program functions shown on the computer's display screen. The program may also guide you through the steps you must take when, for instance, you are entering data. If you make an error, the program should detect it immediately and allow you to correct it without disrupting your previous program's data.

Personal Finance Master allows you to develop a monthly plan by setting up goals for adding to your savings, as well as taking care of normal expenses and credit transactions. You can then analyze your actual versus planned outlays and create a monthly variance report (see Exhibit 4–2). Detailed records can be kept for any type of liability account, including credit cards, loans and personal notes in seven separate accounts. Sample reports (see Exhibits 4–3 through 4–7) from Personal Finance Master are not only representative of the kinds of things this program can produce but serve as examples of what good financial management reports in general should look like. No matter which program you finally choose you should look for similar formats for your data.

Exhibit 4–2. **Personal Finance Master: Jones for 198x (actual/budget report in dollars for January–March)**

```
          ACTUAL/BUDGET REPORT IN $
            FOR JANUARY-MARCH
```

PURPOSE	TOTAL	BUDGET	VARIANCE
1:DEPOSITS/PAYMENTS	17161.94	18000.00	-838.06
2:SPECIAL	2304.00	2000.00	-304.00
3:FOOD	378.31	450.00	71.69
4:CLOTHING	0.00	50.00	50.00
5:HOUSEHOLD	0.00	150.00	150.00
6:IMPROVEMENTS	75.00	100.00	25.00
7:UTILITIES	627.06	650.00	22.94
8:VISA PAYMENTS	2523.28	2500.00	-23.28
9:MC PAYMENTS	1693.59	1000.00	-693.59
10:MORTGAGE	2556.00	2556.00	0.00
11:GAS	485.66	500.00	14.34
12:AUTO EXPENSE	0.00	150.00	150.00
13:PRESCRIPTIONS	0.00	100.00	100.00
14:SUBSCRIPTIONS	125.00	100.00	-25.00
15:MEDICAL	77.00	200.00	123.00
16:DENTAL	4.00	50.00	46.00
17:SCHOOL	3.50	25.00	21.50
18:ENTERTAINMENT	469.68	250.00	-219.68
19:INSURANCE	811.59	800.00	-11.59
20:MISCELLANEOUS	1274.54	1000.00	-274.54
21:VEHICLE TAXES	0.00	100.00	100.00
22:CULO PAYMENT	0.00	540.00	540.00
23:HIBBS PAYMENT	0.00	300.00	300.00
24:PROPERTY TAXES	30.00	30.00	0.00
25:INVESTMENT	500.00	500.00	0.00
26:BUEX	1399.65	1200.00	-199.65
27:BUIN	0.00	0.00	0.00
28:CASH	100.00	500.00	400.00
29:INTEREST	0.00	0.00	0.00
30:AMXP	0.00	450.00	450.00
TOTAL EXPENSE	15437.86	16251.00	813.14
CASH FLOW	1724.08	1749.00	-24.92

The budget module lets you choose the period—from 1 to 12 months—for your budget analysis. The quarterly budget is a good intermediate period for financial planning.

Courtesy of Spectrum Software

Many programs currently on the market have highly specialized capabilities. Super Checkbook III from Powersoft, Inc., for example, includes an "income statement system" that provides the user with the capacity to generate a general ledger for tracking personal finances. This particular program even offers a check writing capability that allows you to print

Exhibit 4–3. Personal Finance Master (identifications)

NO.	STANDARD NAMES		STANDARD PURPOSES
1	GULF	1	DEPOSITS/PAYMENTS
2	UNIQUE LABEL	2	UNIQUE LABEL
3	AMOCO	3	FOOD
4	TEXACO	4	CLOTHING
5	VISA	5	HOUSEHOLD
6	BANK VIRGINIA	6	IMPROVEMENTS
7	PENNEYS	7	UTILITIES
8	SEARS	8	VISA PAYMENTS
9	CHEMICAL BANK	9	MC PAYMENTS
10	CREDIT UNION	10	MORTGAGE
11	PRUDENTIAL	11	GAS
12	USAA	12	AUTO EXPENSE
13	UNION LIFE	13	PRESCRIPTIONS
14	ATLANTA GAS	14	SUBSCRIPTIONS
15	SOUTHERN BELL	15	MEDICAL
16	GA POWER	16	DENTAL
17	FULTON CTY WATER	17	SCHOOL
18	PARKER SANIT	18	ENTERTAINMENT
19	ORTHODONTIST	19	INSURANCE
20	BROOKFIELD WEST	20	MISCELLANEOUS
21	MCCLAIN	21	VEHICLE TAXES
22	WYNN DIXIE	22	CULO PAYMENT
23	PRIME RESERVE	23	HIBBS PAYMENT
24	MERRILL LYNCH	24	PROPERTY TAXES
25	NEW ERA	25	INVESTMENT
26	DREYFUS #9	26	BUEX
27	GOLCONDA	27	BUIN
28	UNITED SERVICES	28	CASH
29	CONSTELLATION	29	INTEREST
30	IBM	30	AMXP
31	HUME	31	
32	STEIN CAPITAL	32	
33	OMNI	33	
34	PACER	34	
35	VAN	35	
36	BOAT	36	
37	PERSONAL PROPERTY	37	
38	COMPUTER	38	
39	TYPEWRITER	39	
40	CHARNITA	40	
41	SHAWNEE	41	
42	SILVER/GOLD	42	
43	HOUSE	43	
44	RICHWAY	44	
45	PEDIATRICIAN	45	
46	FAMILY DR.	46	
47	BIG STAR	47	
48	KROGER	48	
49	DAIRY	49	
50	AMA	50	
51	MORSEMERE	51	
52	AMEX	52	

The standard names and purposes are used to identify transactions by name and purpose within the seven major accounts.

Courtesy of Spectrum Software

Exhibit 4-4. Personal Finance Master (checking February)

```
*****************************************************************************
*                                                                           *
*                         CHECKING FEBRUARY                                 *
*                      PRIOR BALANCE =   2699.90                            *
*                                                                           *
*****************************************************************************
* T  NBR R  DATE NAME              PURPOSE            AMOUNT   BALANCE *
*****************************************************************************
*    1 *    2/1 GULF               GAS                 73.94   2625.96 *
*    2 *    2/1 AMOCO              GAS                114.08   2511.88 *
*    3 *    2/1 BANK VIRGINIA      VISA PAYMENTS      719.99   1791.89 *
*    4 *    2/1 PARKER SANIT       UTILITIES           53.00   1738.89 *
*    5 *    2/1 FULTON CTY WATER   UTILITIES           64.65   1674.24 *
*    6 *    2/1 MCCLAIN            PROPERTY TAXES      30.00   1644.24 *
*    7 *    2/2 GA POWER           UTILITIES           53.65   1590.59 *
*    8 *                           INSURANCE          120.05   1470.54 *
*        2/24 UNIQUE               MORTGAGA           852.00    618.54 *
*   31 *  2/24 UNIQUE LABEL        INSURANCE          139.00    ⁻9.54 *
*   32 *  2/24 VISA                                                  12⁓
*   33    2/24 UNIQUE LABEL        BU⁓               100.95   1130.05 *
*   34 *  2/24 UNIQUE LABEL        BUEX               349.00    781.05 *
*   43 *  2/26 UNIQUE LABEL        DEPOSITS/PAYMENTS 2001.00   2782.05 *
*   44 *  2/26 UNIQUE LABEL        BUEX               100.00   2682.05 *
*   45 *  2/26 UNIQUE LABEL        BUEX                48.00   2634.05 *
*   46 *  2/26 UNIQUE LABEL        BUEX               120.00   2514.05 *
*   42 *  2/28 IBM                 DEPOSITS/PAYMENTS 1414.11   3928.16 *
*****************************************************************************
*            ENDING BALANCE OF * ITEMS ONLY =   4029.11                     *
*****************************************************************************
*                              LEGEND                                       *
*    T = TAX FLAG   R = RECONCILED(*)     NBR = TRANSACTION NUMBER       *
*****************************************************************************
```

The search module lets you look at transactions for selected periods.

Exhibit 4–5. Personal Finance Master (searching)

```
**********************************************************************
*                                                                    *
*                   SEARCH REPORT FOR JANUARY-MARCH                  *
*                      COVERING THESE ACCOUNTS                       *
*                            CHECKING                                *
**********************************************************************
* T   NBR R   DATE NAME              PURPOSE           AMOUNT  BALANCE *
**********************************************************************
*     10 *   1/6 PRUDENTIAL          INSURANCE         135.21   135.21 *
*     14 *   1/6 USAA                INSURANCE          81.05   216.26 *
*      8 *   2/2 USAA                INSURANCE         120.05   336.31 *
*     10 *   2/2 UNION LIFE          INSURANCE         139.00   475.31 *
*     14 *   2/8 UNION LIFE          INSURANCE          41.00   516.31 *
*     28 *  2/24 USAA                INSURANCE         158.20   674.51 *
*      7 *   3/7 PRUDENTIAL          INSURANCE          15.93   690.44 *
*      9 *   3/7 USAA                INSURANCE         100.55   790.99 *
*     16 *  3/11 PRUDENTIAL          INSURANCE          20.60   811.59 *
**********************************************************************
*                            LEGEND                                  *
*    T = TAX FLAG     R = RECONCILED(*)     NBR = TRANSACTION NUMBER  *
**********************************************************************
*********CURRENT SEARCH KEYS***********
*                 MIN       MAX      *
* STANDARD NAMES    11        13      *
* STANDARD PURPOSES .......NONE........*
* DAY OF THE MONTH  .......NONE........*
* TAX FLAG          .......NONE........*
* TRANSACTION NUMBER.......NONE........*
* TRANSACTION AMOUNT.......NONE........*
**************************************
```

The search module allows you to select unique criteria (up to six), including the time interval. In this search, the criterion was all the insurance payments by check made in the first quarter.

checks and vouchers from text files created by the system. Checkbook balancing has certainly come a long way since the early programs of only five years ago.

Systems offered by two other vendors illustrate the wide range of functions and prices available in personal financial software. Murnane and Associates sells its Personal Savings Planning (PSP) series to users of TRS-80 computers, while Howard Software Services offers Creative Fi-

---

Exhibit 4–6. Personal Finance Master (major accounts)

```
            INITIAL BALANCES
      JONES        --198
ACCOUNT NAME       TYPE         BALANCE
1*CHECKING         ASSET          470.00
2*MONEY MARKET     ASSET         2323.00
3*MIXED ASSET      ASSET       181100.00
4*STOCKS/FUNDS     ASSET        17259.00
5*CREDIT CARD      LIABILITY     1019.00
6*LOANS            LIABILITY    71990.00
7*MIXED            LIABILITY    14817.00
-----------------------------------------

INITIAL NET WORTH =            113326.00
```

These are the seven major accounts used within PFM. They give you a starting point for tracking your net worth.

Exhibit 4–7. PFM (ending reports)

```
   NET WORTH REPORT FOR  JONES    --198
                 MARCH
ASSETS
      CHECKING                   2194.08
      MONEY MARKET              59251.85
      MIXED ASSET              195250.00
      STOCKS/FUNDS              18328.00
      -------------------------------

      TOTAL ASSETS             275023.93

LIABILITIES
      CREDIT CARD                1579.75
      LOANS                     68513.01
      MIXED                         0.00
      -------------------------------

      TOTAL LIABILITIES         70092.76

NET WORTH                      204931.17
```

The PFM system looks up the ending balance of all currently defined accounts, sorts them into asset and liability categories, and prepares a report.

Courtesy of Spectrum Software

---

nancing to users of Apple II computers and IBM PCs. PSP I is designed to help you identify realistic financial objectives and to develop savings plans to achieve those objectives. It has modules to handle major purchases, retirement planning, and college expenses. PSP II helps you analyze your life insurance needs by evaluating your existing policies and analyzing alternatives to maximize benefits and minimize costs. PSP III shows you how to develop amortization schedules and calculate payment amounts for loans of any size. All three PSP programs sell for less than $15.

Creative Financing is a comprehensive program for solving complex loan and investment evaluations. At a cost of around $150 it is considerably more expensive than the PSP programs, but its capabilities, in my opinion, justify the price. It allows users to compare different kinds of loans and investments by computing compound annual interest, internal rate of return, and the net present value of an investment. Among the many useful products of this program are:

Computations that project your monthly interest and principal payments for various loan packages.

Annual depreciation schedule calculations.

Calculations that project the yields that could be realized by selling an asset.

In addition, Creative Financing offers an excellent set of business arithmetic functions for calculations that are beyond the capability of a small calculator.

Programs like Creative Financing are useful for all types of everyday arithmetic no matter what you are investing in. They provide a powerful scratch-pad capability that is especially useful if you invest with borrowed money. These are powerful but relatively inexpensive personal financial management tools, and the discipline they impose on you should yield significant improvements in your financial position. That translates into more efficient management and fewer dollars "falling through the cracks." A good starting point would be to contact various software vendors and get their literature. After reviewing the literature and seeing the programs demonstrated, you can decide which program best meets your needs.

ELECTRONIC SPREADSHEETS

As seen previously, electronic worksheets have numerous applications in financial work. No matter which one you select, it can be easily adapted for personal financial management.

Developing an annual cash flow model, for example, is quite simple. The columns are labeled with the months while the rows list specific elements of income and expenses (see Exhibit 4–8). The particular items in your budget can either be included among the broader expense elements, which they fall under, or entered in separate budget file. Either way, data changes can be quickly analyzed. For example, there have been several changes in tax laws that will reduce personal withholding rates over the next several years. If you want to understand the impact of these reductions on your cash flow, you can estimate your income and expenses for

Exhibit 4–8. Personal Cash Flow Statement

MONTHS:	JAN	FEB	MARCH	APRIL	MAY	JUNE	JULY	AUGUST	SEPT	OCT	NOV	DEC	TOTAL
OPEN BALAN	352.00	-45.75	-410.50	-546.25	1581.00	1151.25	1313.50	-132.25	-628.00	-1205.50	1178.75	1407.00	
SALARY	4250.00	4250.00	4250.00	4250.00	4250.00	4250.00	4250.00	4250.00	4250.00	4675.00	4675.00	4975.00	52575.00
DIVIDENDS	0.00	0.00	235.00	0.00	0.00	235.00	0.00	0.00	235.00	0.00	0.00	235.00	940.00
INTEREST	75.00	0.00	0.00	75.00	0.00	0.00	75.00	0.00	0.00	75.00	0.00	0.00	300.00
CAPITAL GA	0.00	0.00	300.00	500.00	0.00	345.00	-575.00	0.00	1275.00	155.00	0.00	335.00	2335.00
OTHER	450.00	0.00	0.00	2500.00	400.00	225.00	0.00	0.00	400.00	2650.00	475.00	0.00	7100.00
TOTAL CASH	5127.00	4204.25	4374.50	6778.75	6231.00	6206.25	5063.50	4117.75	5532.00	6349.50	6328.75	6952.00	67265.25
FOOD	450.00	450.00	450.00	450.00	450.00	450.00	450.00	450.00	450.00	450.00	450.00	450.00	5400.00
CLOTHING	47.50	55.00	12.00	250.00	0.00	45.00	65.00	0.00	50.00	175.00	0.00	25.00	724.50
MORTGAGE	715.00	715.00	715.00	715.00	715.00	715.00	715.00	715.00	715.00	715.00	715.00	715.00	8580.00
UTILITIES	180.00	180.00	180.00	180.00	180.00	180.00	180.00	180.00	180.00	180.00	195.00	195.00	2190.00
MAINTENANC	90.00	0.00	0.00	75.00	225.00	65.00	0.00	0.00	45.00	175.00	0.00	25.00	700.00
HOME FURNI	0.00	0.00	0.00	150.00	44.00	0.00	0.00	0.00	255.00	0.00	0.00	65.00	514.00
CAR EXPENS	75.50	40.00	125.00	45.00	180.00	45.00	225.00	45.00	30.00	127.00	40.00	40.00	1017.50
BOAT EXPEN	0.00	0.00	0.00	0.00	75.00	45.00	75.00	100.00	25.00	0.00	150.00	0.00	470.00
CHARITY	40.00	40.00	40.00	40.00	40.00	40.00	40.00	40.00	40.00	40.00	40.00	40.00	480.00
GIFTS	0.00	10.00	15.00	0.00	25.00	0.00	130.00	45.00	0.00	0.00	135.00	250.00	610.00
RECREATION	64.00	64.00	64.00	64.00	64.00	64.00	64.00	64.00	64.00	64.00	64.00	64.00	768.00
SUBSCRIPTI	8.00	0.00	0.00	27.00	32.00	0.00	8.00	0.00	53.00	95.00	0.00	34.00	257.00
TOTAL LIVI	1670.00	1554.00	1601.00	1996.00	2030.00	1649.00	1952.00	1639.00	1907.00	2021.00	1789.00	1903.00	21711.00
LIFE INSUR	184.00	75.00	125.00	64.00	40.00	105.00	184.00	75.00	125.00	64.00	40.00	105.00	1186.00
HOME INSUR	27.00	27.00	27.00	27.00	27.00	27.00	27.00	27.00	27.00	27.00	27.00	27.00	324.00
CAR INSURA	62.00	62.00	62.00	62.00	62.00	62.00	62.00	62.00	62.00	62.00	62.00	62.00	744.00
BOAT INSUR	0.00	0.00	0.00	130.00	0.00	0.00	0.00	0.00	0.00	0.00	0.00	0.00	130.00
MISC INSUR	0.00	0.00	0.00	0.00	0.00	0.00	0.00	0.00	0.00	0.00	40.00	0.00	40.00
TOTAL INSU	273.00	164.00	214.00	283.00	129.00	194.00	273.00	164.00	214.00	153.00	169.00	153.00	2230.00

MEDICAL EX	90.00	0.00	35.00	45.00	32.00	0.00	0.00	0.00	0.00	0.00	0.00	75.00	277.00
DENTAL EXP	156.00	0.00	75.00	0.00	0.00	50.00	60.00	0.00	35.00	80.00	0.00	0.00	456.00
ORTHODONTI	60.00	60.00	60.00	60.00	60.00	60.00	60.00	60.00	60.00	60.00	60.00	60.00	720.00
EYE CARE	35.00	0.00	0.00	0.00	0.00	0.00	0.00	0.00	0.00	0.00	0.00	0.00	35.00
OTHER HEAL	0.00	10.00	10.00	10.00	10.00	10.00	10.00	10.00	10.00	10.00	10.00	10.00	110.00
TOT HEALTH	341.00	60.00	170.00	105.00	92.00	110.00	120.00	60.00	95.00	140.00	60.00	0.00	1353.00
SPECIAL TR	0.00	0.00	0.00	0.00	0.00	0.00	0.00	0.00	1950.00	0.00	0.00	0.00	1950.00
INVESTMENT	300.00	300.00	300.00	300.00	300.00	300.00	300.00	300.00	300.00	300.00	400.00	400.00	3800.00
LOAN PAYME	185.00	185.00	185.00	185.00	185.00	185.00	185.00	185.00	185.00	185.00	185.00	185.00	2220.00
MISC FINAN	0.00	0.00	0.00	0.00	0.00	0.00	0.00	0.00	0.00	0.00	0.00	0.00	0.00
TOTAL FINA	485.00	485.00	485.00	485.00	485.00	485.00	485.00	485.00	2435.00	485.00	585.00	0.00	7385.00
FED INCOME	1700.00	1700.00	1700.00	1700.00	1700.00	1700.00	1700.00	1700.00	1700.00	1870.00	1870.00	1990.00	21030.00
STATE INC	212.50	212.50	212.50	212.50	212.50	212.50	212.50	212.50	212.50	233.75	233.75	223.75	2603.75
FICA	276.25	276.25	276.25	276.25	276.25	276.25	276.25	276.25	0.00	0.00	0.00	0.00	2210.00
PROPERTY T	120.00	120.00	120.00	120.00	120.00	120.00	120.00	120.00	120.00	120.00	120.00	120.00	1440.00
PERSO PROP	20.00	20.00	20.00	20.00	20.00	20.00	20.00	20.00	20.00	20.00	20.00	20.00	240.00
SALES TAX	75.00	23.00	12.00	0.00	15.00	126.00	37.00	69.00	34.00	128.00	75.00	230.00	824.00
MISCELL. T	0.00	0.00	110.00	0.00	0.00	0.00	0.00	0.00	0.00	0.00	0.00	0.00	110.00
TOTAL TAX	2403.75	2351.75	2450.75	2328.75	2343.75	2454.75	2365.75	2397.75	2086.50	2371.75	2318.75	2583.75	28457.75
BUSINESS E	0.00	400.00	0.00	2500.00	225.00	0.00	400.00	0.00	275.00	0.00	2900.00	400.00	7100.00
COMPUTER C	2400.00	275.00	350.00	654.00	125.00	85.00	50.00	0.00	0.00	210.00	375.00	0.00	4524.00
OTHER	0.00	0.00	0.00	0.00	0.00	0.00	0.00	0.00	0.00	0.00	0.00	0.00	0.00
TOTAL USES	5172.75	4614.75	4920.75	5197.75	5079.75	4892.75	5195.75	4745.75	6737.50	5170.75	4921.75	4486.75	61136.75
													0.00
RESIDUAL	-45.75	-410.50	-546.25	1581.00	1151.25	1313.50	-132.25	-628.00	-1205.50	1178.75	1407.00	2465.25	6128.50

the next several years and then, by making the appropriate adjustments in your withholding rate, recalculate your estimate to observe the effect these changes will have on your bottom line.

Once you have a computer model of your cash flow, updating it is simple. Entering new data and recalculating the model takes only a few seconds. Consequently, in a very short time you can run through many what-if scenarios. If you are planning a major purchase like a car, an appliance, or a house, you can quickly estimate the impact the purchase would have on your cash flow. You may also want to use your computer to test the effects of alternatives to an outright purchase, such as buying on a time payment plan or leasing. Using your computer, you may also find that shifting expense elements within your model may help make room for the purchase. Whatever your decision is, you will know in advance if you can afford the item or not—and under what terms the purchase would best fit your needs and financial resources.

FINANCIAL FORECASTING

To meet your investment goals it is important to be able to forecast your personal financial expectations. Simply knowing how much cash you can get your hands on when you need it can give you an edge over many other investors by enabling you to respond more quickly to changing market conditions. Careful, computerized planning can give you a clear vision of your finances extending far into the future.

It can also help you set up the mechanism to make your financial dreams come true. Suppose, for instance, your plan calls for placing a fixed amount of money each month (dollar averaging) in long-term equity and money funds, and periodically engaging in speculative trading in volatile high-technology stocks. Part one of your plan requires a consistent monthly addition to a pool of money invested in long-term securities while part two requires a random commitment of varying amounts. Clearly you need two entirely different mechanisms to manage your portfolio.

With your computer this is a relatively easy task. Once you have established your cash flow model, you should split your residual, or "saved," funds into two segments. The first will flow directly into purchases of blue-chip stocks and mutual funds, and the second into a special holding fund. This second fund will support your future speculative trading, assuming that you are not always in the market and are spending considerable time poised on the sidelines awaiting the right opportunities. Your speculative fund may be kept in a money fund for quick accessibility. The management of this fund is similar to the cash management accounts available through several brokerage houses. The differences, however, are significant in two ways: you control your money and there is no minimum amount required to establish your fund. This independence from a broker-age house is made possible by your personal computer. You exercise control over the entire financial process from the amount you invest to the use you make of your portfolio earnings.

The next chapters focus on specific computer-aided investments. You may not want to read each chapter, so select the ones that apply to your investment goals. Once you have read the discussions that interest you, read Chapters 9, 10, and 14, which tie the computer-aided investment systems together into a common structure.

APPENDIX

Resource List

Product	Resource	Computer
Household Financial Package	Creative Software 201 San Antonio Circle, #270 Mountain View, CA 94040	VIC-20™[1] TRS-80 PET®[2]
Personal Finance Master	Spectrum Software 142 Carlow P.O. Box 2084 Sunnyvale, CA 94087	Apple II+ IBM Personal Computer
Super Checkbook III	Powersoft, Inc. P.O. Box 157 Pitman, NJ 08071	Apple II+
Creative Financing	Howard Software Services 8008 Girard Avenue Suite 310 La Jolla, CA 92037	Apple II+, IIe/III IBM Personal Computer
Chequemate	Masterworks Software 1823 W. Lomita Blvd. Lomite, CA 90266	Apple II+
Checkbook Balancing	Secure Software Systems, Ltd. P.O. Box 2352 Huntsville, AL 35804	TRS-80

[1] VIC-20 is a trademark of Commodore Business Machines.
[2] PET is a registered trademark of Commodore Business Machines.

Product	*Resource*	*Computer*
Disk-O-Check	High Technology Software Products, Inc. P.O. Box 14665 Oklahoma City, OK 73113	Apple II+
Home Accounting System	SiCom Software Systems P.O. Box 888061 Dunwoody, GA 30076	TRS-80 I
Microhome	Compumax P.O. Box 1139 Palo Alto, CA 94301	Atari
Personal Finance and Record-Keeping	Atari 1265 Borregas P.O. Box 427 Sunnyvale, CA 94086	Atari

Information Utilities

Speakers at investment seminars are often asked, "How can I find the information I need to make really good investment decisions?" The most frequent answer up to now has been such familiar sources as *The Wall Street Journal, Barron's,* brokerage house research newsletters, investment advisory services, and so on. The Public Broadcasting System's "Wall $treet Week" and regional telecasts on local financial matters also are frequently mentioned.

Lately though, investment advisors are also recommending the information services accessible by personal computers or by timesharing terminals. These services include Dow Jones News/Retrieval®, the SOURCE, and CompuServe among many. Their purpose is simple: to provide a resource for locating the kind of information that is necessary to business and personal decision making. And best of all is their extraordinary convenience. Through a telephone hookup all the information you need can be routed directly into your computer.

It is virtually impossible for any of us to sift through, much less read and absorb, all of the financial data available these days. Subscribing to an information service, though, gives you a new way to obtain and quickly sort the data that is pertinent only to your needs. For example, suppose you wanted some recent price/volume and five-year performance data on a particular set of stocks. Done in the traditional way such research could cost you many hours of research time, and most investors don't have the time or the desire to do that much work. An easier way would be to talk to your broker and get his company's suggestions on which stocks look attractive.

For the independent-minded investor, however, there is nothing quite like finding your own winners in the stock market, and—best of all—getting to those stocks before anybody else does. For this, you either need a lot of time to manually sift through all the information available or you need a computerized information retrieval service—so pay close attention to the forthcoming section.

ELECTRONIC LIBRARIES

Information services are basically electronic libraries. You buy your "library card"—your annual subscription to the given service—for an average price of $50. Beyond that, use of the library is on a pay-as-you-go basis. Individuals who don't plan to use the service every day may elect to pay for the service by the minute, as opposed to the typical business user, who will generally pay for the service on an hourly rate to get the best price break. One expense you don't have to worry about is your phone bill. Calls to the service are local, thereby eliminating long-distance rates. The information services use large communications networks that have a series of local outlets, and your telephone call is automatically routed to the nearest network access point.

Data retrieval through these services is easy. You decide which information service you want to use, tell your computer, and it automatically dials the service's phone number and connects you. A simple menu is then displayed on your screen that permits you to quickly select the kinds of financial data you want.

The electronic library is not, however, the entire answer to your information needs. More traditional information sources—business magazines, newspapers, and trade journals—are not to be completely overlooked since they can provide valuable assistance by pointing you in the right general direction. They then give you a clearer idea of the information upon which you want to focus. This minimizes wasted search time and unnecessary retrieval service charges.

The chief usefulness of an information service is that it provides current data on the economic conditions underlying market trends, on the industries that are faring well in the current climate, and on specific stocks that look good. Selectively retrieved financial and market data can alert you to fast-breaking opportunities. Whether you are a professional trader or a private investor, knowing your market indicators and keeping abreast of the signals they are sending will be important when trying to time your trends for maximum profits. Putting this information together, making your preliminary choices, and then discussing them with your broker could lead to some well-informed, highly profitable trades.

THE INFORMATION REVOLUTION

In the United States, private information services have mushroomed in recent years into multi-million dollar operations. Similar growth has taken place overseas, where public information networks have been started in several countries. In many ways, these foreign public information networks are more advanced than those in the United States.

Prestel, the experiment by the British postal service, is an early public information service. For the international investor, Prestel offers business data, commodities information, and shipping schedules (just a few of its services). American users can obtain access to it over Telenet, using an Apple II computer with special software called Appletel, marketed by British Telcom's U.S. marketing arm. Other foreign networks include those in Germany, Canada, and France. Japan is also reported to be working on an advanced public network.

In this country, the generic name for our proposed public information network is "videotex." Several computer hardware vendors offer video terminals for access to videotex information services. For instance, Tandy Corporation, through its Radio Shack stores, offers videotex programs for its TRS-80 microcomputer line as well as for Apple computers. Videotex software is likely to be offered for more personal computers in the next couple of years.

Studies by Payment Systems, Inc., of Atlanta point out that financial planning and budgeting activities have become increasingly important to consumers. According to PSI, it is logical to suppose that the automated system of buying and selling securities that brokers currently use will ultimately be extended to the home, allowing ready access to information that will help individuals make their financial decisions. Financial service companies are under increasing pressure to provide computerized information directly to their customers if they don't want to lose their business to a company that will benefit from this competition and from the expanded information services that it engenders.

DOW JONES NEWS/RETRIEVAL® SERVICE

The Dow Jones News/Retrieval® (DJN/R) service is one of the most widely used sources of online financial data. Obviously, as publishers of *The Wall Street Journal* and of *Barron's,* Dow Jones has access to the financial news in either newspaper, and this information is available via your personal computer. Free Text Search has articles back to mid-1979 and is a feature that is especially beneficial if you are researching a particular company and want to develop a profile of its recent activities. Dow Jones News (another data base) carries 90 days of material by company or news category symbols. Both national and international news stories of significance for the investor are carried. Further, focusing on several companies is also made easy. Extracts of the highly informative 10K reports that corporations file annually with the Securities and Exchange Commission (SEC) and price/volume trends for one or more companies can be quickly retrieved and stored on your personal file of computer disks, allowing you to view it on the display or to have it printed at your convenience.

Exhibits 5–1 through 5–3 show a logical sequence of retrievals from the DJN/R). The objective is to gather fundamental financial data on two companies in the telecommunications industry. The analysis of the industry was done on an IBM Personal Computer linked to the DJN/R computers. The program supporting this exercise was the IBM Dow Jones Reporter.

Several years ago, a joint effort between Dow Jones and Apple Com-

---

Exhibit 5–1.   Sample Data Retrieval from Dow Jones News/Retrieval® (Disclosure II data base)

```
DISCLOSURE CO NO:    G669800000
COMPANY NAME:        GRAPHIC SCANNING CORP
CROSS REFERENCE:     NA
ADDRESS: 329 ALFRED AVENUE
TEANECK
NJ
07666
TELEPHONE: 201-837-5100
INCORPORATION: DE
EXCHANGE: OTH
TICKER SYMBOL: GSCC
FORTUNE NUMBER: NA
CUSIP NUMBER: 0003886868
D-U-N-S NO: 05-522-9777
SIC CODES: 4811 4821 3662
PRIMARY SIC CODE: 4811
DESCRIPTION OF BUSINESS:
A TELECOMMUNICATIONS SERVICE COMPANY, ENGAGED IN PROVIDING A WIDE
VARIETY OF SPECIALIZED DATA AND MESSAGE PROCESSING AND COMMUNICATIONS
SERVICES.
CURRENT OUTSTANDING SHARES:     16,983,752 (SOURCE: 10-Q        10/31/82)
SHARES HELD BY OFF & DIR:                NA
SHAREHOLDERS:                       5,600
EMPLOYEES:                          1,830


FISCAL YEAR END: 06/30
AUDITOR CHANGE: NA
AUDITOR: TOUCHE ROSS & CO.
AUDITOR'S REPORT: UNQUALIFIED
```

Exhibit 5–2. Sample Data Retrieval from Dow Jones News/Retrieval® (Media General provides fundamental corporate data)

```
INTERNATL BUSINESS MACH
-FUNDMNTL DATA- 01/28/83     (170)
REVENUE           (1)
-LAST 12 MOS $34,364 MIL
-LAST FISCAL YEAR $29,070 MIL
-PCT CHANGE LAST QTR 23.1%
-PCT CHANGE YR TO DATE 18.2%
EARNGS 12MOS $4,409.0F MIL
EARNINGS PER SHARE
-LAST 12 MONTHS $7.39
-LAST FISCAL YEAR $7.39
-PCT CHANGE LAST QTR 20.9%
-PCT CHANGE FY TO DATE 20.4%
-PCT CHANGE LAST 12MOS 20.4%
-FIVE YR GROWTH RATE 9.0%


DIVIDENDS         (2)
-CURRENT RATE $3.44
-CURRENT RATE YIELD 3.5%
-5 YR GROWTH RATE 9.7%
-PAYOUT LAST FY 47%
-PAYOUT LAST 5 YEARS 55%
-LAST X-DVD DATE 11-04-82
RATIOS
-PROFIT MARGIN 12.8%
-RETURN ON COMMON EQUITY 21.5%
-RETURN ON TOTAL ASSETS 14.9%
-REVENUE TO ASSETS 116%
-DEBT TO EQUITY 15%
-INTEREST COVERAGE 15.7
-CURRENT RATIO 1.4


SHAREHOLDINGS     (3)
-MARKET VALUE $58,130 MIL
-LTST SHR OUTSTND 596,970,000
-INSIDER NET TRADING 19,000
-SHORT INTEREST RATIO 2.0 DYS
-FISCAL YEAR ENDS 12 MOS
```

puter, Inc. produced two programs designed specifically for retrieving financial news and stock quotes and for updating records of a stock portfolio's performance. These two programs are the Apple Dow Jones News/ Quotes Reporter and the Apple Dow Jones Portfolio Evaluator. The News/Quotes Reporter program allows users of Apple II computers to use the Dow Jones News/Retrieval® service and provides news in 80 separate categories on over 6,000 companies grouped into 50 industries. The headlines of *The Wall Street Journal* and of *Barron's* can be searched

---

Exhibit 5–3. Sample Data Retrieval from Dow Jones News/Retrieval® (the Corporate Earnings Estimator provides financial data for fundamental stock analysis)

```
CORPORATE EARNINGS ESTIMATOR
ZACKS INVESTMENT RESEARCH INC.
          CHICAGO, ILL.
THIS WEEKLY DATABASE PROVIDES
CONSENSUS FORECASTS OF EARNINGS
PER SHARE FOR 2,400 COMPANIES
BASED ON ESTIMATES PROVIDED BY
1,000 RESEARCH ANALYSTS AT MORE
THAN 50 MAJOR BROKERAGE FIRMS
FOR CONSISTENCY, ESTIMATES ARE
CONVERTED TO PRIMARY EARNINGS
BEFORE EXTRAORDINARY ITEMS.
------------------------------
PLEASE ENTER DESIRED STOCK
SYMBOL AND PRESS RETURN

AMERICAN TEL&TE
--FISCAL YEAR ENDS   12/83

EARNINGS PER SHARE ESTIMATES
--MEAN      9.17
--HIGH     10.20
--LOW       8.10
NUMBER OF ANALYSTS   21
P/E RATIO (ESTIMATED EPS)    7.63
PAST EARN PR SH ESTIMATES (MEAN)
--WEEK AGO      9.17
--13 WEEKS AGO     9.49
--26 WEEKS AGO     9.64
------------------------------
PRESS RETURN FOR NEXT PAGE

AMERICAN TEL&TE
--FISCAL YEAR ENDS   12/84

EARNINGS PER SHARE ESTIMATES
--MEAN      9.95
--HIGH     10.10
--LOW       9.80
NUMBER OF ANALYSTS    2
P/E RATIO (ESTIMATED EPS)    7.04
PAST EARN PR SH ESTIMATES (MEAN)
--WEEK AGO      9.95
--13 WEEKS AGO     N/A
--26 WEEKS AGO     N/A
```

---

for stories as old as 90 days. Transcripts from Public Broadcasting's "Wall $treet Week" are also available through the DJN/R using the News/Quotes Reporter.

The purpose of the Portfolio Evaluator is to update your records on your portfolio with information from the current and historical data bases contained in the DJN/R service. With it you can have your complete stock portfolio repriced at the end of the trading day in a matter of seconds.

THE SOURCE

The SOURCE is a service of Source Telecomputing Corporation, a subsidiary of The Reader's Digest Association, Inc., that began operations in 1979. It was originally designed for users of home computers and for people in small businesses. By dialing a local access number, the user gains access to many different computerized pools of information, including all the resources of United Press International. The UPI network can provide up-to-the-second international, national, and local news. If you are interested in the oil industry, for instance, you simply type into the system "UPI N G OIL AND OPEC." This system will then give you every news item containing those words every day or hour, as they are being reported. If commodities trading interests you, type "UPI N G SOYBEANS." The system might respond with eight national stories containing the word "soybean." You can then either read backward or forward to find the specific data you want.

Unistox, another offering of the SOURCE, gives you timely information on stocks, precious metals futures, and foreign currency exchanges. Reports may be requested on all these areas or on just one or two. You may also create your own portfolio and keep it on the disk storage files at the SOURCE. In-depth articles from the Raylux Financial Services also are available. These articles include financial forecasts, investment improvement ideas, and other business and financial information. A typical Unistox report is shown below in Exhibit 5–4.

Exhibit 5–4. Sample Unistox Retrieval

```
            LUMBER FUTURES
            Chicago (UPI)-Lumber futures closing range
            of prices Tuesday.

LUMBER:
Mercex - 100,000 bd ft; 1 per 1000 bd ft

        ###Open      #High       *Low      *Close     *Prev.
May        188.50     188.80     185.30     186.10     190.30
Jly        200.00     201.90     197.60     201.30     202.60
Sep        202.00     204.40     200.80     203.20     204.00
Nov        201.00     201.80     198.80     201.50     201.80
Jan        209.40     209.40     207.00     208.50     209.40
Mar        219.00     219.30     217.00     218.60A    219.40

Open interest: 8,677 off 34. Total volume: 2,928 contracts.
A-Ask.
```

An interesting feature of the SOURCE is the preprogrammed financial routines that are provided for the investor. You type in the data and the programs do the rest. These services include calculation of annuities, present value of cash flows, and loan amortization. (Exhibit 5–5 is an example of a loan amortization.)

Exhibit 5–5. Sample SOURCE Financial Routine

INPUT: R LAMORT

Response: ENTER INTERVAL OF
PRINTOUT DESIRED. I.E., (1) FOR
EVERY MONTH, (6) FOR EVERY SIX
MONTHS, (12) FOR EVERY YEAR.

INPUT: 12

RESPONSE: ENTER PRINCIPAL AMOUNT
IN DOLLARS AND CENTS, INTEREST
RATE IN PERCENT, AND TERM IN YEARS.

EXAMPLE FORMAT (3000,6.5,25)

INPUT: 8000, 14.5,3

Response: PRINCIPAL = $8000
   RATE = 14.5 PERCENT
    PER YEAR
   TERM = 3 YEARS
   MONTHLY PAYMENT
   (PRINCIPAL AND INT-
   EREST) = $275.37

PYMT. NO.	PRIN. PYMT.	INT. PYMT.	TOT. INT.	NEW BAL.
12	203.94	71.43	1011.59	5705.15
24	235.56	39.81	1667.71	3058.83

LAST PAYMENT = $275.29

36	272.00	3.29	1913.24	.00

TOTAL PRINCIPAL
PAYMENTS = $8000.00
TOTAL INTEREST
PAYMENTS = $1913.24
TOTAL PAID = $9913.24

COMPUSERVE

Through the CompuServe's MicroQuote system, users have instant access to up-to-date trading statistics and descriptive information on more than 32,000 stocks, bonds, and options traded on the national exchanges and over-the-counter markets. The system provides such essential details as volumes, dividends, earnings per share, ratings, and total shares outstanding. For those interested in the commodities market, the Micro-Quote system provides information on current prices and news developments affecting commodities. The system also provides users with a general commentary on energy, metals, and agriculture commodities.

In the personal finance arena, CompuServe offers personal money management information for mortgage loans, compound interest calculations, depreciation analysis, and compound growth rates. These facilities are similar to those available through the SOURCE.

These brief descriptions of Dow Jones News/Retrieval®, the SOURCE, and CompuServe should give you a better feeling for the type of data to which you have access via the information services. All provide a broad range of data bases that cover general interest as well as financial topics.

Choosing between the competing services is difficult since one may have information and services that the others don't. The solution to the dilemma can be simple—don't make a choice. Instead, sign up for all the services and any others that provide the data you need. The use of these services is relatively inexpensive once you have the communications equipment on your computer. After paying a small initiation fee, all you have to do is dial the service that has the information you need.

TICKERTEC®

If you need financial and stock market data as soon as it becomes available, you should consider Tickertec®, which puts the familiar stock market tickertape into your home by way of your personal computer. Max Ule & Company has made Tickertec® available for a number of personal computers. The system is unique because it provides up-to-the-minute stock market prices via computer displays. A continuous flow of price and share volume information is received from the low-speed tickertape of the New York and American Stock Exchanges and instantly flashed on the bottom three lines of your computer's display screen (see Exhibit 5–6). The information is reported the same instant it is being displayed on the floors of the exchanges.

With Tickertec® you can monitor the last traded price and total volume of up to 48 specific stocks contained in the basic system. These stocks can be traded in either of two separate lists. Your indicator stocks and your indicators and speculative plays may be kept separate from your main portfolio holdings for monitoring purposes. Simple keyboard commands are all that are needed to recall or change securities in either list. For control purposes, upper and lower limits may be set on each of the securities you have listed to produce a visual indication on the screen when the prices are reached or exceeded.

Exhibit 5–6. Tickertec®

Courtesy of Max Ule & Company, Inc.

Tickertec® is complemented by several related programs. These include:

1. A database retriever to allow users access to the Tickertec data stored on the service's diskette after the market closes.
2. A hard-copy option for printing the entire tickertape or selected stocks on your printer.
3. A portfolio management system that lets you sum up and evaluate your portfolio's performance after the close of the trading day.
4. Stock Market Pulse, which lets you update frequently, and displays the Dow Jones Industrial Average.

What is important about Tickertec® is not only its many individual features but the integrated capabilities it provides. First, it gives you "real-time" data without a 15-minute trading delay. Second, it allows you to retrieve data from the trading day's activities. Third, it automatically updates your portfolio. Each day you know exactly where your holdings stand, and you can plan your next day's trading program accordingly.

NATIONAL MARKET SYSTEM

The ultimate trading system will be a computerized national market system. An extension of brokerage services directly into the home may someday include the capacity to make trades using a personal computer's linkage to a national market system. At the outset this system would probably provide just information and quotes. Eventually, however, it could allow investors to execute buy/sell transactions directly from the home computer's keyboard.

The drive for a national market system is being encouraged by the United States Congress, which in 1975 pressed the Securities and Exchange Commission to develop a computer-based electronic communication system among all the markets. The objective was to integrate the exchanges and the over-the-counter (OTC) market and so-called fourth market (its investors trade securities with each other directly, without a brokerage firm) to facilitate the flow of information and orders and create a more efficient market.

The NYSE and AMEX trade in traditional fashion, with all transactions taking place on the exchange floors. Although brokerage house backoffices are automated, relatively little has been done to computerize the trading floor. Since 1971 the OTC market has used a computer-based system called NASDAQ (National Association of Securities Dealers Automated Quotations) that connects hundreds of broker-dealer firms into one integrated market. NASDAQ has been a great success. In 1981, for instance, its share volume grew 17 percent compared to the NYSE's 5 percent growth and AMEX's 17 percent decline.

In the computerized fourth market, trading goes on without brokers or dealers through a computerized system, Instinet. Institutional investors communicate with the fourth market through their computers and trades take place instantly.

Some believe that a national market system could eventually mean one vast computer-controlled marketplace—consisting of the NYSE, AMEX, OTC, and fourth market—with open books for investors' orders. Investors could ask for information on who is buying and selling specific stocks and at what price, and based on that information execute their trade. That would be going a big step beyond just requesting information from an information service, but in terms of available technology it is not at all a difficult step.

The efficiencies of such an integrated system would be outstanding. Lower cost, faster, and possibly better trades could result, and the quality of investing improved overall. These benefits will accrue to those who invest in a personal computer and gain experience in its use. When the bell rings for the national market system, they will be at the door waiting.

COMMUNICATING

Several specialized computer components are needed to communicate with the information services. These components connect the computer to the telephone line. Earlier, we talked about a modem and a communications attachment for the computer. A third device is a line coupler, which senses the dial tone, dials numbers, answers, and hangs up the phone. An alternative type of coupling device is an acoustic coupler, on which the telephone receiver is placed, in contrast to the line coupler that plugs into the phone jack on your wall. The differences between the two couplers are ones of price, ease of operation, and, sometimes, reliability. Choosing between them is usually dependent on the information source with which you want to communicate.

Your computer vendors can give you details on the specific brand of communications equipment that will best suit your needs. Often they can demonstrate the procedures needed to gain access to the information service while giving you a sampling of the data you can retrieve. Once you buy the requisite hardware you will have to pay an initial charge for using the information utility. The remaining hourly charges—which range from as low as $0.10 per minute in nonprime time (usually 6:00 P.M. to 6:00 A.M.) to $1.50 per minute in prime time depending upon the type of service used—are based on your individual usage.

NEXT UP—TAMING THE STOCK MARKET

Personal computers have become very popular in the complex world of stock evaluation and selection because they are excellent tools for manipulating numbers and comparing many variables. There are several fine software offerings to aid you in choosing your winners and to help you keep track of your portfolio's performance. In the next chapter, we will look at this software as tools for taming the stock market with your computer.

APPENDIX

Bibliography

James, David. "Coming On-Line With the World." *Personal Computing,* April 1982, pp. 36–42, 155.
"Home Terminal Services." Payment Systems, Inc., Atlanta, 1980.
Lee, Susan. "The Battle for a National Market System." *The Wall Street Journal,* June 1, 1982, editorial page.
"Window on the World: The Home Information Revolution." *Business Week,* June 29, 1981, pp. 73–84.
Glossbrenner, Alfred. *The Complete Handbook of Personal Computer Communications.* New York: St. Martin's Press, 1983.

Resource List

Product	*Resource*	*Computer*
	Dow Jones & Company, Inc. P.O. Box 300 Princeton, NJ 08540	*
	The Source Telecomputing Corp. 1616 Anderson Road McLean, VA 22102	*
	CompuServe, Inc. 5000 Arlington Centre Blvd. Columbus, OH 43220	*
	The New York Times Information Service, Inc. Mount Pleasant Office Park 1719-A Route 10 Parsippany, NJ 07054	*
	Data Resources, Inc. 29 Hartwell Avenue Lexington, MA 02173	*
	Dialog Information Services, Inc. 3460 Hillview Avenue Palo Alto, CA 94304	*
Apple/Dow Jones Portfolio Evaluator and Apple/Dow Jones News/Quotes Reporter	Apple Computer, Inc. 10260 Bandley Drive Cupertino, CA 95014	Apple II/II+
Dow Jones Market Analyzer™	Dow Jones & Company, Inc. P.O. Box 300 Princeton, NJ 08540	Apple II+/III
Tickertec®	Max Ule & Co. 6 East 34rd Street New York, NY 10017	TRS-80 CP/M Apple II+
Appletel	Logica, Inc. 666 Third Avenue New York, NY 10017	Apple II+

---

* Information utilities allow the use of a variety of terminals and computers.

Portfolio Evaluation
and Selection

The random walk theory is often used to describe the performance of the stock market. The theory implies that the market responds randomly to economic and market conditions, and that therefore stocks bought randomly should have equal chances of being profitable. If this is true, then why spend time analyzing such things as broad market averages and stock price/volume trends, or concerning ourselves with the ins and outs of company finances?

You have probably heard the story about the college students who blindly threw darts at a newspaper stock table and bought whatever stocks the darts hit. Those stocks did no better and no worse than the market averages. The dart-throwing experiment is supposed to demonstrate that any random selection of stocks will produce the same overall result: a duplication of the average market performance. You can prove this to yourself by trying your own dart-throwing exercise with the NYSE/AMEX/OTC listings and tracking the stocks over several months. But how many investors will be satisfied if their stock portfolios merely equal the performance of such broad market indices as the Standard & Poor's 500? Specific stocks can track well above (or below) the market averages, based on circumstances and conditions unique to those stocks or their specific industry. The trick is to sort out the stocks that will leave the market averages far behind.

A LESSON FROM NAVAL WARFARE

The selection of a fast-track stock in today's economic uncertainties is analogous to shooting down enemy planes from a moving ship. The enemy planes are your stocks, the moving ship is your financial position, the ocean represents the general markets, and the weather is the general economy. In the old days massive firepower was used to bring down enemy planes, a nonselective and blanket approach analogous to buying a random group of stocks in the hope of finding a fast one among them.

Today, technology has vastly changed the science of naval warfare. Radar and laser-guided missiles are computer controlled from aboard ship. The computer is the element that ties together the ship, its missiles, and the environment. It calculates the changing position of the ship amid shifting weather patterns and ocean conditions, and its relationship to the approaching enemy planes. By tracking the incoming enemy planes and carefully timing the firing of his missiles, the ship's captain is able to maximize his chance of knocking down his target—a situation analogous to picking the right stock in a turbulent market. The ship's fire control computers can guide missile firings in almost all types of conditions. Similarly, a computer-controlled stock evaluation program should allow you to accurately select and track your stock in any economic climate or market conditions.

MARKETS IN TURMOIL

Between the late 1940s and early 1960s, stock markets were fairly stable, reflecting gradual economic expansion and minimal inflation (see Exhibit 6–1). The period from the early 1960s to early 80s, however, showed a marked departure from the previous period of relative placidity. In the last two decades there have been five major stock slumps in which Dow Jones averages plummeted by as much as 33 percent.

In the past 20 years the U.S. economy has been battered by everything from the inflation spawned by the Vietnam War to the exorbitant increases in the price of petroleum engineered by the OPEC oil cartel. Most recently, the economy has been thrown into a series of punishing reversals by record-breaking interest rates. In light of the turbulence of the last 20 years, do we have any reason to expect a return to stability in the future?

Many knowledgeable forecastors have difficulty predicting more than six months into the future with any certainty, and that makes it tougher to assess which stocks we should be buying over the next three to five years. In a climate like this, we must look out for our investing health. I'm convinced that writing our own investment prescription in these volatile times is something we can all do with the help of computers.

Exhibit 6–1. Dow Jones Industrial Average: Recent History

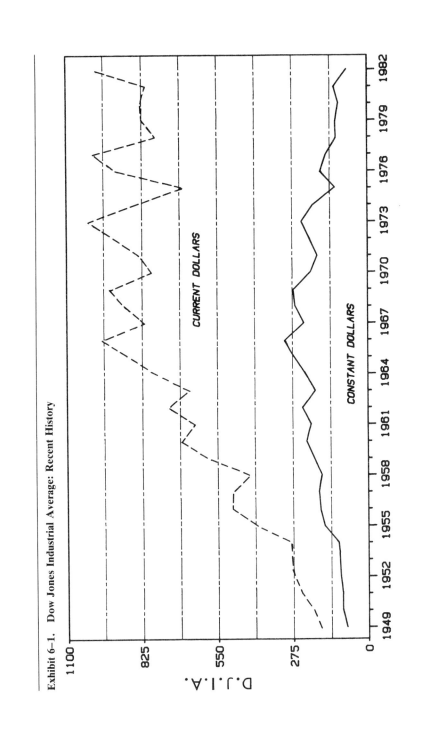

The traditional strategy of buying blue-chip stocks and holding them for years through business peaks and troughs has severely punished many investors in recent years. The key to an effective strategy is timing. Many investment advisors and market seers are advocating market timing as a strategy to minimize losses and maximize gains by anticipating price trends.

The information the nonprofessional needs to select market timing points is usually too difficult to get or to keep track of. Losing track of the information necessary for good timing is like having your alarm clock stop running in the middle of the night. It doesn't ring in the morning when you need it.

What you need is a more automatic way to uncover the timing data, store it, and retrieve it in time to make a profitable investment decision. The computer is just such an intelligent clock. It can assist you in setting the trading alarm, and it won't forget to alert you when the time is right to trade. You can set this alarm for one or for many holdings. The alarm settings are usually called "market timing indicators," or "indicators" for short. They are simply a kind of data easily read by a computer—provided that the indicator can be expressed numerically.

An example of how market timing works is the following scenario. Suppose you had decided to invest in the stock market in 1960. Between then and 1982 you would have had five ideal occasions to buy stocks—namely, second quarter 1962; third quarter 1966; second quarter 1970; third quarter 1974, and first quarter 1978. Each of these points came in advance of major stock market rallies. The sixth buy point has proven to be the third quarter, 1982. However, there were six sell opportunities in the same period: fourth quarter 1961; fourth quarter 1965; fourth quarter 1968; fourth quarter 1972; fourth quarter 1976; and first quarter 1981. Both the buy and sell opportunities are plotted on Exhibit 6–2.

These are roughly four-year cycles from peak to peak and trough to trough. This pattern coincides with what many view as a constant pattern of four-year business cycles. Advocates of this theory point out there has

Exhibit 6–2.   Stock Market Timing

Buy		*Sell*	
Quarter	*Year*	*Quarter*	*Year*
—	—	4th	1961
2d	1962	4th	1965
3d	1966	4th	1968
2d	1970	4th	1972
3d	1974	4th	1976
1st	1978	1st	1981
3d	1982	—	—

Source: Growth Fund Research, Yreka, Calif.

been a market bottom approximately every four years since the early 1930s. The underlying cause of the cycle is open to question, but many people point to the major influence of the federal government on the economy. They maintain that Presidents have generally initiated hardnosed economic programs early in their terms, but about 30 months prior to election they used their powers to inject new life into the economy hoping to produce the maximum amount of prosperity by election time. The four-year business cycle and presidential election cycle are plotted on Exhibit 6–3. As you can see, there is a high correlation.

Exhibit 6–3. Four-Year Cycles (S&P performance, 1935–1981)

Mid-Term		Preelection		Election		Postelection	
		1935	+ 41.4	1936	+ 27.9	1937	− 38.6
1938	+ 24.4	1939	− 5.5	1940	− 15.3	1941	− 17.9
1942	+ 12.4	1943	+ 19.4	1944	+ 13.8	1945	+ 30.7
1946	− 11.9	1947	0	1948	− 0.7	1949	+ 10.3
1950	+ 21.8	1951	+ 16.5	1952	+ 11.8	1953	− 6.6
1954	+ 45.0	1955	+ 26.4	1956	+ 2.6	1957	− 14.3
1958	+ 38.1	1959	+ 8.5	1960	− 3.0	1961	+ 28.1
1962	− 11.8	1963	+ 18.9	1964	+ 13.0	1965	+ 9.1
1966	− 13.1	1967	+ 20.1	1968	+ 7.7	1969	− 11.4
1970	+ 0.1	1971	+ 10.8	1972	+ 15.6	1973	− 17.4
1974	− 29.7	1975	+ 31.5	1976	+ 19.1	1977	− 11.5
1978	+ 1.1	1979	+ 12.3	1980	+ 25.8	1981	− 11.3
Avg. =	+ 7.0		+ 16.7		+ 9.9		− 4.7

Markets generally make a major low early in a mid-term election year. They exhibit strength in pre-presidential election and in election years when positive economic events are emphasized, and the markets weaken in post-presidential election years when undesirable economic programs are usually instituted.

Courtesy of Growth Fund Guide, Growth Fund Research, Yreka, Calif.

A number of respected market watchers have long believed that the four-year cycle is only a smaller version of much longer cycles. Two important studies on this have been made in the recent past that have defined so-called long waves outlining economic periods lasting from 48 to 60 years; and, 10-year cycles that show a repetitive pattern in industrial stock prices.

Nicholas D. Kondratieff, a controversial Russian economist, in the mid-1920s developed the theory of long cyclical economic movements in capitalist societies. He believed these waves dominated the shorter cycles. Kondratieff's long-wave theory suggests there is a coincidental relationship among wars, social and political trends, and economics. As he saw it, a typical long wave consists of three parts: an initial period of 20 to

30 years of sustained growth, a transition phase of recession and recovery, and a 7-to-10-year period of stability followed by a 20-to-30-year down wave that begins with a depression. In U.S. history there have been three complete long waves. We are now in the fourth (see Exhibit 6–4).

The theory of 10-year cycles was first demonstrated by Edgar Lawrence Smith. He concluded these decennial periods were related to a

Exhibit 6–4. Long Waves

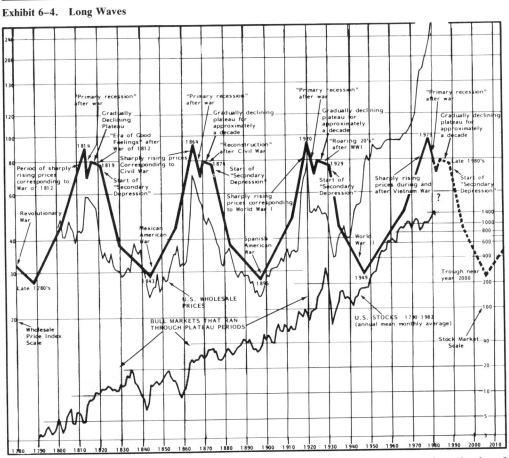

Source: The Kondratieff Wave Cycle and Wholesale Price Index portion of this chart is an adaptation and update of material originally presented in *Media General Financial Weekly* (P.O. Box 26565, Richmond, VA 23261). See issues 8/2/72 and 6/3/74. The lower stock market portion of this chart is an adaptation and update of material originally presented in *Cycles* Magazine, issue of February 1965 (Foundation for the Study of Cycles, 124 S. Highland, Pittsburgh, PA 15205). The series used for the stock market chart is: 1790–1831 Bank & Insurance Companies, 1831–1854 Cleveland Trust Rail Stocks, 1954–1871 Clement-Burgess Composite Index, 1871–1897; Cowles Index of Industrial Stocks, 1897–1965 Dow Jones Industrial Averaging, and 1965–1982 New York Stock Exchange Composite Index.

Courtesy: Growth Fund Research, Yreka, Calif.

Exhibit 6–5. Ten-Year Pattern of Dow Jones Industrial Average, 1887–1982

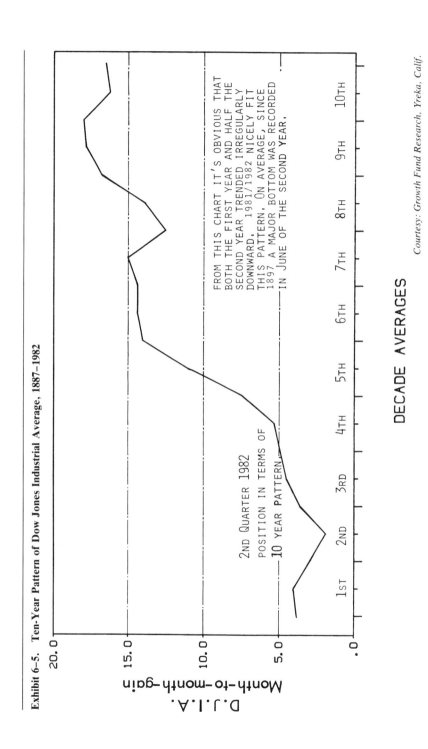

DECADE AVERAGES

FROM THIS CHART IT'S OBVIOUS THAT
BOTH THE FIRST YEAR AND HALF THE
SECOND YEAR TRENDED IRREGULARLY
DOWNWARD. 1981/1982 NICELY FIT
THIS PATTERN. ON AVERAGE, SINCE
1897 A MAJOR BOTTOM WAS RECORDED
IN JUNE OF THE SECOND YEAR.

2ND QUARTER 1982
POSITION IN TERMS OF
10 YEAR PATTERN.

D.J.I.A.   Month-to-month-gain

20.0
15.0
10.0
5.0
.0

1ST 2ND 3RD 4TH 5TH 6TH 7TH 8TH 9TH 10TH

Courtesy: Growth Fund Research, Yreka, Calif.

gradual rhythmic change in the biological and psychological nature of man. Exhibit 6–5 plots the 10-year cycle based on the DJIA from 1897 to 1982.

Technical Analysis and Market Indicators

The importance of the preceding discussions of business, presidential election, Kondratieff, and 10-year cycles is to suggest that perhaps the market is not as random as it might appear to be to the casual observer. These cycles appear to represent predictable behavior. Predictable market movements are something we should be able to handle with our computer, but what we need is a formula for recognizing patterns in these movements. Based on this formula we should then be able to establish key points within the patterns that can be used as buy/sell indicators. This is what technical analysis is all about.

Many technical analysts believe that the fundamentals of corporate and general economic performance are irrelevant because the market has already absorbed and adjusted for the information. The items that the technical analysts follow most carefully are momentum and trend; that is, the behavior of the market's internal mechanism. This includes stock prices over time, volumes achieved, checkpoints passed, and resistance and support levels broken through. There is no mystery to stock market patterns once you understand the underlying cycles that affect their behavior. The trick is to spot the trends and time the reversals.

Market indicators fall into the following three general categories:

1. **Fundamentals**—expectations of the economy's performance based on trends in corporate profits, interest rates, and inflation. Profit trends are the most important since they have a basic influence on dividend and stock prices. Rising interest rates usually push stock prices lower. Conversely, falling inflation or interest rates generally presage market rallies—provided the market is convinced that these two bullish trends will be lasting.

2. **Psychological factors**—best deduced from the pronouncements of the market advisory services. If most are bearish, expect a market upturn (the old "it is always darkest just before the dawn" theory still holds true).

3. **Technical indicators**—statistics that define stock price/volume patterns of behavior, such as:

a. Ticker tape action. In many brokers' opinions this is the best day-to-day measure of the real pulse of the market. It shows concentrations of interest in certain stock groups, institutional activity and big block trading, and stocks breaking out of resistance levels or falling through support levels. It lets you follow your favorite stock and watch it go up or down on daily volume.

b. The Federal Reserve (the Fed) Buy Rule. According to this rule, whenever the Fed eases the monetary climate by decreasing one of the three basic policy rates under its jurisdiction two times in succession, conditions are favorable for a subsequent increase in stock prices.

Conversely, the *Fed Sell Rule* states that, whenever monetary tightening is caused by an increase in one of the three basic rates three successive times, investors should expect a stock market decline in the near future. The reasoning behind these rules is simple: money fuels the stock market and the Fed controls money. (The most frequently used of the Fed's three basic policy tools is the discount rate. The other two are the bank reserve requirements and stock margin requirements.)

c. The Dow Jones Industrial Average. It is a composite index of stock prices of 30 top industrial companies, and is the most familiar and most often quoted index of stock market performance. It is generally recognized, however, that the Dow is not the best indicator of the overall health of the stock market since secondary stocks are likely to turn down as a group well before the big blue-chip stocks that make up the Dow.

d. The advance/decline line. This is an average of the ratio of the stocks advancing to those declining. Advocates of the A/D line believe it shows the true direction of the market because it mirrors the performance of all stocks on the exchanges and in the computerized stock services (see Exhibit 6–6).

e. The mutual funds cash assets ratio. This ratio indicates how much untapped buying power lies in investment companies. Generally, the average is about 9 percent. A ratio higher than this indicates that investment companies have excess cash to buy stocks of interest to them. This may place considerable upward push on the prices of the stocks being bought.

f. Short interest ratios. These show the relationship of short interest (the amount of stock borrowed and sold short in the expectation of a market decline) to average daily trading volume. The concept is simple: if the monthly short interest ratio rises significantly, it is a bullish indicator. Short selling is a buy signal if you view short interest as a future commitment to buy because sooner or later short sellers must buy stock to cover their positions. That pool of potential demand constitutes a floor under the market or an individual stock (see Exhibit 6–7).

g. Overbought/oversold indicators. These measure whether stocks have moved out of line with their long-term price levels. For example, if 70 percent of stocks are selling above these levels, then they are considered "overbought." Conversely, if fewer than 30 percent of stocks are selling above the average, the market is considered "oversold" (see Exhibit 6–8).

h. Volume analysis. It is a technique that relies on classic price trend charting. Plotting years of price movements reveals recurring patterns. The most famous is the "head and shoulders" pattern, which consists of

Exhibit 6–6. Cumulative Advance/Decline Indicator

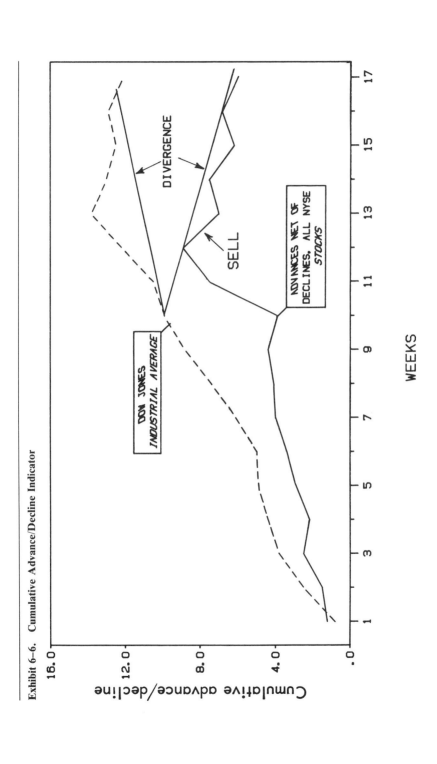

Exhibit 6–7. Short Interest Ratios

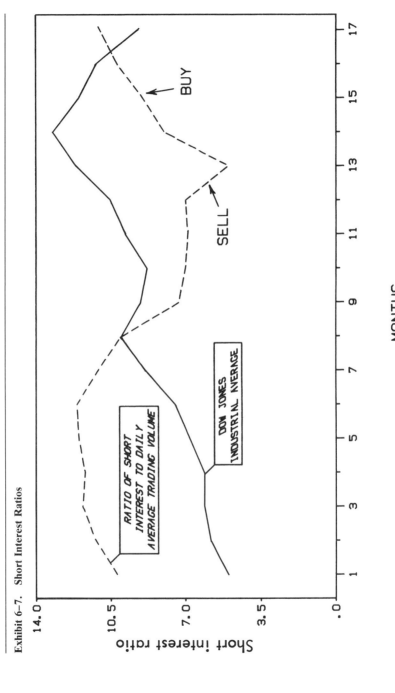

Exhibit 6—8. Overbought/Oversold Indicator

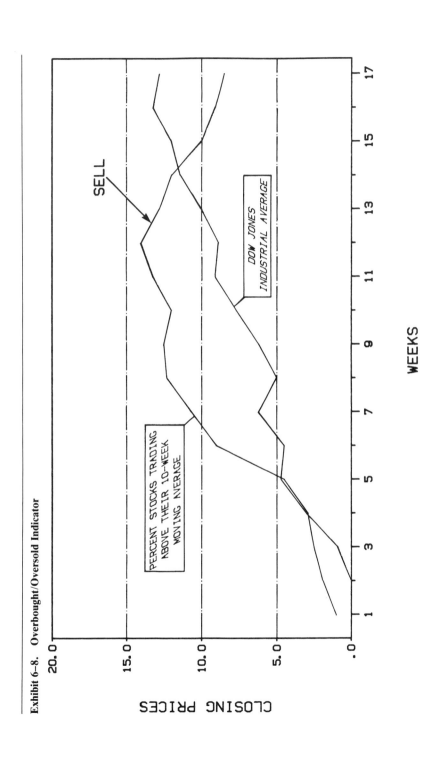

three peaks in prices with the central peak higher, forming the head. That's traditionally a signal for a major market decline.

i. Other technical indicators. These include the Standard & Poor's composite index of 500 stocks, discounted cash flow, on-balance volume measures, beta analysis, and acceleration, to name a few.

The technical indicators and indexes described above are not difficult to understand. If you have a basic knowledge of their meaning you will be better able to understand most of the stock evaluation and tracking programs available for your computer. This understanding should help you to make more profitable trading decisions with the computer as an aid. Depending upon the program you eventually select and its technical methodology, you should look into the details of the indicators it uses.

FUNDAMENTAL STOCK ANALYSIS

Before we start looking at the different computer programs for charting indicators presently on the market there is one more area for you to consider: fundamental analysis of a specific company. Technical analysis of the market's historical and current trends is extremely useful for zeroing in on a target industry or a group of stocks that look like they are on a fast track.

Fundamental analysis lets you go one step further by helping you select the particular firm within an industry or stock grouping that should do well, based on a combination of factors unique to that company. Your objective should be to establish the stock's value. How is it priced in relation to the market, and how does its price-earnings ratio compare to those of other stocks within its industry? How can you decide whether a stock is currently undervalued, overvalued, or right where it should be? But first, consider these factors:

Earnings growth—past, present, and projected.

Return on equity.

Competitive position in the industry.

Balance sheet strength.

Amount of dividend (if any) and prospects for dividend growth.

Product development.

Management quality.

Growth orientation.

Profitability.

Investor perception.

These are only some of the factors you may need to consider. Perhaps you can pick the best stocks by considering only a few factors. Nevertheless, fundamental analysis provides the rifle shot you need to single out profitable stocks for your portfolio. The vast bulk of data you need for this kind of analysis may be retrieved from one of the information services we discussed earlier. What information is not there can probably be supplied by your broker, who can also offer his experience and thoughts about a personal computer as an aid to improving your portfolio performance.

Dow Jones Market Microscope

This program from National Softworks and Dow Jones & Company, Inc., can significantly aid you in establishing fundamental stock screens similar to those discussed earlier. It allows you to specify up to 20 or 68 fundamental indicators (plus price and volume information), and then use these indicators to rank your lists of stocks or industry group for buying and selling. It requires the use of an Apple computer (either models II, II+, or III).

The Market Microscope has the capability of ranking information from up to 20 lists of stocks or industry groups. Each of these groups may contain up to 50 items on each disk. You can then determine support and resistance levels for stocks within the lists, and assign threshold prices above and below these levels. The program will automatically alert you when an updated stock price reaches a set critical point determined by the assigned values. A complete set of ranking reports helps you manage your fundamental portfolio analysis.

The fundamental stock data you need is collected from the Dow Jones News/Retrieval databases. Upon retrieving the desired information, it is stored on a data disk. When you are offline (not connected to the database), the information is used for investment evaluation with either the screening or price alert portions of the Market Microscope.

The two databases within Dow Jones News/Retrieval® that can provide you with fundamental data are Media General and the Corporate Earnings Estimator. The former provides information on the NYSE, AMEX, and selected OTC companies. Included are earnings, dividends, price-earnings ratios, revenues, shareholdings, ratios, and stock price and performance relative to the market indicators. The Corporate Earnings Estimator, on the other hand, includes consensus forecasts of earnings per share for 2,400 companies based on estimates provided by top analysts at major brokerage firms.

ME AND MY BROKER

If you are serious enough about investing to buy a personal computer to aid you, you should take the time to make maximum use of it. This means doing your own fundamental, technical, or cash flow analyses. Your broker can be very helpful in supplying you with specific leads. These may be of considerable or of no interest to you. Using your computer you can quickly sort out the useful from the useless. Once you have chosen the best issues for you, track and evaluate them for a while before actually committing your hard-earned dollars. After you have tracked several selected items and screened them to your satisfaction, make your decision to either buy or sell or do nothing at all.

Your broker can help alert you to situations that may become important, but it is up to you to determine your own best interests and then to make the decision to invest or not. The computer can help you in this by greatly enhancing the quality and profitability of your investment decisions. Because of this, your broker's judgment may be quite valuable. The final selection of stocks in your portfolio is a judgmental decision. If you have sufficient experience to look at the data and determine which stocks will lead to profits and which will lead to problems, then you can make good decisions on your own. If, however, your experience is limited, or the particular industry group you are considering is foreign to you, a broker or investment advisor may provide invaluable guidance.

A COMPUTERIZED STOCK PORTFOLIO

The previous discussions about market cycles, market timing indicators, and fundamental analysis should give you a better understanding of the factors to consider in selecting stocks and measuring their performance. This information, combined with a set of well-planned financial objectives, accessibility to an information service, and a working relationship with your broker should leave you superbly prepared to make the maximum use of the computer programs available. The remainder of this chapter will focus on these programs.

At present many excellent portfolio tracking programs are on the market. Most of these fall into one of two categories: record-keeping/updating and technical analysis/updating. The former provides a set of "books" easily updated either manually or via information services, while the latter has true technical analysis employing a wide variety of technical indicators. In both categories far too many programs are available to describe in detail here. What follows is a sample of the programs presently on the market. They may not be the best ones available, but they are representative of the type of programs you should consider for yourself. Keep in mind that existing programs are constantly being updated and new ones are being offered.

PORTFOLIO TRACKING PROGRAMS

In the record-keeping/updating category are such programs as the Dow Jones Market Manager, Portfolio Master, PEAR Systems, Market Analyst, and Portware for Apple computers; Stockpak for TRS-80 computers; and the Personal Investor for the IBM Personal Computer.

Dow Jones Market Manager

This program is a portfolio management tool that provides an accounting and control system for one or more portfolios. It is offered by Micro Business Systems, Inc., and Dow Jones & Company, Inc. It requires an Apple II or II+ computer.

The Market Manager has the capability to control up to 26 different portfolios with a maximum of 150 tax records. These records—for both realized long- and short-term gains or losses—are maintained within the gain/loss file. You also have the capability to track the total worth of a portfolio, including a cash balance that may be adjusted for cash received and cash withdrawn. The cash balance is stored by the program and printed on the Holdings by Portfolio report. It is automatically adjusted every time a security is bought or sold.

Security pricing may be done by an automatic or manual process. Selecting automatic pricing causes the program to dial the Dow Jones News/Retrieval database. It then retrieves, displays, and stores prices for the securities. Any security left unpriced after the automatic retrieval process causes the program to switch to the manual pricing mode. It displays these securities and prompts you for the new prices.

The Market Manager matches sell transactions with previously entered buy transactions. In similar fashion, it matches buy transactions with previously entered short-sell transactions. After you enter a closing transaction, the program scans the current positions to determine if there is sufficient quantity in the portfolio selected to satisfy this transaction. Once all the buys and sells are matched, your projected profits and losses are displayed.

Four types of reports provide a hard-copy display of your portfolio. These include: Holdings by Portfolio, Holdings by Symbol, Realized Gains/Losses, and Year-to-Date Transactions (see Figures 6–9 through 6–12).

Portfolio Master

Portfolio Master from Investor's Software is a report-based tracking system for keeping your portfolio up to date. Like many similar programs, it is designed as a portfolio management tool and uses the Dow Jones News/Retrieval® service to place at your fingertips the latest market prices. You can also enter prices manually. For many investors, the less-expensive manual method is more than adequate.

One of the keys to profitably managing your portfolio is knowing its

Exhibit 6–9. Dow Jones Market Manager (Holdings by Portfolio)

TODAY'S DATE   12/08/82

C O D E	SYMBOL	T Y P E	B SS	DATE	QUANT	$COST	PRICE	$VALUE	PRICE	UNREALIZD GAIN/LOSS	L S
								:TRANSACTION:	12/08/82		
A	AAPL	S	B	3/15/82	100	1,528	15.28	3,312	33⅛	1,784	S
A	AAPL	S	B	3/15/82	200	3,080	15.40	6,625	33⅛	3,545	S
A	AAPL	S	B	3/17/82	200	2,853	14.26	6,625	33⅛	3,772	S
*TOTAL AAPL					500	7,461		16,562		9,101	
A	DEC	S	B	1/15/82	50	4,128	82.56	5,450	109	1,322	S
A	DEC	S	B	1/27/82	25	2,159	86.36	2,725	109	566	S
*TOTAL DEC					75	6,287		8,175		1,888	
A	DJ	S	B	11/20/81	100	5,118	51.18	6,975	69¾	1,857	L
A	DJ	S	B	11/23/81	200	10,201	51.00	31,950	69¾	3,749	L
A	DJ	S	B	11/24/81	100	5,025	50.25	6,975	69¾	1,950	L
*TOTAL DJ					400	20,344		27,900		7,556	
A	IBM	S	B	5/20/82	100	6,313	63.13	9,450	94½	3,137	S
A	IBM	S	B	5/20/82	50	3,182	63.64	4,725	94½	1,543	S
A	IBM	S	B	6/01/82	50	3,108	62.16	4,725	94½	1,617	S
*TOTAL IBM					200	12,603		18,900		6,297	
VALUED SECURITIES LONG					1,175	46,695		71,537		24,842	
VALUED SECURITIES SHORT					0	0		0		0	
CASH BALANCE = 3305											

Courtesy of Micro Business Systems, Inc. and Dow Jones & Company, Inc.

Exhibit 6–10. Dow Jones Market Manager (Holdings by Symbol)

TODAY'S DATE   12/08/82

C D D E	SYMBOL	T Y P E	B SS	DATE	QUANT	$COST	PRICE	$VALUE	PRICE	UNREALIZD GAIN/LOSS	L S
								:TRANSACTION:	12/08/82		
A	IBM	S	B	5/20/82	100	6,313	63.13	9,450	94½	3,137	S
Q	IBM	S	B	6/01/82	50	3,182	63.64	4,725	94½	1,543	S
Q	IBM	S	B	6/01/82	50	3,108	62.16	4,725	94½	1,617	S
Q	IBM	S	B	6/01/82	100	6,313	63.13	9,450	94½	3,137	S
X	IBM	S	B	6/01/82	50	3,108	62.16	4,725	94½	1,617	S
X	IBM	S	B	5/20/82	100	6,313	63.13	9,450	94½	3,137	S
X	IBM	S	B	5/20/82	50	3,182	63.64	4,725	94½	1,543	S
VALUED SECURITIES LONG					500	31,519		47,250		15,731	
VALUED SECURITIES SHORT					0	0		0		0	

Courtesy of Micro Business Systems, Inc. and Dow Jones & Company, Inc.

Exhibit 6–11. Dow Jones Market Manager (Realized Gains/Losses)

C O D E	SYMBOL	QTY	PURCHASE DATE	PRICE	$COST	SALE DATE	PRICE	PROCEEDS	GAIN/LOSS	L/S
A	DJ	100	11/23/81	51.01	5101	12/07/82	70.23	7023	1922	L
A	AAPL	100	3/15/82	15.40	1540	12/07/82	33.45	3345	1805	S
A	DEC	50	1/15/82	82.56	4128	12/07/82	111.36	5568	1440	S
A	DEC	25	1/27/82	86.36	2159	12/07/82	111.36	2784	625	S
A	IBM	50	5/20/82	63.64	3182	12/07/82	94.56	4728	1546	S
A	IBM	50	6/01/82	62.16	3108	12/07/82	94.56	4728	1620	S
TOTALS:		375			19218			28176	8958	

Courtesy of Micro Business Systems, Inc. and Dow Jones & Company, Inc.

Exhibit 6–12. Dow Jones Market Manager (Year-to-Date Transactions)

TODAYS DATE   12/08/82

DATE	CODE	TRANSACTION	DESCRIPTION				AMOUNT
11/20/81	A	BUY	100	DJ	@	51.18	5118
11/23/81	A	BUY	200	DJ	@	51.00	10201
11/24/82	A	BUY	100	DJ	@	50.25	5025
1/15/82	A	BUY	50	DEC	@	82.56	4128
1/27/82	A	BUY	25	DEC	@	86.36	2159
3/15/82	A	BUY	100	AAPL	@	15.28	1528
3/15/82	A	BUY	200	AAPL	@	15.40	3080
3/17/82	A	BUY	200	AAPL	@	14.26	2853
5/20/82	A	BUY	100	IBM	@	63.13	6313
5/20/82	A	BUY	50	IBM	@	63.64	3182
6/01/82	A	BUY	50	IBM	@	62.16	3108
12/08/82	A	CHANGE	100	DJ	@	50.25	5025
11/01/81	A	CASH	INITIAL	ENTRY			50000
12/07/82	A	SELL	100	DJ	@	70.23	7023
12/07/82	A	SELL	100	AAPL	@	33.45	3345
12/07/82	A	SELL	50	DEC	@	111.36	5568
12/07/82	A	SELL	25	DEC	@	111.36	2784
12/07/82	A	SELL	50	IBM	@	94.56	4728
12/07/82	A	SELL	50	IBM	@	94.56	4728

Courtesy of Micro Business Systems, Inc. and Dow Jones & Company, Inc.

composition and balance at all times. Portfolio Master lets you display the current value of each holding, its percentage "weight" in the portfolio, and the total current value of the entire portfolio. If you find that certain securities become too heavily weighted, you may decide that they should be thinned to rebalance the total mix. This can be an excellent check on your portfolio's diversity.

Portfolio Master brings the computer's benefits to the investor in spades. One of the program's strong points is the visibility it gives to the performance of your securities. Portfolio Master provides you with a series of listings that reflect your portfolio's contents viewed from seven different statistical perspectives:

1. *Portfolio listing:* automatically sorts securities by type or alphabetically, or by date of purchase.

2. *Portfolio profit and loss:* calculates short-term and long-term gains for each, holding up to 100 line items.

3. *Category listing:* furnishes dollar totals and weights for each type of security.

Exhibit 6–13.   Portfolio Master: Profit and Loss

```
                        MODEL
               PORTFOLIO PROFIT AND LOSS
                    AS OF 06/10/81
                                          GAIN/LOSS
   # SHS      NAME      COST    PRICE    SHRT  LONG
-----------------------------------------------------
    200     AVP        38.98   41.50            503
    100     GM         55.73   58.38      264
    100     IBM       236.42  233.38           -305
   1000     WDEPY       9.44   18.88           9438
    300     PPLB       22.25   26.25     1199
     10  C  DOWFF       1.53    2.00      467
     10  P  BATG        3.72    3.25     -473
   1000  E  ATTR        1.00    3.50     2500
   1000  W  LEH         9.16    9.25       93
    200  S  XON        70.62   65.88      948
     10  M  IP.K       89.23   81.13     -811


   TOTAL LONG TERM GAIN                        9637
   TOTAL SHORT TERM GAIN                 4191

   NET GAIN IN PORTFOLIO                       13828
-----------------------------------------------------
```

This display shows the *cost* of each holding and the *price* on the date in the heading. The last two columns show the *gain* or *loss*—with *short* term appearing in the next-to-last column and *long* term in the last column. Losses are shown as minus numbers.

Courtesy of Investors Software

4. *Sales table:* records all sales, calculates realized gains or losses for the long or short term, and displays their running totals on a year-to-year comparison basis.

5. *Basis table:* displays cost and purchase date of each holding.

6. *Maturity and expiration table:* furnishes the crucial dates for bonds, T-bills, calls, puts, rights, and warrants.

7. *Description table:* gives the full description of each security.

For convenience and record-keeping, Portfolio Master provides up to seven on-screen, 40-column reports (see Exhibits 6–13 to 6–19). Complementing these are three 80-column printouts (see Exhibits 6–20 and 6–21); the third chart shows the high, low, and last volume quotes received from Dow Jones News/Retrieval®.

You can store any number of portfolios on your disk file. They may all be yours or they may belong to others, such as clients, friends, or relatives. All are available for immediate reference. An interesting additional feature of Portfolio Master is its ability to help you evaluate the performance of your investment advisor. You can do this with Portfolio Master by storing the advisor's recommendations along with the price and date of the recommendations.

Exhibit 6–14. Portfolio Master: Basis Table

```
                    MODEL
                 BASIS TABLE
               AS OF 06/10/81
```

# SHS		NAME	COST	DATE	AMOUNT
200		AVP	38.98	05/26/80	7796
100		GM	55.73	10/15/80	5573
100		IBM	236.42	07/28/78	23642
1000		WDEPY	9.44	06/06/78	9437
300		PPLB	22.25	11/12/80	6675
10	C	DOWFF	1.53	05/26/81	1532
10	P	BATG	3.72	04/04/81	3722
1000	E	ATTR	1.00	03/09/81	1000
1000	W	LEH	9.16	07/07/80	9156
200	S	XON	70.62	04/04/81	14123
10	M	IP.K	89.23	09/10/80	8923
25000		T-BILL			23785

```
     TOTAL COST OF SECURITIES:  101242
```

The *basis table* shows the *cost* per share (or per right, call, etc.) and the *date* of purchase. For shorts, the *basis table* shows the date the stock was sold short and the sale price.

Exhibit 6–15. Portfolio Master: Listing by Weight

```
                  MODEL
            PORTFOLIO LISTING
              AS OF Ø6/1Ø/
```

# SHS		NAME	PRICE	AMOUNT	%WGT
2ØØ		AVP	41.5Ø	83ØØ	4.6
1ØØ		GM	58.38	5837	3.2
1ØØ		IBM	233.38	23337	12.9
1ØØØ		WDEPY	18.88	18875	1Ø.5
3ØØ		PPLB	26.25	7875	4.4
1Ø	C	DOWFF	2.ØØ	2ØØØ	1.1
1Ø	P	BATG	3.25	325Ø	1.8
1ØØØ	E	ATTR	3.5Ø	35ØØ	1.9
1ØØØ	W	LEH	9.25	925Ø	5.1
2ØØ	S	XON	65.88	13175	7.3
1Ø	M	IP.K	81.13	8112	4.5
25ØØØ		T-BILL		23785	13.2
		CASH		52948	29.4
TOTAL		PORTFOLIO VALUE		168Ø18	

The "%WGT" column is a calculation of the percentage of each holding in the total value of the portfolio. This enables you to see how risk is distributed. Code flags appear between "#SHS" and "NAME," and indicate the type of security. Common/preferred stocks have no code flags.

Exhibit 6–16. Portfolio Master: Listing by Security

```
                  MODEL
            PORTFOLIO LISTING
                  BY
            SECURITY CATEGORY
              AS OF Ø6/1Ø/
```

CATEGORY	TOTAL	%WGT
COMMON STOCK	5635Ø	31.3
PREFERRED STOCK	7875	4.4
OPTIONS	1175Ø	6.5
RIGHTS	35ØØ	1.9
WARRANTS	925Ø	5.1
SHORT SALES	13175	7.3
BONDS	8112	4.5
CASH/EQ	23785	13.2
CASH	52948	29.4
TOTAL VALUE	168Ø18	

This report is sorted by the weighting of the holding.

Courtesy of Investors Software

Exhibit 6–17. Portfolio Master: Listing by Descriptions

```
              MODEL
        PORTFOLIO DESCRIPTIONS
-------------------------------------------

SYMBOL      DESCRIPTION
-------------------------------------------

AVP         AVON PRODUCTS
GM          GENERAL MOTORS
IBM         INTERNATIONAL BUS. MACH.
WDEPY       WESTERN DEEP LEVELS
PPLB        PA PWR & LGT 4.50 PFD
DOWFF       DOW CHEM JUN 30 CALLS
BATG        BOEING AUG 35 PUTS
ATTR        AMERICAN TELEPHONE RIGHTS
LEH         LEHIGH CORP WARRANTS
XON         EXXON CORP
IP.K        INTL PAPER 8.85 OF 95
T-BILL
-------------------------------------------
```

You have the choice of listing security *descriptions* for either the *portfolio* or the *sales table*. The *description* generally will be the name of the company.

Exhibit 6–18. Portfolio Master: Sales Table

```
              MODEL
           SALES TABLE
          AS OF 06/10/
-----------------------------------------------

# SHS    NAME      PRICE    DATE      AMOUNT
-----------------------------------------------

  200    SLS       33.38  06/06/81     6675
         BASIS     35.77  02/02/80     7153
         LONG TERM LOSS...          -477.87

   10 C MLI         3.77  06/09/81     3765
         BASIS      2.55  03/03/81     2552
         SHORT TERM GAIN...         1212.95

   10 M CIW        92.03  06/10/81     9202
         BASIS     88.85  07/07/79     8885
         LONG TERM GAIN...           317.78

NET LONG TERM LOSS                    -161
NET SHORT TERM GAIN                   1212

TOTAL NET GAIN                        1052
-----------------------------------------------
```

The *sales table* keeps a record for you of securities sold and shorts covered. The first line of the listing shows the *number* of shares sold, the *name* of the security, the selling *price,* and the *date* of sale. The second line shows the *basis* (cost *price* and purchase *date*). The third line shows the *long*-term or *short*-term *gain* or *loss* for that item. Short sale profit or loss always will be in the short-term column.

Courtesy of Investors Software

Exhibit 6–19.   Portfolio Master: Maturities and Expirations

```
                     MODEL
          MATURITY/EXPIRATION TABLE
                 AS OF 06/10/
        ----------------------------------------
        # SHS        NAME       EXPIRES    MATURES
        ----------------------------------------
        CALLS
            10  C    DOWFF      06/20/81
        PUTS
            10  P    BATG       08/20/81
        RIGHTS
          1000  E    ATTR       06/06/81
        WARRANTS
          1000  W    LEH        12/01/84
        BONDS
            10  M    IP.K                  08/01/95
        CASH/EQS
         25000       T-BILL                07/25/81
        ----------------------------------------
```

The display shows the expiration dates of calls, puts, rights, and warrants, and the maturity dates of bonds and T-bills.

Courtesy of Investors Software

PEAR

The Portfolio Evaluation and Reporting System from PEAR Systems is geared to the needs of the professional stockbroker or investment advisor to give statistical support for his or her client presentations. It relies on 80-column reports to display portfolio appraisals, unrealized and realized capital gains and losses, security cross-references, and investment income (see Exhibits 6–22 through 6–26).

An interesting feature of the PEAR program is its organization of data into two separate files—namely, securities and portfolio position. Both files allow you to focus your attention on either individual securities or on a whole portfolio. Using identification numbers, you can gear one set of files to the other, which allows you to enter or update securities information on a specific security in one file and have it automatically adjusted in all the other files in which it appears.

PEAR Systems has recently developed a measurement program called the PEARformance Measurement System. The objective is to apply the power of VisiCalc to the problem of measuring investment portfolio performance. It is based on the principle of "time-weighted total return performance," an advanced technique used by many large institutional investors.

PEAR Systems recommends the PEARformance Measurement only if you are knowledgeable in VisiCalc. For those of you who may have used VisiCalc in previous exercises this should not be a problem. For those

Exhibit 6–20. Portfolio Master: A Schedule

MODEL

SCHEDULE OF CAPITAL GAINS AND LOSSES

AS OF 06/12/

PAGE 1

	BASIS DATE	CLOSING DATE	BASIS AMOUNT	CLOSING AMOUNT	SHORT TERM	LONG TERM
200	SHARES	SO. LOUISIANA SYSTEMS				
	02/02/80	06/06/81	7153.20	6675.33		-477.87
10	CALLS	MOUNTAIN LAND INC				
	03/03/81	06/09/81	2552.30	3765.25	1212.95	
10	BONDS	CLEVELAND IRON WORKS				
	07/07/79	06/10/81	8885.10	9202.88		317.78

NET REALIZED SHORT TERM GAIN.......................$ 1212.95

NET REALIZED LONG TERM LOSS........................$ -160.09

TOTAL NET REALIZED GAIN............................$ 1052.86

This printout, called "Schedule of Capital Gains and Losses," is an expanded version of the sales table. Security descriptions are used instead of symbols unless the description is blank. Then, symbols will be printed.

Courtesy of Investors Software

Exhibit 6–21. Condensing Three Reports

MODEL

PORTFOLIO PROFIT & LOSS
AS OF 06/12/

# UNITS	NAME	BASIS DATE	BASIS	06/10/8 PRICE	AMOUNT	GAIN OR LOSS SHORT	LONG	% CHG
200	AVP	05/26/80	38.98	41.50	8300		503	6.5
100	GM	10/15/80	55.73	58.38	5837	264		4.8
100	IBM	07/28/78	236.42	233.38	23337		-305	-1.3
1000	WDEPY	06/06/78	9.44	18.88	18875		9438	100.0
300	PPLB	11/12/80	22.25	26.25	7875	1199		18.0
10	C DOWFF	05/26/81	1.53	2.00	2000	467		30.5
10	P BATG	04/04/81	3.72	3.25	3250	-473		-12.7
1000	R ATTR	03/09/81	1.00	3.50	3500	2500		250.0
1000	W LEH	07/07/80	9.16	9.25	9250	93		1.0
200	S XON	04/04/81	70.62	65.88	948	948		6.7
10	M IP.K	09/10/80	89.23	81.13	8112	-811		-9.1
$25000	T-BILL	(MATURES: 07/25/81)			23785			

```
CASH..........................$   52948
TOTAL PORTFOLIO COST..........$  154189
TOTAL PORTFOLIO VALUE.........$  168018          9.0

NET UNREALIZED SHORT TERM GAIN......       4191
NET UNREALIZED LONG TERM GAIN......$       9637
TOTAL NET UNREALIZED GAIN......$          13829
```

This report is a condensation of three reports from the *display/print menu: Portfolio Listing, Portfolio Profit and Loss, and Basis Table.*

Exhibit 6-22. PEAR Appraisal

```
||||||||||||||||||||||||||||||||||||||||||||||||||||||||||||||||||||||||||||||||||||||||||||||||||||||||||||||||||||||
PAGE 1                                       PEAR SYSTEM DEMO                                                 10/31/
                                          PORTFOLIO APPRAISAL
SOC.SEC.#123-45-6789                          JOHN E. CASH                                               ACCT.#123456
||||||||||||||||||||||||||||||||||||||||||||||||||||||||||||||||||||||||||||||||||||||||||||||||||||||||||||||||||||||
```

SHARES OR PAR VALUE	SECURITY	UNIT COST	INVENTORY	CURRENT PRICE	CURRENT MARKET VALUE	INT/DIV RATE	ANNUAL INCOME	YIELD %	% OF TYPE OR TOTAL
1,000	AMER BROADCASTING	0.03	33	35.000	35,000	2.00	2,000	5.71	7.6
1,400	DOME PETROLEUM	35.50	49,695	57.000	79,800	0.00	0	0.00	17.3
3,000	GEORGIA PACIFIC	28.20	84,614	25.750	77,250	1.20	3,600	4.66	16.7
1,685	GRACE W.R.	26.85	45,250	49.625	83,618	2.30	3,875	4.63	18.1
3,000	NL INDUSTRIES	17.31	51,938	62.250	186,750	1.20	3,600	1.93	40.4
TOTAL COMMON STOCKS			231,530		462,418		13,075	2.83	54.6
800	ARCATA CV.A	26.98	21,584	27.750	22,200	2.16	1,728	7.78	52.1
600	JOHNSON CTRL CV.B	35.36	21,214	34.000	20,400	2.00	1,200	5.88	47.9
TOTAL PREFERRED STOCKS			42,798		42,600		2,928	6.87	5.0
30	ENGLHRD JAN 60 CALL	5.14	15,422	3.250	9,750	0.00	0	0.00	36.4
10	HMSTK JAN 66 5/8CALL	13.58	13,577	17.000	17,000	0.00	0	0.00	63.6
TOTAL OPTIONS			29,000		26,750		0	0.00	3.2
50,000	BENEFICIAL CORP DEB. 8% 06/15/01	100.00	50,000	78.500	39,250	80.00	4,000	10.58	50.6
50,000	PFIZER DEB. 9.25% 08/15/00	99.50	49,750	76.500	38,250	92.50	4,625	12.48	49.4
TOTAL CORPORATE BONDS			99,750		77,500		8,625	11.13	9.2
25,000	BOSTON MASS. G.O. 6.25% 08/01/97	98.05	24,512	76.000	19,000	62.50	1,562	9.06	44.8
30,000	LITTLE ROCK ARK. 7.3% 09/01/11	87.00	26,100	78.000	23,400	73.00	2,190	9.52	55.2
TOTAL MUNICIPAL BONDS			50,612		42,400		3,752	8.85	5.0
75,000	GEN'L MOT ACCEPT 13.5% 11/27/80	100.00	75,000	100.000	75,000	135.00	10,125	13.50	60.0
50,000	GEN'L MOT ACCEPT 13.25% 11/07/80	100.00	50,000	100.000	50,000	132.50	6,625	13.25	40.0
TOTAL COMMERCIAL PAPER			125,000		125,000		16,750	13.40	14.8
50,000	U.S.TREASURY 9.75% 05/31/81	101.75	50,875	97.250	48,625	97.50	4,875	14.84	100.0
TOTAL U.S.TREASURIES			50,875		48,625		4,875	10.03	5.7
21,000	NAT'L LIQUID RESERVE	1.00	21,000	1.000	21,000	0.10	2,163	10.30	100.0
TOTAL LIQUID ASSETS			21,000		21,000		2,163	10.30	2.5
TOTAL PORTFOLIO			650,566		846,293		52,169	6.16	100.0

Portfolio Appraisal—Your clients will appreciate the easy legibility and completeness of this summary report, which includes full security descriptions, percent breakdown within and by security type, and yield to maturity for fixed income securities.

The PEAR System requires an Apple II computer with 48 Kilobytes of memory, dual 5¼ inch disk drives, a monitor, and a 132 column printer. To implement the automatic pricing feature, a D.C. Hayes Micromodem, (or Apple Communications Card and acoustic coupler) and a Dow Jones password are also required.

Courtesy of PEAR Systems

Exhibit 6–23. PEAR Profitability Picture

```
::::::::::::::::::::::::::::::::::::::::::::::::::::::::::::::::::::::::::::::::::::::::::::::::::::::::::::
PAGE 1                                    PEAR SYSTEM DEMO                                    10/31/
                                 UNREALIZED CAPITAL GAINS AND LOSSES
SOC.SEC.#123-45-6789                        JOHN E. CASH                              ACCT.#123456
::::::::::::::::::::::::::::::::::::::::::::::::::::::::::::::::::::::::::::::::::::::::::::::::::::::::::::
```

SHARES OR PAR VALUE	SECURITY	PURCHASE DATE	COST	MARKET PRICE	MARKET VALUE	SHORT TERM GAIN(LOSS)	LONG TERM GAIN(LOSS)
1,000	AMER BROADCASTING	01/01/80	33.00	35.000	35,000.00	34,967.00	
1,000	DOME PETROLEUM	02/21/80	35,969.17	57.000	57,000.00	21,030.83	
400	DOME PETROLEUM	02/25/80	13,726.00	57.000	22,800.00	9,074.00	
1,500	GEORGIA PACIFIC	10/03/79	41,799.00	25.750	38,625.00		(3,174.00)
1,500	GEORGIA PACIFIC	10/01/79	42,815.00	25.750	38,625.00		(4,190.00)
1,685	GRACE W.R.	03/13/78	45,250.00	49.625	83,618.12		38,368.12
3,000	NL INDUSTRIES	12/16/77	51,938.10	62.250	186,750.00		134,811.90
800	ARCATA CV.A	12/14/78	21,584.00	27.750	22,200.00		616.00
600	JOHNSON CTRL CV.B	12/17/79	21,214.00	34.000	20,400.00	(814.00)	
30	ENGLHRD JAN 60 CALL	09/19/80	15,422.35	3.250	9,750.00	(5,672.35)	
10	HMSTK JAN 66 5/8CALL	09/26/80	13,577.42	17.000	17,000.00	3,422.58	
50,000	BENEFICIAL CORP DEB. 8% 06/15/01	06/15/76	50,000.00	78.500	39,250.00		(10,750.00)
50,000	PFIZER DEB. 9.25% 08/15/00	01/01/70	49,750.00	76.500	38,250.00		(11,500.00)
25,000	BOSTON MASS. G.O. 6.25% 08/01/97	11/14/69	24,512.50	76.000	19,000.00		(5,512.50)
30,000	LITTLE ROCK ARK. 7.3% 09/01/11	12/12/79	26,100.00	78.000	23,400.00	(2,700.00)	
75,000	GEN'L MOT ACCEPT 13.5% 11/27/80	10/14/80	75,000.00	100.000	75,000.00	0.00	
50,000	GEN'L MOT ACCEPT 13.25% 11/07/80	10/14/80	50,000.00	100.000	50,000.00	(0.00)	
25,000	U.S.TREASURY 9.75% 05/31/81	07/11/79	25,500.00	97.250	24,312.50		(1,187.50)
25,000	U.S.TREASURY 9.75% 05/31/81	07/10/79	25,375.00	97.250	24,312.50		(1,062.50)
21,000	NAT'L LIQUID RESERVE	01/01/80	21,000.00	1.000	21,000.00	0.00	
		TOTALS	650,565.54		846,293.12	59,308.06	136,419.52

Unrealized Capital Gains and Losses—Update your securities prices with the Dow Jones Quotation Service, then get a complete, accurate and current picture of each client's profitability down to the individual position, organized by long and short term gains.

Courtesy of PEAR Systems

Exhibit 6-24. PEAR Cross-Reference

```
SECURITY CROSS-REFERENCE REPORT---                          APRIL 1,                              PAGE 2
!!!!!!!!!!!!!!!!!!!!!!!!!!!!!!!!!!!!!!!!!!!!!!!!!!!!!!!!!!!!!!!!!!!!!!!!!!!!!!!!!!!!!!!!!!!!!!!!!!!!!!!!
                               SHS/M    DATE      BOUGHT    DATE      SOLD
AMSTAR CORP.       1ASR
--------------------
HARRY L. SMITH......................... 200    11/12/80....... 28.58


APPLE COMPUTER INC.  1AAPL
--------------------
HARRY L. SMITH......................... 200    12/26/80....... 36.02


APPLICON INC.      1APPL
--------------------
JAMES E. CARTER........................ 200    12/04/80....... 42.62    01/07/81....... 38.39
HARRIET B. STOWE....................... 100    12/08/80....... 37.87    01/09/81....... 38.48
JOAN OF ARK FOUNDATION................. 100    12/05/80....... 41.87
HARRY L. SMITH......................... 200    03/02/81....... 33.00
HARRY L. SMITH......................... 200    12/17/80....... 40.31    01/06/81....... 45.10


ARIZ. PUB. SERVICE   1AZP
--------------------
MS. MORTIMER SMERD..................... 300    05/24/79....... 18.76    01/15/81....... 17.42
JOHN E. CASH........................... 300    01/01/81....... 17.62    01/16/81....... 17.42


ARMCO INC. CV. PREF. 1AS+
--------------------
MS. MORTIMER SMERD..................... 200    06/14/79....... 28.87


ATLANTIC SERVICES    1@ATSV
--------------------
JOHN L. SULLIVAN....................... 500    01/01/81........ 0.00


BACHE GROUP INC.   1BAC
--------------------
J.P. MORGAN ESQ........................ 110    05/21/80........ 8.27


BACHE GROUP WTS.   1BACI
--------------------
JAMES B. RICH.......................... 200    01/09/81....... 10.11    03/24/81....... 12.88
CHARLES X. CHANG....................... 200    01/06/81....... 11.38


BALLY MFG.         1BLY
--------------------
HARRY L. SMITH......................... 400    03/02/81....... 18.55


BASIC RESOURCES INTL 1BASRF
--------------------
MR. M. ALI............................. 100    11/26/80....... 11.28
MR. R. REAGAN.......................... 500    01/21/80....... 12.38
I. PERLMAN - PENSION PLAN.............. 200    03/04/80....... 16.57
```

Security Cross-Reference Report—At the push of a button, PEAR generates a complete listing of all positions on the system by security. You can forget about tedious calculations of average costs, double posting of transactions, and embarrassing audits of your records.

Courtesy of PEAR Systems

Exhibit 6–25. PEAR Historical Records

```
!!!!!!!!!!!!!!!!!!!!!!!!!!!!!!!!!!!!!!!!!!!!!!!!!!!!!!!!!!!!!!!!!!!!!!!!!!!!!!!!!!!!!!!!!!!!!!!!!!!!!!!!!!!!
PAGE 1                               PEAR SYSTEM DEMO                              01/01/   TO 12/31/
                              REALIZED CAPITAL GAINS AND LOSSES
SOC.SEC.#123-45-6789                     JOHN E. CASH                              ACCT.#123456
!!!!!!!!!!!!!!!!!!!!!!!!!!!!!!!!!!!!!!!!!!!!!!!!!!!!!!!!!!!!!!!!!!!!!!!!!!!!!!!!!!!!!!!!!!!!!!!!!!!!!!!!!!!!
```

SHARES OR PAR VALUE	SECURITY	PURCHASE DATE	SALE DATE	COST	PROCEEDS +NYS TAX	SHORT TERM GAIN(LOSS)	LONG TERM GAIN(LOSS)	NYS TAX
300	ARIZ. PUB. SERVICE	01/01/81	01/16/81	5,287.50	5,226.40	(61.10)		0.00
200	ALEXANDERS	11/06/80	01/29/81	2,644.24	2,660.49	16.25		0.00
200	PENN. PWR. LGT.	11/27/79	02/01/81	3,701.00	3,179.95		(521.05)	0.00
20	PACIFIC POWER & LGT.	05/01/80	02/02/81	342.00	387.00	45.00		0.00
200	PACIFIC POWER & LGT.	01/16/80	02/02/81	3,750.00	3,873.10		123.10	0.00
100	GRAPHIC SCANNING	11/17/80	02/19/81	3,188.78	3,094.79	(93.99)		0.00
300	MCI COMM. CV.PREF.	10/02/79	03/04/81	3,122.46	5,337.23		2,214.77	0.00
300	AM INTERNATIONAL	11/18/80	03/04/81	4,561.95	4,408.72	(153.23)		0.00
400	CITY FED. N.J.	10/22/80	03/11/81	5,179.80	3,610.42	(1,569.38)		0.00
200	SYKES DATATRONICS	10/16/80	03/23/81	4,598.51	7,981.02	3,382.51		0.00
	TOTALS.....			36,376.24		1,566.06		0.00
					39,759.12		1,816.82	

Realized Capital Gains and Losses—The benefits of recording transactions that include historical cost basis become apparent when you need tax reports for your clients. When you enter sell tickets, the information has already been created to generate each client's realized gain and loss reports for any period desired. Historical gain and loss records can be reorganized at year end by use of a few simple commands. You also have the option of recording New York State Taxes in order to save your client's money at tax time.

Courtesy of PEAR Systems

Exhibit 6-26. PEAR Income Data

```
!!!!!!!!!!!!!!!!!!!!!!!!!!!!!!!!!!!!!!!!!!!!!!!!!!!!!!!!!!!!!!!!!!!!!!!!!!!!!!!!!!!!!!!!!!!!!!!!!!!!!!!!!!
PAGE 1                              PEAR SYSTEM DEMO                          06/30/   TO 06/30/
                            STATEMENT OF INVESTMENT INCOME
SOC.SEC.#123-45-6789                    JOHN E. CASH                              ACCT.#123456
!!!!!!!!!!!!!!!!!!!!!!!!!!!!!!!!!!!!!!!!!!!!!!!!!!!!!!!!!!!!!!!!!!!!!!!!!!!!!!!!!!!!!!!!!!!!!!!!!!!!!!!!!!

                      SECURITY DESCRIPTION              INCOME

                      AMER.EL.PWR.                      552.00
                      CASTLE & COOKE                    160.00
                      EAGLE PICHER IND.                 192.00
                      OCCIDENTAL PETE.                  457.50
                      UPJOHN CO.                        450.00

                 TOTAL COMMON STOCKS                  1,811.50




                      ALLIS CHALMERS     10.35%  06/01/99    220.70
                      ALUM. CO. CV. BOND  5.25%  09/15/91     52.50
                      PITTSTON CP. CV.DEB. 9.2%  07/01/04    324.75

                 TOTAL CORPORATE BONDS                 597.95




                      U.S. TREA. NOTES   12.625% 10/31/81    242.50
                      U.S. TREA. NOTES    9.125% 06/30/81     36.50

                 TOTAL U.S.TREASURIES                  279.00

                 TOTAL PORTFOLIO                     2,688.45
```

Statement of Investment Income—During the year, enter income data from your monthly statements on PEAR and avoid concern about the accuracy of manually reconstructed income schedules at year end. You can also generate income summaries for any period desired—a particular month, week, or a non-calendar fiscal year.

The PEAR System also generates complete status reports when it automatically splits a stock and accounts for fractional shares, when it generates a cross reference report for an individual security, when it backs up your files, when it lists portfolio holdings by symbol and description, and when it deletes a specific security.

who have not, it still shouldn't be too much of a hurdle since VisiCalc is relatively easy to use.

Portware

An interesting set of programs is in Portware from the company of the same name. The series includes Portrate, Portrac, Portrend, and Portcom.

Portrate is a unique planning aid covered in Chapter 3 that helps you make or improve upon your strategic decisions by evaluating portfolio quality, risk, yield, price-earnings, industries, diversification, income and cash flow, and liquidity.

Portrac helps you keep complete records of your transactions and portfolio status with up-to-date data on portfolio value, cost, acquisition dates, realized gains/losses, expirations/maturities, cash analysis, and audit trails (see Exhibit 6–27).

Portrend helps track and compare portfolio and market income return, principal return, and total return to measure your performance (see Exhibit 6–28).

Portcom, the fourth module in the Portware series, provides access to the Dow Jones News/Retrieval® service. It automatically logs-on to the DJN/R service, retrieves and stores quotes, and updates portfolio files. Using Portcom, any number of lists up to 200 securities in length may be created and stored. These may be a mixture of stocks, bonds, options, and mutual funds, as well as U.S. notes and bonds.

The *Portware* series is interesting because it brings together several key elements of investing. Starting at the planning stage, you can evaluate several alternative hypothetical portfolios against your own needs and objectives using Portrate. Then Portrac and Portrend provide the portfolio management tools, and finally, there is Portcom to bring you the most current market data.

Stockpak

Stockpak is offered by Standard & Poor's for Radio Shack's TRS-80 microcomputers. Stockpak provides 30 key facts for each of the 900 most actively traded common stocks. These facts are updated monthly by S&P. The Portfolio Management section lets you record your stock purchases and sales and keep close track of your overall account (see Exhibit 6–29). The system also provides the investor with a variety of criteria for screening all 900 stocks. For example, if you wanted to screen only growth stocks within a particular industry, with specific yields, earnings, price ranges, capitalization, and so forth, you could easily set up the

Exhibit 6–27. Sample Portrac

```
           SAMPLE PORTRAC 1981
           PORTFOLIO VALUATION
               06/29/81
----------------------------------------
# SHS    NAME      PRICE      AMOUNT
----------------------------------------
 800     AMBRDS    43. 38      34700
 500     AT&T      57. 13      28562
1000     DENMFG    23. 50      23500
2000     FLAPW     15. 13      30250
 500     GTNONK    43. 88      21937
1561     KEYBANK   14. 00      21854
 300     PACPW     21. 00       6300
1000     PSVNH     16. 25      16250
1000     PSVNM     24. 25      24250
1000     ROBTSN    27. 63      27625
 400     ROYLD     32. 75      13100
 468     SFEIND    26. 25      12285
1000     TENNECO   38. 13      38125
 500     TRAVLRS   48. 25      24125
1000     BOS1. 17   8. 63       8625
  10 C   IBMJN       . 25        250
  20 P   MMMAL      4. 75       9500
 100 W   TW WT      9. 63        962
   5 S   TICKI      1. 50       -750
 500 S   XEROX     51. 75     -25875
  20 M   BELLPA    62. 00      12400
         T-BILL                10000
         CASH BALANCE          98798

TOTAL PORTFOLIO VALUE         436774
THERE ARE 23 ITEMS LISTED.
----------------------------------------
```

```
           SAMPLE PORTRAC 1981
           PORTFOLIO VALUATION
                   BY
            SECURITY CATEGORY
               06/29/81
----------------------------------------
CATEGORY              TOTAL      %WGT
----------------------------------------
LONG POSITIONS:

COMMON STOCK         322864     73. 9
PREFERRED STOCK        8625      2. 0
OPTIONS                9750      2. 2
WARRANTS                962       . 2
BONDS                 12400      2. 8
T-BILLS               10000      2. 3
CASH                  98798     22. 6

TOTAL LONG           463399    100. 0

TOTAL SHORT          -26625

TOTAL VALUE          436774
----------------------------------------
```

Exhibit 6–27 (*concluded*)

```
        SAMPLE PORTRAC
        REALIZED GAINS/LOSSES
        ----------------------

# SHS    NAME    PRICE    DATE     AMOUNT
------------------------------------------
1000    BOSE PR   7. 66   05/13/81    7663
        BASIS    10. 00   09/19/75   10000
            LONG  TERM LOSS......    -2337

 500  S TRVLRS    6. 41   06/12/81    3204
        BASIS     3. 87   03/24/81    1932
            SHORT TERM LOSS......    -1271

 500  S TRVLRS     . 75   07/09/81     375
        BASIS     1. 40   06/12/81     699
            SHORT TERM GAIN......     324

NET LONG TERM  LOSS       -2337
NET SHORT TERM LOSS                   -948

TOTAL NET LOSS                       -3285
```

```
            SAMPLE PORTRAC 198
               AUDIT TRAIL
    DATE        ITEM      AMOUNT      BALANCE
---------------------------------------------
08/15/81 PURCHASE    26345. 00    72453. 00
08/15/81 SALE        14230. 00    86683. 00
08/15/81 DIVIDEND     3445. 00    90128. 00
08/15/81 CONTRIB    125000. 00   215128. 00
08/15/81 INC W/D      2333. 00   212795. 00
08/15/81 PURCHASE    26345. 00    72453. 00
08/15/81 PURCHASE    25343. 00    73455. 00
08/15/81 PURCHASE    26343. 00    72455. 00
08/17/81 PURCHASE    48885. 00    49913. 00
08/17/81 SALE        47556. 00    97469. 00
08/17/81 DIVIDEND     3445. 00   100914. 00
08/17/81 INC W/D      2150. 00    98764. 00
08/17/81 CONTRIB     85000. 00   183764. 00
```

Courtesy of Portware, Inc.

screening criteria with a few keystrokes, making portfolio creation much easier and faster.

Stockpak comes in two parts—the actual system software and an annual subscription service. The first part contains four software components: (1) the Portfolio Management System, (2) Screen and Select software, (3) Report Writer programs (see Exhibit 6–30), and (4) a sample

Exhibit 6-28. Sample Portrend

```
         SAMPLE PORTREND 198
    PRINCIPAL PERFORMANCE MONITOR
          JAN TO AUG 1981
-------------------------------------
                ADJUSTED  ---RETURN %---
MONTH   VALUE     VALUE   MONTH   ANNUAL
-------------------------------------
  AUG   425056   426230   -4. 0   -39. 0
  JUL   443824   443722   -1. 3   -15. 4
  JUN   449909   448429    2. 4    32. 9
  MAY   437793   438967     . 2     2. 5
  APR   438052   437950     . 8    10. 1
  MAR   434421   436441    3. 0    43. 9
  FEB   423183   421812    2. 7    37. 7
  JAN   410555   410453    2. 0    28. 1
  DEC   401981


PERIOD RETURN          5. 7%
ANNUALIZED PERIOD RETURN        8. 8%
```

```
         SAMPLE PORTREND 198
     INCOME PERFORMANCE MONITOR
          JAN TO AUG 1981
-------------------------------------
                AVERAGE   ---YIELD %---
MONTH   INCOME  PORT VAL  MONTH   ANNUAL
-------------------------------------
  AUG    2626    435027     . 6     7. 4
  JUL    3902    446815     . 8    10. 9
  JUN    5280    443111    1. 1    15. 2
  MAY    2626    438509     . 5     7. 4
  APR    3902    436185     . 8    11. 2
  MAR    5280    429812    1. 2    15. 7
  FEB    2626    416183     . 6     7. 8
  JAN    3902    406217     . 9    12. 1


PERIOD YIELD          7. 1%
ANNUALIZED PERIOD YIELD       10. 9%
```

database containing 900 companies with 30 data items per company. The annual subscription service entitles you to receive each month a new disk with updated information. A newsletter is also sent to subscribers to guide them in the use of Stockpak under changing market conditions.

Unlike the preceding portfolio management programs, Stockpak does

Exhibit 6–28 (*concluded*)

SAMPLE PORTREND 198
MARKET DATA

LINE/ MONTH	VALUE	% YIELD	T-BILL RATE	PORT BETA
1/DEC	969	5. 70	15. 03	0. 00
2/JAN	947	5. 80	15. 41	. 60
3/FEB	975	5. 60	14. 23	. 60
4/MAR	1004	5. 40	12. 64	. 60
5/APR	998	5. 40	14. 40	. 60
6/MAY	992	5. 50	16. 41	. 60
7/JUN	977	5. 60	14. 69	. 60
8/JUL	945	5. 80	15. 23	. 60
9/AUG	881	6. 30	15. 70	. 60

MARKET PERFORMANCE MONITOR
JAN TO AUG 198

MONTH	VALUE	% RETURN INCOME	TOTAL
AUG	881	. 52	-6. 4
JUL	945	. 48	-2. 8
JUN	977	. 46	-1. 0
MAY	992	. 45	-. 1
APR	998	. 45	-. 1
MAR	1004	. 45	3. 3
FEB	975	. 46	3. 3
JAN	947	. 48	-1. 8
DEC	969		

PERIOD RETURN   -5. 9%
ANNUALIZED PERIOD RETURN   -8. 7%

SAMPLE PORTREND 198
MGMT PERFORMANCE MONITOR
JAN TO AUG 1981

	PERIOD	ANNUAL
	% RETURN	
MARKET RETURN	-5. 9	-8. 7
MARKET RETURN AT PORTFOLIO BETA(. 60)	. 5	1. 0
PORTFOLIO RETURN	13. 3	20. 6
MGMT PERFORMANCE	12. 7	19. 5

Courtesy of Portware, Inc.

Exhibit 6–29.   Stockpak PMS System

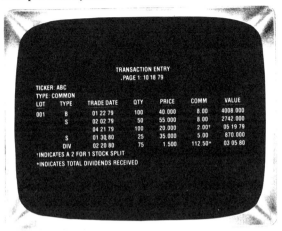

This is a record of all user-entered transactions on ABC Corporation common stock from the Portfolio Management System. The system will automatically track and list B (buys), S (sells), / (stock splits), DIV (dividends) and commissions for you. It also computes all the arithmetic functions necessary to manage and evaluate your holdings based on transactions you ask the system to perform.

The net position report from the Portfolio Management System provides a summary of all securities followed in regards to current value, net gains and losses and unrealized gains/losses. Other Portfolio reports list short and long-term gains and losses, dividends and profits received, eligibility for long-term gains or losses for tax consideration, rate of return analysis and current status of each security.

Courtesy of Standard & Poor's Corp.

Exhibit 6–30. Stockpak Report Writer System

OIL & GAS (LOW PE)

DATA DATE: 01 31 80
DATE RUN: 01 31 80

TIK	PRICE	EPSEST	PE(EST)	DIVIDEND	YIELD	RANK
SUN	81.000	11.77	6.88	3.000	3.7	A
XON	60.875	9.74	6.25	4.800	7.9	A+
MOB	58.375	9.48	6.16	3.000	5.1	A+
SD	62.250	10.44	5.96	3.200	5.1	A+
GO	39.250	6.78	5.79	2.250	5.7	A−
SC	32.750	6.00	5.46	1.160	3.5	A
TX	34.875	6.48	5.38	2.400	6.9	A−
API.A	40.750	7.77	5.24	2.500	6.1	B+
TSO	20.750	4.03	5.15	0.000	0.0	B
OXY	28.500	7.00	4.07	1.500	5.3	B
RD	82.125	25.00	3.28	5.530	6.7	A
BP	32.750	10.00	3.28	0.806	2.5	—
TOTALS						
AVERAGE			5.24			

This is a report created from the STOCKPAK Report Writer System using the results of a user-defined screening of the data base. The screening process used a criteria set called: Oil and Gas stocks with Price/Earnings Ratios of less than 7 Based on Estimated Earnings Per Share. The user-created report shown here lists 12 Oil and Gas stocks yielded from the screening. Note the capability which allows you to sort these stocks in descending order by the Price/Earnings Ratio based on Estimated Earnings.

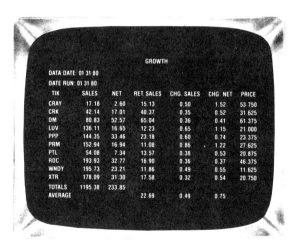

GROWTH

DATA DATE: 01 31 80
DATE RUN: 01 31 80

TIK	SALES	NET	RET. SALES	CHG. SALES	CHG. NET	PRICE
CRAY	17.18	2.60	15.13	0.50	1.52	53.750
CRK	42.14	17.01	40.37	0.35	0.52	31.625
DM	80.83	52.57	65.04	0.36	0.41	61.375
LUV	136.11	16.65	12.23	0.65	1.15	21.000
PPP	144.35	33.46	23.18	0.60	0.74	23.375
PRM	152.94	16.94	11.08	0.86	1.22	27.625
PTL	54.08	7.34	13.57	0.38	0.53	20.875
RDC	193.93	32.77	16.90	0.36	0.37	46.375
WNDY	195.73	23.21	11.86	0.49	0.55	11.625
XTR	178.09	31.30	17.58	0.32	0.54	20.750
TOTALS	1195.38	233.85				
AVERAGE			22.69	0.49	0.75	

This is another user-created report from the STOCKPAK Report Writer System. A pre-defined screen of the data base in the Screen and Select portion of the system has located companies with net sales of less than 200 million, return on sales greater than 10%, and with an increase in both sales and net income of at least 30% from the previous year. The report shown here displays all user-selected information on each company. The system allows you to total or average any column of numeric data.

Courtesy of Standard & Poor's Corp.

not have access to either Dow Jones News/Retrieval® or any other on-line information utility, but for many investors the monthly updates are more than adequate. This is one of the decisions you have to make. Ask yourself, "Do I really need a constant and up-to-the-second flow of stock market data or can I live with periodic updates?" The cost of on-line data is certainly much higher than either monthly, disk-borne updates, or manual entry of data. Though there are many benefits to retrieving data from an information utility, the fact remains that it may not suit your particular style of investment management or your investing budget.

Personal Investor Program

An interesting program from PBL Corporation is the Personal Investor. Unique to this program is the detailed tax report it produces (see Exhibit 6–31) that gives you all the pertinent information you need to file your tax return. We discussed earlier how important taxes are to your ultimate investing profit. It is not only important to consider the effect of taxes when planning your portfolio but also when reporting your profits to Uncle Sam. With the Personal Investor you can automatically maintain your tax data as a byproduct of the investment bookkeeping process.

Other reports you can produce using the Personal Investor program include portfolio description and price, stock gains or losses, and a tally of dividends (see Exhibit 6–32). This system was designed expressly for the individual investor, whereas some of the other systems we have discussed could be used by either pros or amateurs. The data-entry screens and reports are relatively simple and well laid out, and consequently more easily understood.

Market Analyst

Market Analyst from Anidata is the program that allows the individual investor to bridge the gap between portfolio management and technical analysis by offering both functions in one neat package. This program also gives you the freedom to communicate with not only the Dow Jones News/Retrieval® service but with the SOURCE and CompuServe as well. If you can't get the information you need from one service, then you can turn to another.

Some of the features of the subprograms within Market Analyst include the following:

1. *Portfolio Manager:*
   Maintains multiple portfolios on separate disks.
   Indicates short-term and about-to-turn positions.
   Updates current prices easily.

Exhibit 6–31. PBL Tax Program

Date 3/13/82

Sym	Date of Purchase	Date Sold	Number of Shares	Purchase Cost	Proceeds from Sale	Profit/<Loss> Short Term	Profit/<Loss> Long Term	Commissions On Purchase	Commissions On Sale	Price/Share Total	Price/Share Of Purchase	Price/Share Of Sale
GM	7/15/82	11/17/82	75.0000	921.63	1076.62	154.99		9.13	10.88	20.01	12 5/32	14 1/2
IBM	1/17/81	3/1/82	20.0000	1282.45	1225.12	<57.33>		12.45	12.38	24.83	63 1/2	61 7/8
KO	12/14/79	3/8/82	120.0000	3423.56	3727.35		303.79	33.56	37.65	71.21	28 1/4	31 3/8
AAPL	3/3/82	3/10/82	150.0000	2272.50	2585.40	312.90		22.50	20.85	43.35	15	17 3/8
GM	3/8/74	1/5/82	100.0000	2790.13	4063.15		1273.02	27.63	49.35	76.98	27 5/8	41 1/8
GM	3/8/74	3/10/82	50.0000	1395.06	1957.22		562.16	13.81	17.78	31.59	27 5/8	39 1/2
Total				12085.33	14634.86	410.56	2138.97	119.08	148.89	267.97		

Total Profit/<Loss> of 2549.53

Courtesy of PBL Corp.

Exhibit 6–32. PBL Personal Investor

DESCRIPTION AND PRICE

Sym	Stock Name	Purchase Date	No. of Shares	Purchase Price	Last Price	Commission
GM	General Motors	3/8/74	150.0000	27 5/8	39 1/2	41.44
GM	General Motors	7/15/82	100.0000	39 1/2	39 1/2	39.50
IBM	Intn'l Business Mach	3/3/82	500.0000	57 1/4	59 1/8	314.87
IBM	Intn'l Business Mach	1/17/81	80.0000	63 1/2	59 1/8	49.78
KO	Coca Cola Co.	12/14/79	80.0000	28 1/4	31 3/8	22.37
CMB	Chase Manhattan	7/15/81	150.0000	58	57 1/8	87.00
CMB	Chase Manhattan	3/9/82	200.0000	56 3/8	57 1/8	56.37
AAPL	Apple Computer Co.	1/1/79	70.0000	21	16 1/2	14.70
AAPL	Apple Computer Co.	3/3/82	150.0000	15	16 1/2	22.50

STOCK GAIN / <LOSS>

Symbol	Name	Purchase Cost	Current Value	Gain / <LOSS>	
				Short Term	Long Term
GM	General Motors	4185.19	5925.00		1739.81
GM	General Motors	3989.50	3950.00	<39.50>	
IBM	Intn'l Business Mach.	28939.87	29562.50	622.63	
IBM	Intn'l Business Mach.	5129.78	4730.00		<399.78>
KO	Coca Cola Co.	2282.37	2510.00		227.63
CMB	Chase Manhattan	8787.00	8568.75	<218.25>	
CMB	Chase Manhattan	11331.37	11425.00	93.63	
AAPL	Apple Computer Co.	1484.70	1155.00		<329.70>
AAPL	Apple Computer Co.	2272.50	2475.00	202.50	
		68402.28	70301.25	661.01	1237.96
	Total Gain/<Loss> of Stock is				1898.97

STOCK DIVIDENDS

Symbol	Name	Xdividend Date	Quarterly Dividend	Annual Dividend	Yield	
					Purchase Cost	Last Price
GM	General Motors	2/5/82	0.6000	2.4000	8.7%	6.1%
GM	General Motors	2/5/82	0.6000	2.4000	6.1%	6.1%
IBM	Intn'l Business Mach.	2/4/82	0.8600	3.4400	6.0%	5.8%
IBM	Intn'l Business Mach.	2/4/82	0.8600	3.4400	5.4%	5.8%
KO	Coca Cola Co.	3/9/82	0.6200	2.4800	8.8%	7.9%
CMB	Chase Manhatten	1/26/82	0.8500	3.4000	5.9%	6.0%
CMB	Chase Manhatten	1/26/82	0.8500	3.4000	6.0%	6.0%

Courtesy of PBL Corp.

Prints reports for tax accounting.

Reports and evaluates gains and losses, market value, liquid value, current yield, averaged cost, and term.

2. *News, Views, & Quotes:*

Holds 30 pages of text in memory, thereby allowing offline data review and thus saving you money on connect costs.

Mini-screen editor facilitates screen reading.

Maintains a list of frequently called numbers.

3. *Technical Analyst:*

Provides semilogarithmic or linear scales.

Lets you select a time frame for analysis up to six months of daily data.

Provides several market indicators on split-screen charts allowing you to track and compare.

These are only a few of the many programs available to automate your portfolio. Many others have features that are different, in some cases uniquely so. You should review the whole wide array of programs for the special feature that fits your portfolio management technique. Although this will be a time-consuming task, it should prove worthwhile. You might also talk to users of programs that interest you and find out why they chose the program and if they're satisfied. Consultations with user groups may be useful, too.

Some companies offer a demonstration diskette for little or no cost. Try out the demonstrator and get a feel for the program's methodology, then ask the vendor any questions you may have. Check out the company's references and make your decision.

TECHNICAL ANALYSIS AIDS

Four technical analysis programs are available for your computer that are outstanding, namely: Dow Jones Market Analyzer™, On-Balance Volume™ Charting, Stock/Market Tracker, and Compu Trac. They provide a range of tools that can meet the demands of even the most ardent technical analysis. Some of the indicators and statistical methods may be beyond the understanding of amateur investors. Nevertheless, it is not imperative that you understand the program's methodology to benefit from its output.

In the previous chapter, we discussed three programs used to quickly retrieve stock data from the various information services. While two of those programs are strictly limited to retrieving financial data and portfolio management, one, the Dow Jones Market Analyzer™ (DJMA), provides aids for technical analysis as well. It is, however, just one of several technical analysis programs that gives you the ability to gather historical data on stocks and quickly produce sets of charts for subsequent analysis. The DJMA charts make use of the market timing indicators we discussed earlier. These charting aids can relieve you of the tedium of constructing the charts yourself, freeing you to spend more of your time analyzing data.

A word of caution is necessary at this point since there is no magic to these indicators. By themselves they only point out trends and possible directions in stock prices and volumes. It is up to you to understand the interpretation of these indicators and apply them. Previous market experience will be helpful in understanding and maximizing the benefits of whatever system you use.

DOW JONES MARKET ANALYZER®

There are two parts to the DJMA. The first uses the computer as a "smart" terminal—one that can sift and sort the data contained in the DJN/R service—and the second part uses it as a powerful tool for technical analysis. Having already covered its smart terminal mode, let us now turn to the use of the DJMA for technical analysis.

Technical Analysis.   This is an attempt to describe the patterns in the movement of stock prices and volume, movements that usually result from an imbalance between supply and demand. Market indicators give us a feel for this imbalance and help us improve our timing into and out of the market. The DJMA lets you quickly retrieve historical and current data, and plot performance charts. In that way you can track as many stocks as you wish before actually choosing the one or ones you wish to buy or sell.

All of the indicators used for individual graphs fall into one of four general categories: moving averages, support/resistance lines, volume indicators, and oscillator charts. For comparing the price action of two different stocks, the DJMA and similar programs allow you to plot their performance against each other on one graph.

The usefulness of moving averages as trend indicators is that they provide a way to smooth out the discontinuities in daily price changes in the stock. Three types of moving averages are used in the DJMA: simple, weighted, and exponential. The *simple moving average* indicates the trend of closing stock prices over some specified time, giving the same weight to the early days as it does to the most recent days. A *weighted average,* however, gives more emphasis to the most recent closing prices. *Exponential moving averages* give the most weight to the more recent closing prices but consider all closing prices over a given period.

When the closing price of a stock is above the moving average, it is considered an indicator of bullish tendencies, while prices below the moving average are thought of as bearish signs. Indicators of future stock movements can also be derived from comparisons of two moving averages—a simple and an exponential. If the exponential is above the simple moving average, it may be interpreted as a departure from the stock's previous trading pattern. This is because the exponential moving average amplifies recent price tendencies more than the simple moving average.

The Dow Jones Market Analyzer also allows you to construct a *trading band* around any moving average. You can chart plus or minus bands around a simple moving average for a 12-day period, and if the price moves above or below this band you can expect that a correction is probably imminent.

Trading bands may help you to develop a system for making better investment decisions. Suppose you are evaluating a stock and have constructed a 10 percent trading band around either side of its moving average. Your sell signal occurs when the stock breaks through the upper 10 percent band. A corresponding buy signal occurs when it falls 10 percent below the average. As we noted earlier, *support/resistance lines* provide an indication of the general levels at which a stock price may be supported or will meet resistance as it attempts to move down or up. The types of S/R line provided by the DJMA include horizontal and trend lines, linear trading bands, and *1/3 and 2/3 speed* resistance lines. Each is based on historical trading patterns. Normally, when a stock price falls to the support level, demand for the stock appears to drive the price back up. A resistance line is a horizontal line above the stock price that works in reverse.

Trend lines may also be used as support and resistance lines. The purpose of trend lines instead of the standard S/R horizontal lines is to allow more flexibility in the direction of prices. If a support trend line is sloping upward and the prices stay above this line, then the stock's price is also in an upward tendency. If, however, the stock's price breaks the trend line and is accompanied by large volume, you can expect the stock to find new support and resistance levels.

Several volume indicators are available with the DJMA, including the following:

Negative and positive volume indicators.

Cumulative volume indicator.

Price/volume trend.

Daily volume indicator.

Many investors consider volume measurements essential to recognizing patterns of stock accumulation and distribution. When trend breakouts occur, they frequently increase the trading volumes associated with them. Thus sharply higher trading volume in a specific stock may be a harbinger of important shifts in stock prices.

The negative and positive volume indicators for a given stock are curves which can show relationships between rises and falls in its volume and trends in its price. Normally, positive volume indicators (PVIs) increase since increases in volume generally signal a rise in prices, while NVIs trend downward. Deviations from this normal volume/price relationship may be a warning of changes.

The cumulative volume indicator (CVI) is a running total of excess volume over down-volume during a specific period. CVI can be interpreted in relation to a given stock over time. For example, if a stock closes at $32 per share at a daily volume of 22,500 shares, then the stock would have to be traded daily at this volume to maintain the price.

The Dow Jones Market Analyzer™ also includes oscillator charting. Oscillators display certain differences not readily observable in the charts. The construction of momentum curves is done with oscillator charts. They are essentially the comparison of a stock's moving average with the oscillator's own moving average.

One unique and highly useful feature of the DJMA is comparison charting, which gives the investor the capability to compare multiple stock investments starting with an arbitrary point to assess how a given stock is performing relative to an industry or group of stocks.

A relative strength chart is also a type of comparison chart. It shows how a stock stacks up relative to an index like the DJIA, the S&P 500, or any other index you might choose. If your stock is rising faster than the index, it is certainly worth holding on to. If, on the other hand, it has dropped 10 percent while the index has only dropped 5 percent, then it may be time to reevaluate your position. (Exhibit 6–33 illustrates some of these graphical methods.)

Finally, if you have a favorite indicator, the DJMA lets you include it as part of its "user-jump" routine. This lets you incorporate it into the DJMA for personalized charts. The printer you use may require special prompting to print these charts, but a special program for driving the printer can also be included in the user-jump routine.

There are many other facilities of the Dow Jones Market Analyzer™, but the ones I have chosen to describe are basic to the program's operation. If your interest lies with other indicators, then perhaps a different program will satisfy your needs.

OBV Charting

At the heart of the OBV Charting system by Stock Market Software are the on-balance charting techniques developed by Joseph E. Granville. Technical analysts familiar with these concepts should find this program a significant improvement over manual charting methods because the calculations for charting indicators are completed automatically. The pro-

Exhibit 6–33. Dow Jones Market Analyzer™

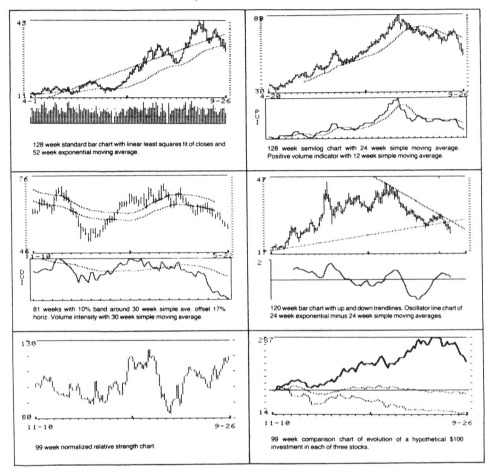

128 week standard bar chart with linear least squares fit of closes and 52 week exponential moving average.

128 week semilog chart with 24 week simple moving average. Positive volume indicator with 12 week simple moving average.

81 weeks with 10% band around 30 week simple ave. offset 17% horiz. Volume intensity with 30 week simple moving average.

120 week bar chart with up and down trendlines. Oscillator line chart of 24 week exponential minus 24 week simple moving averages.

99 week normalized relative strength chart.

99 week comparison chart of evolution of a hypothetical $100 investment in each of three stocks.

gram's charts show OBV, price, and variable moving averages, along with the CLX, NFI, and CCLX indicators (see Exhibits 6–34 through 6–37) for any stock or group of stocks.[1] The data for these charting programs can be obtained from any one of three different sources: CompuServe, Warner Computing Service, or the Dow Jones News/Retrieval® service. Two access programs are available for communicating with the information utilities: OBV Microlog permits retrieval of historical data from CompuServe's Microquote, while the OBV Dowlog lets you gather daily stock

---

[1] CLX, NFI, and CCLX are trademarks of Granville, Inc. Definitions for these terms are shown in the Appendix to this chapter.

Exhibit 6–34.   On-Balance Volume Charting

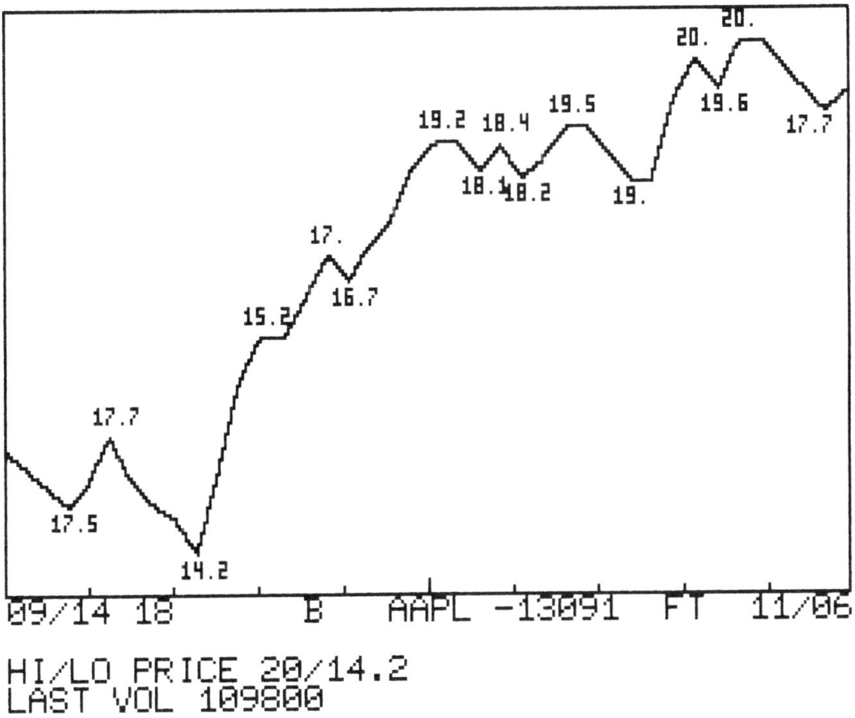

Courtesy of Stock Market Software

data from the DJN/R. You may read statistics on bonds, options, treasury notes, and mutual funds from the data banks, too. OBV Charting can be used for any one of these chores. All you have to do is tell it what type of security you want to chart.

Stock Tracker and Market Tracker

These tracking methods were designed and used by David Howard, a well-known and highly successful investment advisor, for several years before being computerized and offered to the public by H&H Trading Company. Contrary to what the name implies, Stock Tracker is designed for the trader in either stocks or commodities. Each day it will tell you whether to buy, sell, or hold your position. Trading signals are set up for a short-term basis (days or weeks) for stock options, and on an intermediate term (several weeks or months) for stocks and commodities. Long-term stock investments may be timed for periods longer than one year.

Exhibit 6–35. On-Balance Volume Charting

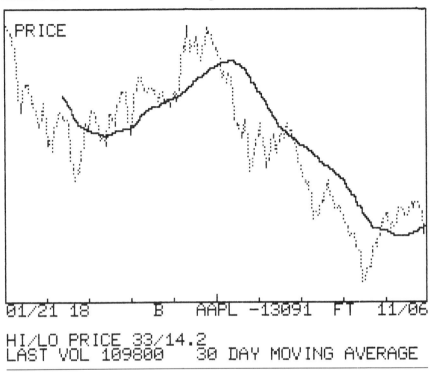

HI/LO PRICE 33/14.2
LAST VOL 109800   30 DAY MOVING AVERAGE

Courtesy of Stock Market Software

The Stock Tracker system needs to accumulate about two calendar months of historical data before it can issue trading signals. The required data consists of the date of the trade, daily closing prices and sales volumes, and the split ratio when and if a stock splits. This data may be entered manually or via the Dow Jones terminal program. The number of securities you can track is only limited by the number of disks you have available. Although the methodology used in Stock Tracker is based on the principles of Joseph Granville, it incorporates several major differences and should not be considered the same as On-Balance Volume.

Market Tracker is designed for use with Stock Tracker. It uses six technical market indicators to arrive at its Intermediate Composite Market Index:

A 5-day moving average of new highs and lows.

A 10-day advance/decline line.

A 30-day most-active oscillator.

Exhibit 6–36. On-Balance Volume Charting

Courtesy of Stock Market Software

The Dow Industrials chart pattern and trendline.

Short interest ratio.

A version of Granville's Climax Indicator.

These indicators create intermediate-term buy and sell signals for the market as a whole, not for specific stocks. You can selectively use Market Tracker signals to override Stock Tracker recommendations for an individual security. (The Market Grapher program provides a graphing capability to Market Tracker.)

Compu Trac

In 1979, a group of professional stock and commodity traders searching for a way to speed their technical market analysis formed something called the "Personal Computer Technical Analysis Group" (TAG). Today they claim to offer the largest collection of stock and commodity programs for the Apple computer. TAG also provides database manage-

Exhibit 6–37.   On-Balance Volume Charting

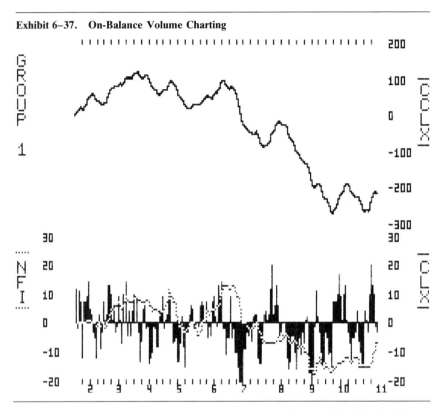

Courtesy of Stock Market Software

ment, including data acquisition of commodity, stock, and option information.

The collection of programs offered by TAG is Compu Trac, and it is a library of technical analysis programs that offers features for automatic data collection, bar and point-and-figure charts, statistical studies, account posting, record-keeping, and precision graphic printouts. The Compu Trac programs are complex but comprehensive. Nearly all of its technical analysis programs may be used for either stocks or commodities. (A more detailed discussion of these programs is in Chapter 12, Commodities and Options Trading.)

LOOKING BACK—AND AHEAD

Stock evaluation and selection is surely the heart of computer-aided investing; there are more programs available for stock investing than for any other single computer investing activity. In this short space I have attempted to describe the challenges of stock market investing and to show how the computer can help you discern patterns in the market to make better decisions. Your computerized investing system should include not only portfolio management and technical analysis programs but personal finance and planning elements as well. The interrelationship among these parts is very important to the success of your total program. The question you must always ask yourself is this: "Has my net worth increased as a result of my investing efforts?" By plugging your stock market successes or failures back into your original plan and measuring the impact on your personal finances, you will know if a change in direction or strategy is called for.

APPENDIX

On-Balance Volume™ Definitions*

1. *On-Balance Volume™* OBV™ is a running total of daily volume figures for a particular stock that can be plotted to form a line on a graph. If the OBV is superimposed on a price line and the OBV line is diverging upward, then this is a desirable situation called, a "positive slingshot." The converse is also true. However, if the stock's price is moving the same as the OBV, then future price fluctuations are indeterminate.

2. *On-Balance Volume breakouts* are used to determine the trend of the OBV. When the OBV line rises above the closest previous OBV high, the stock has recorded an upside breakout. This is an "UP" condition. A "DOWN" designation is given whenever the OBV falls below the closest previous low of the stock's OBV.

3. *Field Trends* describe the general direction of the stock's prices. The field trend is determined by examining a series of breakouts. The series is characterized by any number of UP or DOWN designations, not necessarily consecutive.

For example:

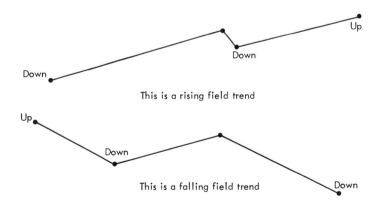

This is a rising field trend

This is a falling field trend

---

* Note: the terms "Granville," "Climax Indicator," "On-Balance Volume," "Net Field Trend," and the initials "CLX," "OBV," and "NFI" are trademarks of Granville, Inc., and should be used only to identify its services.

4. *Climax Indicator* (CLX) is the total number of upside breakouts in the 30 Dow Jones stocks (or any user-defined group of stocks) minus the total number of downside breakouts. The CLX is one of the indicators used to determine the tops and bottoms in the Dow Jones Industrial Average.

5. The *Net Field Trend Indicator* is the total number of Dow Jones stocks (or user-defined groups of stocks) in rising field trends minus the total in falling field trends.

Bibliography

Edgerton, Jerry. "How You Can Forecast the Market." *Money,* June 1982, pp. 40–42.

Hagin, Robert. *The Dow Jones-Irwin Guide to Modern Portfolio Theory.* Homewood, Ill.: Dow Jones-Irwin, 1979.

"How to Read Stock Market Indicators." *Business Week,* December 8, 1980, pp. 112–14.

"How to Get Started in Stocks." *Business Week,* August 4, 1980, pp. 78–81.

Rolo, Charles J. "Anticipating Major Ups and Downs." *Money,* June 1982, pp. 44–50.

Ryan, Paul. "Intelligent Investment Management by Computer." *Personal Computing,* January 1982, pp. 97–99.

Shafer, Edward D. "Being Bullish with Personal Computers." *Personal Computing,* July 1981, pp. 75–81.

Shaffer, Richard A. "Personal Computers are Becoming More Useful to Many Investors for Managing of Portfolios." *The Wall Street Journal,* December 29, 1980.

Sloan, Allan. "When to Sell a Stock." *Money,* June 1982, pp. 73–74.

"Stock Selection, Timing and Techniques." New York: Merrill Lynch Pierce Fenner & Smith, September 1978.

Resource List

Name	Resource	Computer
Portware	Portware, Inc. 1234 Tucker Edina, MN 98765	Apple II+
Wall Streeter	Microlab 2310 Stokie Valley Road Highland Park, IL 60035	CP/M-Based
Stock-Focus	Centennial Software 410 17th St. Suite 1375 Denver, CO 80202	Apple II+ IBM Personal Computer TRS-80
Market Charter and Market Analyzer	RTR Software, Inc. 1147 Baltimore Drive El Paso, TX 79902	Apple II+

Name	Resource	Computer
On-Balance Volume Charting	Stock Market Software 44 Front Street Ashland, MA 01721	Apple II +
Stock Pak	Standard & Poor's Corp. Personal Computer Division 25 Broadway New York, NY 10004	TRS-80
Forecaster	META Software Engineering 4737 Trumbull St. Albuquerque, NM 87108	TRS-80
Computing Investor Series	MicroComputing Research 29 Estancia Marana, AZ 85238	Apple II +
Portfolio Master	Investor's Software P.O. Box 2605 San Francisco, CA 94162	Apple II +
PEAR	PEAR Systems P.O. Box 2605 Stamford, CT 06903	Apple II +
Stock Tracker and Market Tracker	H & H Trading Company P.O. Box 549 Clayton, CA 94517	Apple II +
Compu Trac	Compu Trac, Inc. P.O. Box 15951 New Orleans, LA 70175	Apple II +
Stock Management	Atari Program Exchange Atari, Inc. P.O. Box 3705 Santa Clara, CA 95055	Atari 800
The Personal Investor	PBL Corporation 605 Harmony Cr. Dr. Wayzata, MN 55391	Apple II + IBM Personal Computer
Market Analyst	Anidata 613 Jaeger Ct. Sicklerville, NJ 08081	Apple II +
Market Analyzer	N2 Computing 5318 Forest Ridge Road Silverton, OR 97381	Apple II + /III
Dow Jones Market Analyzer™	Dow Jones & Company, Inc. P.O. Box 300 Princeton, NJ 08540	Apple II + /III
Dow Jones Market Manager	Dow Jones & Company, Inc. P.O. Box 300 Princeton, NJ 08540	Apple II + /III

Name	*Resource*	*Computer*
Dow Jones Market Microscope	Dow Jones & Company, Inc. P.O. Box 300 Princeton, NJ 08540	Apple II + /III
Portfolio Accounting- and-Reporting System	Software Resources Inc. 186 Alewife Brook Parkway Suite 310 Cambridge, MA 02138	IBM Personal Computer
Wall Street Plotter	Dickens Data Systems, Inc. Suite A 3050 Holcomb Bridge Road Norcross, GA 30071	Apple II +

Debt Securities Analysis

Debt securities differ significantly from stocks in that they are interest-bearing IOUs, as opposed to dividend-yielding shares in a company. Traditionally, debt securities have been a key ingredient of a balanced portfolio, complementing one's investments. Investment strategies traditionally call for moving into stocks when the stock market is at a low and into bonds when the market is high. The fluctuations in the value of stocks and bonds are not, however, always consistent with this predictable teeter-totter pattern.

There are other myths about bonds that have been dispelled in recent years. Some of these myths include the beliefs that:

1. *Bonds are stable investments.* In the past few years, high inflation and wildly gyrating interest rates have thrown bond prices into a deep slump. Vast amounts of money have been lost as bond rallies have been closely followed by major sell-offs. All of this has come at a time when bonds have offered investors their highest "real return" (the interest rate minus the rate of inflation) returns in history.

2. *Investments in short-term debt issues are safe for long-term investors.* The short-term market is extremely volatile in terms of yield, though not price. At best investors may find such short-term investments as money funds or certificates of deposit to be simply short- to medium-term

parking places for their funds while they sit on the sideline waiting for the markets to settle down.

3. *Interest rate predictions are scientific.* No matter how much data an analyst has that might bear on the future course of interest rates, he or she still doesn't have it all. There are simply too many economic as well as geopolitical and sociopolitical variables that can affect forecasts. Wars, social upheaval, and natural disasters are totally unpredictable, and many of these variables affect monetary and fiscal policy, which directly determines interest rates.

Investment in the debt securities market requires some of the same analytical tools that are used for stock portfolio evaluation, and here again the computer can be particularly helpful. Yield determination, for example, requires complex calculations, and tax impact and convertibility benefits must also be factored into your decision equation. The job of gathering information is as important for various debt securities as it is for stocks, and your research can be enhanced by data from an information service. The management of your bond portfolio can be aided by one of the portfolio management programs discussed in Chapter 6. Your personal computer can help you in locating current market data, computing yields, tracking performance, and keeping complete records. Before we look at these computer techniques, however, we need to understand the types of debt securities available.

DEBT SECURITIES MARKET

Debt securities are usually categorized by their type, issuer, and term. (Table 7–1 shows the characteristics of a variety of debt securities.) As an investor, one of the attractive features of most debt securities is liquidity—the ability to quickly convert your holdings to cash. Another inviting feature in the interest paid on debt issues. The interest paid over the life of the security, plus any appreciation in price between when you bought it and its maturity date, is called the yield to maturity. For example, suppose you bought a newly issued bond maturing in 20 years, paying 10 percent interest per year. Over the 20-year-period (assuming you hold the bond until maturity) your income from the investment will consist solely of the interest. There will be no capital gains. However, suppose you bought the same bond some time after it was issued, when you noticed that it was selling on the market for 15 percent less than its issuing price (i.e., $85 for a $100 bond). If you hold that bond to maturity, you will be paid at par for the bond (i.e., $100). This means you will receive the 15 percent differential in price as a capital gain on maturity—in addition to the 10 percent annual interest. The combined total of appreciation and interest is the yield to maturity.

But besides the yield to maturity mathematics, you will also need to

Table 7-1. Characteristics of Debt Securities

Type	Description	Maturity	Liquidity	Minimum Purchase	Issuer
Banker's acceptance	A security representing an interest in a specific financial transaction	Short	Poor	$100k	Bank
Bond	A debt between the issuer and borrower often secured by specific assets	Long	Good	<=$1,000	Corp. Govt. Munic.
Certificate of deposit	A guaranteed certificate in varying terms	Long, medium, or short	Poor	$5,000	Bank
Commercial paper	An IOU usually maturing within 270 days	Short	Fair	$100k	Corp.
Convertible bond	A debenture that can be converted into a stated number of shares of its stocks	Long	Good	<=$1,000	Corp.
Debenture	A bond that is not secured by a specific asset, but backed by the issuer's general credits	Long	Good	<=$1,000	Corp.
Equipment trust certificate	A security issued by a RR to finance the purchase of rolling stock	Long	Fair	$5,000	Corp.
Municipal bond	A bond issued by a govt. (e.g., state, city, or agency)	Long and medium	Good	<=$1,000	Munic.
Note	A short-term bond maturing in less than 5 years	Short	Fair	$10k	Corp. Munic.
Treasury bill	A U.S. govt. obligation	Short	Good	$10k	U.S. govt.
Treasury bond	A bond issued by the U.S. Treasury	Long and medium	Good	$10k	U.S. govt.

calculate the aftertax impact. The bond's appreciation is taxed as a long-term capital gain, and the interest as ordinary income. These calculations are complex and until recently they have been difficult for the average investor to perform. Previously, he or she had to consult bond books that provided yield to maturity tables, or use special calculators. Nowadays your personal computer can help you through these computations in several ways, giving you the choice of using packaged bond analysis programs, an information service that provides these kinds of calculations, or a program of your own creation to handle them.

THE CASE FOR CONVERTIBLES

Convertible bonds are—in many a knowledgeable person's opinion—an ideal investment. Convertibles are debentures (a bond not secured by a particular asset but backed by the general credit worthiness of the issuing corporation) that may be converted into shares of the issuing company's stock at a predetermined rate within a specified time. These securities offer fixed interest, with the possibility that the company's underlying stock will rise in price. If this occurs, you may convert your bonds into stock and take advantage of the stock's appreciation, thus you can earn interest over time while waiting for a rise in stock price.

The choice of convertible bonds requires an analysis of both the company's stock and the bond's return. The two basic questions to ask when investing in convertibles are: (1) how attractive is the issue in terms of conversion value; that is, how much will you be paying per share of the company's stock? (2) how does the value of the convertible debenture rank relative to other comparable securities? Ideally, you won't want to pay much of a premium for the convertibility feature through either a premium tacked on to the purchase price or through lower interest rates.

Other avenues for investing in debt securities include speculating with low-quality bonds or investing in tax-exempt municipal or government issues, as well as in shorter-term vehicles like T-bills and notes.

RATING BONDS

Bonds are rated according to the credit standing of the bond issuer. The two rating services, Moody's Investors Service and Standard & Poor's Corporation, provide ratings[1] from the top down as follows:

Moody:	Aaa	Aa	A1	A	Baa1	Baa
S & P:	AAA	AA"*	A"	BBB"		

* " = + or −.

Bonds issued by companies or municipalities that have a low credit standing will obviously be rated lower in quality. Usually the lower the bond rating, the higher the interest rate offered. Many of the lower-rated bonds can be trading for 85 percent of their par value only one year from

---

[1] Other types of debt issues are also rated by these services, although a different grading system is used.

maturity. You have, therefore, an attractive opportunity for capital gains—provided you are willing to take the added risks. Buying bonds on a margin (putting up only a fraction of the purchase price) can provide you nice leverage, but the selection of low-rated discount bonds can be tricky, so you will want to minimize the risk on this type of speculative investment.

Although your research will have to be extensive, your computer can ease some of this burden. You can get bond data from the Dow Jones News/Retrieval® service quickly and easily. What you should then consider is writing a small program to screen those bonds that meet your criteria. Perhaps you can find a company that has prospered because of the money it was able to raise through an earlier bond issue. It will still have to pay off the bondholders at maturity, but because of the improved health of the company it has an excellent chance to repay the bond's face value in full. It may be a company that has been successfully reorganized and has now accumulated the funds to pay off its creditors—including you. And remember, since bonds are in a sense senior to stocks, the issuer is legally obligated to pay bondholders before stockholders—an extra element of security if worse comes to worse.

Investing in municipal bonds can be quite advantageous to the high-income taxpayer since interest on these bonds is exempt from federal and usually from state taxes. The object is to locate a high-rated issue, determine its yield, and compare it to a taxable corporate bond. This comparison must take into account your marginal tax rate. Municipal bond brokers often have tables comparing municipals' interest against corporate bonds for several taxable income ranges. These charts are all right for judging the possible tax benefits of munis over corporates, but you need to look at your actual marginal tax rate to determine precisely if munis are better for you than corporates. One way to do this with your computer is by tax planning. (In Chapter 8 there is information about how to keep a running tally of your marginal tax rate throughout the year so you can quickly assess whether municipal bonds are for you or not.)

COMPUTER TECHNIQUES

The selection and evaluation of bonds for your portfolio follows a path similar to the one used for stocks. You must first gather good data on the bonds and their issuers. A variety of sources is available to help you with this task. Besides the tried and true methods of searching through brokers' recommendations, libraries, investment advisory newsletters, and newspapers, you can also use your computer to gather information from the information services, nearly all of which provide bond data. As we pointed out earlier, many of the portfolio management programs have a built-in capacity to reach one or more of these database services, so you can collect bond history, record it in your disk library, and later extract it for subsequent evaluation.

With bonds, as with other types of investments, the central question to ask yourself is, "How do I get the most for my money?" To answer that, focus your attention on the three basic elements present in any debt security: yield, quality, and maturity. By considering these elements you should be able to determine the kinds of securities you need to fulfill your investing objectives. To achieve the best fit between those objectives and the bonds you buy, you will want to know four things:

1. What will my marginal tax bracket be during the time I own these bonds?
2. What are my objectives?
   a. Maximum safety of capital?
   b. Maximum current income?
   c. Moderate income and a chance for capital gain?
3. How long do I want to commit my money.
4. What yield can I expect if any minimum requirement is 10 percent?

A few other pertinent points should be kept in mind, too. One of these is quality. The higher the quality of the bond, the lower its yield. Quality may also influence the volatility of a bond's market price and therefore its market risk. When interest rates are rising while the economy is slowing down, the prices of lower-quality bonds are likely to fall more rapidly than those of higher-quality bonds. You need to decide how much yield you are prepared to give up in exchange for quality.

If you seek capital appreciation, there are rules of thumb on the ways that bond prices behave. Their behavior is largely a function of the complex interaction of maturities and coupon (interest) rates. Low-coupon debt securities move up faster than high-coupon securities when interest rates drop, and a bond with more years left in it will swing wider than one with a shorter maturity. When rates are high, 20-year bonds with low coupons will be hard to find. A reasonable choice is a bond with seven or eight years remaining that is selling for about 70 percent of its face value. By the way, those bonds are often protected from calls by their low market price (a "call" is the redemption by the issuer of a bond prior to maturity). Bonds are called when prices rise and rates fall, thus allowing the issuer to retire its higher cost debt cheaply. Redemption is usually at par plus a premium equal to one year's coupon (interest payment). Calls are undesirable for the bondholder because they can cost the investor's yield. The yield to maturity calculations can be negated if your bond is called, and in that case, the yield you thought you were getting just won't be there. You should consider the possibility of a call as you work through your bond analysis, particularly if there is no redemption protection. This is a good opportunity to exercise some "what if" cases on your computer.

Let's look at some specific ways that the computer can help you with this bond analysis.

THREE WAYS TO ANALYZE BONDS

Suppose you wanted to evaluate six discount bonds maturing in 10 years and paying a 10, 11, or 12 percent coupon rate. Your objective is to realize a capital gain at maturity of from 10 to 15 percent, and thus to have a yield to maturity in the range of 18 to 20 percent.

There are several ways to make a computer evaluation of bonds. First, you could enter data about each bond into a computer program and run it six times to determine the yield to maturity on each security. A simple pencil and paper comparison between these six yields allows you to rank them accordingly. If you need additional information about the issuing companies you can use an information service to conduct a fundamental analysis of the issuer.

A second approach to ranking bonds is to use an electronic spreadsheet program. You could set up your sheets to handle multiple entries so the program could automatically rank the bonds from best to worst, based not only on yield calculations but also on quality ratings, call protection, and any other criteria you think pertinent. You may want to quantify these criteria to make your comparisons easier to program.

The third computer method uses existing programs designed specifically for bond analysis.

The Bond Yielder, offered by CE Software, makes calculations useful to brokers, insurance companies, and other financial institutions. Individual investors can also profit from its ability to compute yields on municipals, corporate bonds and warrants, bank notes, treasury bills, certificates of deposit, and discounted bonds. Table 7–2 lists the types of bonds and their definition and Table 7–3 shows the various inputs and outputs by bond type. Exhibit 7–1 shows a sample calculation from the Bond Yielder.

Table 7–2. Types of Bonds

Type 1 Securities: these include municipal bonds, federal agency securities, and corporate bonds with periodic interest payments on a 30/360 basis.

Type 2 Securities: these include U.S. Treasury notes and bonds with periodic interest payments on an actual or actual day basis.

Type 3 Securities: these are notes and warrants with interest payment at maturity utilizing a 30/360 day basis.

Type 4 Securities: These are securities, such as certificates of deposit or commercial paper, with interest payment at maturity utilizing an actual or 360-day basis.

Type 5 Securities: These include discount securities, like U.S. Treasury bills, sold on a discount basis without an interest coupon and utilizing an actual or 360-day basis.

Source: from the Bond Yielder.   *Courtesy of CE Software*

Table 7–3. Bond Inputs and Outputs

Input/Output	Type of Security				
	1	2	3	4	5
Input:					
1. Bond type	1	2	3	4	5
2. Face interest rate	X	X	X	X	
3. Semiannual or annual coupon schedule	X	X			
4. Maturity date:					
Last coupon date	X	X			
Issue date			X	X	
5. Settlement date	X	X	X	X	X
6. Income-tax rate	X	X	X	X	X
Capital gains rate	X	X	X	X	
7. Redemption value	X	X	X	X	X
Output:					
1. Yield given price	X	X	X	X	
2. Price given yield	X	X	X	X	X
3. Yield to maturity	X	X	X	X	X
Price from yield aftertax	X	X	X	X	X

Courtesy of CE Software

Exhibit 7–1. Sample Bond Calculation* (from the Bond Yielder)

MUNI/AGENCY/AGENCY TYPE BOND WITH SEMIANNUAL COUPONS

COUPON RATE = 12.35%
MATURITY DATE: 01/01/1985
SETTLEMENT DATE: 06/01/82

CALCULATIONS ASSUME A 20% CAPITAL GAINS RATE
    AND A 50% INCOME TAX RATE

PRICE = 85.075%
YIELD TO MATURITY: 20.0055%
CURRENT YIELD = 14.517%
YIELD AFTER TAX = 18.9529%
EQUIVALENT TAXABLE RETURN = 40.011%

ACCRUED INTEREST PER $1000 = 51.458333
TOTAL DUE PER $1000 = 902.20833

A good feature of the Bond Yielder is the "change" function. You may use it to simply correct data entry mistakes or, more important, to ask some hypothetical questions of the bond you are analyzing.

Changing environments can have dramatic effects on bond yields. For example, suppose the bond calculated in Exhibit 7–1 was called a year early at 101.5 percent. What would this do to the bond's yield to maturity? To find out, you must change the maturity date to 01/01/1984, and then recalculate the yields based on this maturity date. The redemption value must be also changed to 101.5. Calculating once more, the Bond Yielder gives the new call yields. Since the new call yield is higher at 25.1374 percent, you would not be hurt should the call option be exercised.

ANALYZING CONVERTIBLES

If you decide to invest in convertible debentures, you will need some special techniques to help you evaluate those that are best for your strategy. When evaluating convertibles your primary concern should be for the growth potential of the company issuing them. This means going through the same examination of a company that you would if you were buying its stock. Analyzing convertibles by computer is a merging of stock market analysis, yield computations, and fundamental company evaluation and entails several essential questions:

Has the common stock peaked in price?
Is there a change in the conversion rate coming up that will change the price of a convertible?
Is a call possible?
What is the general outlook for the stock market?
How long does the conversion privilege last?

The last item is important because the stock price may take longer than the conversion period to rise sufficiently to return the yield you are anticipating. It should be obvious that one of the best times to buy convertibles is when the stock market is depressed but headed for a rally.

A SUMMARY

Bonds and other debt securities pose some difficult challenges for the investor. Determining whether they are right for you will be a complex mix of fundamental company analysis, yield computations, and quality assessments supplemented by stock market technical analysis. The computer can be an invaluable aid in gathering the requisite data, calculating yields, and managing your bond portfolio. The necessary calculations can be handled either by the available programs or by programs of your own design.

APPENDIX

Bibliography

"Bonds: Playing for Capital Gains & Yield." *Business Week,* February 16, 1981, pp. 110–13.

Homer, Sidney. *The Great American Bond Market*. Homewood, Ill.: Dow Jones-Irwin, 1978.

Merrill Lynch, Pierce, Fenner & Smith. "The Bond Book." New York. 1974.

Successful Investing and Money Management. Chapters 10, 11. Toronto: Northington Limited, 1974.

Resource List

Product	Resource	Computer
Bond Yielder	CE Software 801-73rd Street Des Moines, IA 50312	Apple II+/III

Tax Planning and Preparation

Is the secret to accumulating a large personal fortune one of working harder and earning more, or is it simply by making better use of the income and savings you already possess? You probably know several people with incomes similar to yours who seem to have more money to spend than you do. What's their secret? Perhaps they bought stock in Silicon Valley when chips were cheap. More likely, though, they have found a way to maximize the efficiency of their financial resources. One important way to do this is with better management of your taxable income.

Most of us would prefer to forget about taxes until April 15, but since the only real measure of profits is in aftertax dollars our tax situation is of necessity a year-round concern. Taxes have a different impact on each of our investments, so each investment requires a separate strategy. For instance, dividends from corporate bonds or preferred stocks are handled in a straightforward manner and taxed as additions to ordinary income like salary or wages. Capital gains and losses, though, are a more complex issue. For one thing, they may be long or short term (more or less than one year), and for another, their tax treatment varies with the type of investment—be it stocks, bonds, money market, real estate, and so on.

Real estate is permitted several special tax preferences. The government has long encouraged property ownership and development by showering it with tax advantages. Interest payments on loans taken to buy property are tax deductible, and so is a percentage of the value of any buildings on the property, which are assumed to depreciate each year. Even a home—not normally considered an investment because you don't plan to sell it just to make a profit—carries significant tax benefits.

To encourage investments in such things as agriculture and oil drilling, Congress over the years has heightened the attractiveness of these investment activities by legislating specific tax breaks. Generally, what these breaks offer the investor is an opportunity to shelter earned income from Uncle Sam. Depending on the kind of shelter, several different considerations have to be made in their tax treatment. They are usually worth more to a high tax bracket investor, for example, because they operate by producing tax losses in the early years of their life.

The Economic Recovery Tax Act (ERTA) of 1981 significantly reduced the appeal of tax shelters by greatly easing the tax burden on the top brackets. For example, at the very top the marginal rate of taxation will drop from 70 percent to 50 percent by 1984. Thus, shelters will become more useful for the investment they represent than for their income-sheltering value.

ERTA and, to a lesser extent, the Tax Equity and Fiscal Responsibility Act (TEFRA) of 1982 have considerably changed the way investors need to think about the effect of taxes on their profits. Under these tax laws tax planning is for everyone, not just the rich, because they offer to all investors the opportunity to profit from long-range planning in many areas. And to help you with your planning, there are new tax planning tools available in the form of excellent personal computer tax-planning and preparation programs.

Computer programs for handling taxes have been on the market for several years. Until recently, however, most were either too complicated or too costly for the average individual and were designed primarily for accountants and lawyers. Fortunately, the explosion in personal computer sales has provided more than enough incentive for software houses to design and develop simple, easy-to-use tax programs. At the same time, the cost of these programs has been lowered far enough to be within the financial reach of the average investor. Better yet, these microcomputer tax programs are every bit as powerful as their more costly and complex predecessors. They may even be better, and they are certainly easier to use. These new programs can complete a variety of tax forms and schedules—from the Short Form 1040a for nonitemizers to up to 19 different IRS forms and all schedules.

INVESTOR'S TAX CONSIDERATIONS

Several times in this book I have suggested ways in which your computer can help you make your cash flow more visible and thus help you keep better track of it. One of the largest components of any cash flow picture is taxes. Reducing taxes by legally avoiding them is very important to your investing health. ERTA and TEFRA are ways the government is helping you do this, but there are so many benefits in these legislative packages that you must familiarize yourself with them early and keep reviewing them to be sure that you are getting the maximum tax breaks. Knowing what is available should help you determine if you need professional advice or not. If you do seek expert advice, it makes sense to have an idea of what the law can do for you first.

Investors should look at several areas within ERTA for benefits:

Long-term capital gains.

Tax shelters.

An investment in your own free-lance business.

Participation in an individual retirement account (IRA) or Keogh plan.

Estate planning.

Real estate opportunities.

Before we review the available tax-planning and preparation techniques, a few definitions are necessary. Some confusion exists about the meaning of some words, such as taxable income, tax brackets, and total tax. For instance, if your gross salary and wages total $50,000, it is important to recognize that this is not your "taxable income." The difference between your total and taxable incomes is the amount of your deductions. The greater the difference between the two, the less tax you pay. It is the taxable income that determines your tax bracket. Your tax bracket refers to the rate at which your last dollar of income is taxed. If you pay 35 percent on your last dollar of income, that is your "marginal tax rate." You should also remember that even after you total your tax bill, you still have one more thing to consider—your tax credits. A dollar of tax credits offsets a dollar of taxes. Thus credits carry a bigger punch in reducing taxes than do deductions. The value of deductions depends on your marginal tax. Your tax savings from a deduction is always far less than the deduction itself.

TAX PLANNING

It is difficult to overestimate the importance of planning for profits. Without a doubt, planning is the key to successful investing. Similarly, the key to good planning is to pay careful and constant attention to tax considerations. It is not necessary, however, to be a tax expert to achieve major gains from this type of planning. The average investor is well aware of the impact of taxes on his or her investments. Most of us understand the effects of such things as long-term versus short-term capital gains, tax shelters, tax-deferred bonds, and the like. If we are not sure of the immediate impact on a current investment decision, we can call our tax advisor for insights. The use of a tax-planning program for your personal computer is another way to save time while becoming more independent, too. With your computer you can weigh one or more of your investment options and look at the changes they would produce on the bottom line of your estimated tax bill. Some packages allow you to view this tax effect over periods up to four years into the future.

There are a couple of excellent choices when it comes to tax planning by computer—programs for tax preparation and programs for tax planning. Programs in the former group allow you to complete an estimated federal tax return and modify it, on the one hand, by changing Schedule D (Capital Gains and Losses) and watching the change in the tax due (line 35, Form 1040, before special credits). On the other hand, tax-planning programs like the Personal Tax Plan (PTP) from Aardvark Software are designed for federal income-tax planning. As such, they print no forms or schedules but results, with all the alternatives side by side (see Exhibit 8–1). These programs deal only with gross totals, not the myriad individual calculations needed to arrive at them. Therefore, if you decide that one of the alternative filings your program indicates would be more beneficial to you than your original return, you must transfer the numbers to the Form 1040 by hand.

A companion program for the professional financial advisor or tax counselor is the Individual Tax Plan (ITP), also from Aardvark. Both the ITP and PTP provide a simple format that enables tax professionals to study five alternatives at a time. Like other tax programs, these packages produce automatic calculations for federal tax liability, income averaging, maximum tax on earned income, minimum and alternative minimum taxes, and capital gains and losses. The Individual Tax Plan, since it is for professionals, has additional features for use in support of a client base.

TAX PREPARATION

Using a computerized tax-preparation aid for planning is an excellent means of keeping abreast of your tax status during the course of the year. You can, for example, enter tax deductions into the applicable schedules or forms as they occur. This method has several important advantages:

1. By recording your tax deductions as they occur you may find it easier to keep track of them. It saves you the trouble of having to look through piles of papers at the end of the year in search of notes you wrote about your tax deductions, some of which you may even have lost over the years. Record-keeping for itemized deductions can be an immense time-saver.

2. You can quickly quantify the tax impact on your investment deci-

Exhibit 8-1. Personal Tax Plan

```
GEORGE AND MARY BROWN
JANUARY 30, 198
```

	PROJECTION 1983	PROJECTION 1984	PROJECTION 1985	PROJECTION 1986
FILING STATUS	JOINT	JOINT	JOINT	JOINT
NUMBER OF EXEMPTIONS	5	5	5	5
WAGES,SALARIES	35,000	39,000	43,200	47,620
INTEREST AFTER EXCLUSION	300	375	450	525
DIVIDENDS AFTER EXCL.	0	0	0	0
CAPITAL GAIN/LOSS	4,000	0	0	0
PARTNERSHIP INCOME/LOSS	0	0	0	0
OTHER INCOME/LOSS	1,500	2,250	3,000	3,750
	------	------	------	-------
TOTAL INCOME	40,800	41,625	46,650	51,895
ADJUSTMENTS TO INCOME	2,250	3,200	3,400	3,600
	------	-------	-------	-------
ADJUSTED GROSS INCOME	38,550	38,425	43,250	48,295
DEDUCTIONS				
MEDICAL & DENTAL EXP.	543	547	402	251
STATE & LOCAL INC TAXES	3,000	3,500	4,000	4,500
OTHER TAXES	1,250	1,400	1,568	1,756
INTEREST EXPENSE	3,500	3,500	3,500	3,500
CHARITABLE CONTRIB.	400	400	400	400
CASUALTY LOSS	0	0	0	0
MISCELLANEOUS	750	750	750	750
	------	------	------	------
TOTAL DEDUCTIONS	9,443	10,097	10,620	11,157
ZERO BRACKET AMOUNT	3,400	3,400	3,400	3,400
	-------	-------	------	------
EXCESS ITEMIZED DED.	6,043	6,697	7,220	7,757
SUBTOTAL	32,507	31,728	36,030	40,538
EXEMPTIONS	5,000	5,000	5,000	5,000
	-------	-------	-------	-------
TAXABLE INCOME	27,507	26,728	31,030	35,538
	-------	-------	-------	-------
TAX - TAX TABLES/XYZ	4,885	4,209	5,105	6,381
TAX - QUAL.CAP.GAINS	:::N/A	:::N/A	:::N/A	:::N/A
TAX - INCOME AVERAGING	4,606	4,145	5,073	6,369
TAX - MAXIMUM TAX	:::N/A	:::N/A	:::N/A	:::N/A
TAX SELECTED	4,606	4,145	5,073	6,369
ADDITIONAL TAXES	0	0	0	0
	------	------	------	------
GROSS REGULAR TAX	4,606	4,145	5,073	6,369
CREDITS	0	0	0	0
	------	------	-------	------
NET REGULAR TAX	4,606	4,145	5,073	6,369
MINIMUM TAX	0	0	0	0
ALTERNATIVE MIN.TAX	0	0	0	0
OTHER TAXES	0	0	0	0
	-----	-----	-----	-----
TOTAL TAX LIABILITY	4,606	4,145	5,073	6,369
FEDERAL PAYMENTS	4,950	5,544	6,209	6,954
BALANCE DUE (REFUND)	-344	-1,399	-1,136	-585
TAX BRACKET	22	23	25	28

```
::: NOT APPLICABLE
```

Courtesy of Aardvark Software, Inc.

Exhibit 8–2. The "Tax Preparer"

```
FORM 1040         U.S. INDIVIDUAL INCOME TAX RETURN              1981
TAX YEAR - BEGINNING DATE...............: JAN 1;1983
TAX YEAR - ENDING DATE..................: DEC 31;1983
*********************************************************************
    >>> THIS FORM CANNOT BE FILED WITH THE I.R.S!   FOR RULES <<<
    >>> ON FORM 1040 PRINTOUTS, SEE CH. 5 OF THE T.P. MANUAL! <<<
*********************************************************************
1ST NAME & INIT - YOU & SPOUSE.........: PETER & EMILY MOSS
LAST NAME..............................: MOSS
YOUR SOCIAL SECURITY NUMBER............: 765-34-1234
SPOUSE'S SOCIAL SECURITY NO............: 432-54-6787
YOUR OCCUPATION........................: LANDSCAPE ENGR.
SPOUSE'S OCCUPATION....................: HOMEMAKER
PRESENT HOME ADDRESS(#&STREET).........: 125 MOWER ST
CITY...STATE...ZIP CODE.................: LAWN; PA 17000
$1 TO PRES ELECT CAMPAIGN FUND.........? YES
$1 TO SAME FROM SPOUSE.................? YES
***** FILING STATUS... **********************************************
1.   SINGLE............................?  NO
2.   MARRIED FILING JOINTLY............? YES
3.   MARRIED FILING SEPARATELY.........?  NO
4.   HEAD OF HOUSEHOLD.................?  NO
....NAME OF QUALIFYING PERSON.........:
5.   QUALIFYING WIDOW(ER)..............?  NO
....YEAR SPOUSE DIED..................:
***** EXEMPTIONS... *************************************************
6A. CLAIM FOR SELF.....................? YES
....65 OR OVER.........................?  NO
....BLIND..............................?  NO
6B. CLAIM FOR SPOUSE...................? YES
....65 OR OVER.........................?  NO
....BLIND..............................?  NO
6AB.EXEMP'S FOR SELF & SPOUSE..........................6AB.      2.
6C. # DEP'NT CHILDREN CLAIMED........................... 6C.      2.
....FIRST NAMES OF CHILDREN...........: JACK & JILL
6D. NUMBER OF OTHER DEPENDENTS......................... 6D.
6E. TOTAL # OF EXEMP'S CLAIMED......................... 6E.      4.
***** INCOME... *****************************************************
7.   WAGES; SALARIES; TIPS; ETC........................  7.   52,350.
8A. INTEREST INCOME (SCHED B)........................... 8A.     500.
8B. DIVIDENDS (SCHED B)................................. 8B.   2,300.
8C. TOTAL INTEREST & DIVIDENDS......................... 8C.   2,800.
8D. EXCLUSION.......................................... 8D.     400.
8E. TOTAL TAXABLE INT & DIV'ND......................... 8E.   2,400.
9.   STATE & LOCAL TAX REFUNDS.........................  9.     450.
10. ALIMONY RECEIVED.................................. 10.
11. BUSINESS INCOME (SCHED C)......................... 11.   3,112.
12. CAPITAL GAINS (SCHED D)........................... 12.  -3,000.
13. TAXABLE CAP GAINS (NOT D)......................... 13.
14. SUPPLEMENTAL GAINS (4797)......................... 14.
15. TAXABLE PENS'NS (NOT L#16)........................ 15.
16A.PENS'NS; ANNUITIES RECV'D.........................16A.
16B.TAXABLE PENS'NS; ANNUITIES........................16B.
17. RENTS;ROYALTIES;ETC(SCH E)........................ 17.
18. FARM INCOME (SCHED F)............................. 18.
19A.UNEMPL'NT COMP RECEIVED...........................19A.
19B.TAXABLE UNEMPLOYMENT COMP.........................19B.
20. OTHER INCOME (ITEMIZED)........................... 20.

     FORM 1040 CONTINUED ON PAGE 2
```

sions by entering the alternate investing results data in Schedule D and recalculating your taxes.

3. Finally, when April 15 approaches, all your records will be in one place for filing. You can either print out the forms, transcribe the numbers onto the IRS forms and schedules, or send facsimile forms and schedules to your tax person for a review. (Exhibits 8–2 and 8–3 show samples of several completed forms from the "Tax Preparer" by Howard Software Services.)

Exhibit 8–2 (continued)

```
FORM 1040   (CONT'D)    PAGE 2                              1981
(FORM 1040)
PETER & EMILY MOSS MOSS                          SSN 765-34-1234
****************************************************************
...........NATURE AND SOURCE.........:
21. TOTAL INCOME(LINE 7 TO 20).................... 21.   55,312.
***** ADJUSTMENTS TO INCOME... *********************************
22. MOVING EXPENSE (FORM 3903)................... 22.
23. EMPLOYEE BUS EXPENSE(2106)................... 23.
24. PAYMENTS TO AN I.R.A......................... 24.    2,250.
25. PAYMENTS TO A KEOGH PLAN..................... 25.
26. INTEREST PENALTY............................. 26.
27. ALIMONY PAID................................. 27.
28. DISABILITY INC EXCL (2440).................. 28.
29. OTHER ADJUSTMENTS............................ 29.
...................(EXPLAIN).........:
30. TOTAL ADJUSTMENTS (22TO29)................... 30.    2,250.
***** ADJUSTED GROSS INCOME... *********************************
31. ADJUSTED GROSS INCOME........................ 31.   53,062.
***** TAX COMPUTATION... ***************************************
32A.ADJ'D GROSS FROM LINE 31.....................32A.   53,062.
32B.ITEMIZED DEDUCTIONS(SCH A)...................32B.   15,630.
32C.ADJ'D GROSS LESS DED'NS......................32C.   37,432.
33. $1000 TIMES EXEMPS (L#6E.)................... 33.    4,000.
34. TAXABLE INCOME 32C LESS 33................... 34.   33,432.
35. TAX......................................... 35.    7,411.
....COMPUTED FROM TAX TABLES...........? YES
....FROM TAX RATE SCH X;Y OR Z.........?   NO
....FROM SCHEDULE D....................?   NO
....FROM SCHEDULE G....................?   NO
....FROM FORM 4726.....................?   NO
36. ADDITIONAL TAXES............................. 36.
....FROM FORM 4970.....................?   NO
....FROM FORM 4972.....................?   NO
....FROM FORM 5544.....................?   NO
....FROM SECTION 72(M)(5)..............?   NO
37. TOTAL (LINE 35 PLUS 36)...................... 37.    7,411.
***** CREDITS... ***********************************************
38. CREDIT FOR CONTR TO CAND'S................... 38.
39. CREDIT FOR ELDERLY (R&RP).................... 39.
40. CREDIT - CHILD CARE (2441)................... 40.
41. INVEST'NT TAX CREDIT(3468)................... 41.
42. FOREIGN TAX CREDIT (1116).................... 42.
43. WORK INCENT CREDIT (4874).................... 43.
44. JOBS CREDIT (FORM 4884)...................... 44.
45. RES'L ENERGY CREDIT (5695)................... 45.
46. TOTAL CREDITS............................... 46.
47. BALANCE (LINE 37 MINUS 46)................... 47.    7,411.
***** OTHER TAXES... *******************************************
48. SELF-EMPLOY'NT TAX(SCH SE)................... 48.
49A.MINIMUM TAX (FORM 4625).....................49A.
49B.ALT MIN TAX (FORM 6251).....................49B.
50. TAX INV CRED RECOMP (4255)................... 50.
51A.FICA - UNREP'D TIPS(4137)...................51A.
51B.UNC'TED FICA/RRTA ON TIPS...................51B.
52. TAX ON IRA (FORM 5329)....................... 52.
53. ADV EARNED INC CRED RCVD.................... 53.
54. TOTAL (LINE 47 THROUGH 53).................. 54.    7,411.

    FORM 1040 CONTINUED ON PAGE 3
```

FORM 1040 CONTINUED ON PAGE 3

If you choose not to complete the various schedules and forms but have them automatically posted to your form 1040, you can insert estimated numbers for lines 8a, 8b, 11, 12, 17, and 18. (These lines would normally be posted from Schedules B through F.) The tax on line 35 is computed using one of five methods you can choose from. These include: the tax table; tax rate schedule X, Y, or Z; Schedules D or G; and form 4726. One of the keys to successful preparation of taxes, whether by hand or by

Exhibit 8–2 (*concluded*)

```
FORM 1040   (CONT'D)    PAGE 3                                          1981
(FORM 1040)
PETER & EMILY MOSS MOSS                                   SSN 765-34-1234
*********************************************************************
***** PAYMENTS...  **************************************************
55. TOTAL FED INC TAX WITHHELD.......................... 55.      7,500.
56. EST'D TAX PMTS & PAST CRED.......................... 56.
57. EARNED INCOME CREDIT................................ 57.
58. AMOUNT PAID WITH FORM 4868.......................... 58.
59. EXCESS FICA/RRTA WITHHELD........................... 59.
60. CREDIT FOR SPEC TAX (4136).......................... 60.
61. REG'D INV CO CREDIT (2439).......................... 61.
62. TOTAL (LINE 55 THROUGH 61).......................... 62.      7,500.
***** REFUND OR BALANCE DUE...  *************************************
63. AMOUNT OVERPAID..................................... 63.         89.
64. AMT OF 63 TO BE REFUNDED............................ 64.         89.
65. AMT TO APPLY TO EST'D TAX........................... 65.
66. BALANCE DUE......................................... 66.
....AMOUNT FROM FORM 2210...............................
```

Courtesy of Howard Software Services

computer, is to follow the necessary "road map." Some forms or schedules must be completed before others. An example is shown in Exhibit 8–4.

Using the "Tax Preparer" for planning is not advised if what you really need are reports that analyze alternative investing schemes and their effect on your bottom line. For this type of analysis you must develop comparative worksheets upon which to enter your changing tax data. This worksheet approach can be done either manually or electronically, but electronic worksheets would provide a fine way to set up certain comparisons. Reports can be easily prepared with the electronic worksheet, and—if you have a suitable program and printer—bar charts would graphically illustrate the different tax effects of your various investment alternatives.

Atsuko Computing International has a tax-planning and preparation package, Taxman-82, which uses electronic worksheets in place of forms and schedules. It provides templates for use with both VisiCalc and SuperCalc—programs renowned for their ability to permit the user to interact extensively with them.

Taxman-82 extends this interactive environment into the tax arena. It prepares pages 1 and 2 of Form 1040, 11 different schedules, and 31 other IRS forms. Once the calculations are completed and the results made final, it is up to you to manually transfer them to the proper tax forms. An interesting feature of Taxman-82 is its exploratory questionnaire. By answering a series of simple yes-or-no questions, you can automatically select the tax forms necessary for your use.

The only difference between tax planning and preparation is the production of the IRS forms and schedules. It makes a lot of sense to buy a

Exhibit 8-3. Itemizing

```
SCHEDULE A                       ITEMIZED DEDUCTIONS                    1981 * 07
(FORM 1040)                                      OMB NO. 1545-0074
PETER & EMILY MOSS                                         SSN 765-34-1234
***************************************************************************
***** MEDICAL AND DENTAL EXPENSES *****************************************
1.   HALF OF MED INS PREMIUMS............................  1.
2.   TOTAL MEDICINE & DRUGS EXP.........................  2.
3.   1% OF FORM 1040 LINE 31............................  3.         502.
4.   NET MEDICINE & DRUGS DED'N.........................  4.
5.   BAL OF MED INS PREMIUMS............................  5.
6A.  DOCTORS; DENTISTS; NURSES..........................  6A.
6B.  HOSPITAL EXPENSES..................................  6B.
6C.  TRANSPORTATION.....................................  6C.
6D.  OTHER (ITEMIZED)...................................  6D.
7.   TOTAL MEDICAL EXPENSES.............................  7.
8.   3% OF FORM 1040 LINE 31............................  8.       1,505.
9.   NET MEDICAL EXP DED'N..............................  9.
10.  TOTAL MEDICAL EXP DED'N............................ 10.
***** TAXES **************************************************************
11.  STATE & LOCAL INCOME TAXES......................... 11.        750.
12.  REAL ESTATE TAXES.................................. 12.      2,550.
13A. GENERAL SALES TAX..................................13A.        600.
13B. GEN'L SALES-MOTOR VEHICLE..........................13B.        250.
14.  PERSONAL PROPERTY TAX.............................. 14.         45.
15.  OTHER TAXES (ITEMIZED)............................. 15.         60.
16.  TOTAL TAXES....................................... 16.       4,255.
***** INTEREST EXPENSE ***************************************************
17.  HOME MORTGAGE INTEREST............................. 17.     11,000.
18.  CREDIT & CHARGE CARD INT.......................... 18.        800.
19.  OTHER INT EXP (ITEMIZED).......................... 19.        750.
20.  TOTAL INTEREST EXPENSE............................ 20.     12,550.
***** CONTRIBUTIONS ******************************************************
21A. CASH CONT'NS UNDER $3000..........................21A.      1,500.
21B. CASH CONT'NS $3000 OR MORE........................21B.
22.  NON-CASH CONTRIBUTIONS............................ 22.
23.  CARRYOVER FROM PRIOR YEARS........................ 23.
24.  TOTAL CONTRIBUTIONS............................... 24.      1,500.
***** CASUALTY OR THEFT LOSS(ES) *****************************************
25.  LOSS BEFORE REIMBURSEMENT.......................... 25.        750.
26.  INSURANCE REIMBURSEMENT............................ 26.        300.
27.  NET UNINSURED LOSS................................. 27.        450.
28.  MIN OF $100 & LINE 27............................. 28.        100.
29.  TOTAL CASUALTY/THEFT LOSS.......................... 29.        350.
***** MISCELLANEOUS DEDUCTIONS *******************************************
30A. UNION DUES........................................30A.
30B. TAX RETURN PREPARATION FEE........................30B.        125.
31.  OTHER MISC ITEMIZED DED'NS........................ 31.        250.
32.  TOTAL MISCELLANEOUS DED'NS........................ 32.        375.
***** SUMMARY OF ITEMIZED DEDUCTIONS *************************************
33.  TOTAL MEDICAL AND DENTAL.......................... 33.
34.  TOTAL TAXES....................................... 34.      4,255.
35.  TOTAL INTEREST................................... 35.     12,550.
36.  TOTAL CONTRIBUTIONS............................... 36.      1,500.
37.  TOTAL CASUALTY/THEFT LOSS.......................... 37.        350.
38.  TOTAL MISCELLANEOUS............................... 38.        375.
39.  TOTAL DEDUCTIONS................................. 39.     19,030.
40.  ZERO BRACKET AMOUNT.............................. 40.      3,400.
41.  EXCESS ITEMIZED DEDUCTIONS....................... 41.     15,630.
```

These facsimile printouts are from the "Tax Preparer" from Howard Software Services. They illustrate the use of this program both as a tax planning and a preparation aid.

tax-preparation program if you use it for ongoing tax planning as well as year-end forms preparation. Improved aftertax profits from careful planning can easily pay for the program.

There are several good tax packages on the market. Your choice depends on such considerations as the kinds of work you need done, the types of forms or schedules you customarily need, and the number of

Exhibit 8–3 (*continued*)

```
SCHEDULE B                  INTEREST AND DIVIDEND INCOME            1981
(FORM 1040)                            OMB NO. 1545-0074
PETER & EMILY MOSS                                 SSN 765-34-1234
*********************************************************************
***** PART I - INTEREST INCOME **************************************
1A. INTEREST INCOME (ITEMIZED)........................... 1A.       500.
1B. TOTAL INTEREST...................................... 1B.       500.
1C. ALL-SAVERS INT (ITEMIZED)........................... 1C.
1D. TOTAL ALL-SAVERS INTEREST........................... 1D.
1E. ALL-SAVERS EXCLUSION................................ 1E.
1F. TAXABLE ALL-SAVERS INCOME .......................... 1F.
2.  TOTAL INTEREST INCOME............................... 2.        500.
***** PART II - DIVIDEND INCOME ************************************
3.  GROSS DIVIDENDS (ITEMIZED).......................... 3.      2,500.
4.  TOTAL DIVIDENDS FOR LINE3........................... 4.      2,500.
5.  CAPITAL GAIN DISTRIBUTIONS.......................... 5.        200.
6.  NONTAXABLE DISTRIBUTIONS............................ 6.
7.  TOTAL NONTAXABLE DIVIDENDS.......................... 7.        200.
8.  TOTAL DIVIDEND INCOME............................... 8.      2,300.
***** PART III-FOREIGN ACCOUNTS & TRUSTS **************************
9.  ANY FOREIGN ACCOUNTS................? NO
10. GRANTOR/TRANSFEROR-FOREIGN.........? NO
```

```
SCHEDULE C    PROFIT (OR LOSS) FROM BUSINESS OR PROFESSION   1981 * 08
(FORM 1040)                            OMB NO. 1545-0074
PETER & EMILY MOSS                                 SSN 765-34-1234
*********************************************************************
A.  MAIN BUSINESS ACTIVITY.............: LANDSCAPING
....................PRODUCT .........:
B.  BUSINESS NAME.....................: MOSS LTD
C.  EMPLOYER I.D. NO. ................: 12345
D.  BUSINESS ADDRESS(#&STREET)........: 100 TRACTOR DRIVE
....CITY...STATE...ZIP CODE..........: LAWN; PA 17000
E.  ACCOUNTING METHOD -- CASH.........? YES
...................ACCRUAL..........? NO
...................OTHER............? NO
...................(SPECIFY).........:
F.  INVEN'Y VAL'N MTHD - COST.........? NO
.... LOWER OF COST OR MARKET.........? NO
...................... OTHER.........? YES
................. (EXPLAIN).........:
G.  CHANGE IN MTHD DURING YEAR.........? NO
H.  HOME OFFICE EXP'S DEDUCTED.........? YES
***** PART I - INCOME **********************************************
1A. GROSS RECEIPTS OR SALES............................. 1A.     7,000.
1B. RETURNS AND ALLOWANCES.............................. 1B.
1C. BALANCE (LINE 1A LESS 1B) .......................... 1C.     7,000.
2.  COSTS (FROM SCHED C-1).............................. 2.
3.  GROSS PROFIT (L 1C LESS 2).......................... 3.      7,000.
4A. WINDFALL PROFIT TAX CREDIT.......................... 4A.
4B. OTHER INCOME....................................... 4B.
5.  TOTAL INCOME (LNS 3;4A&4B).......................... 5.      7,000.
***** PART II - DEDUCTIONS *****************************************
6.  ADVERTISING.......           : 29A.WAGES..............
7.  AMORTIZATION......           : 29B.JOBS CREDIT........
8.  BAD DEBTS FR SALES           : 29C.WIN CREDIT.........
9.  BANK CHARGES......           : 29D.TOTAL CREDITS......
10. VEHICLE EXPENSES...          : 29E.WAGES LESS CREDITS.
11. COMMISSIONS.......           : 30. WINFL TAX (1981)...
12. DEPLETION.........           : 31. OTHER EXPENSES.....
13. DEPREC. (SCHED C-2)    1,463. :   A
14. DUES AND PUBL'TIONS     250. :   B
15. EMPLOYEE BENEFITS..           :   C
16. FREIGHT (NOT C-2)..           :   D
17. INSURANCE.........      200. :   E
18. INTRST ON BUS. DEBT           :   F
19. LAUNDRY/CLEANING...           :   G
20. LEGAL SERVICES.....     200. :   H
21. OFFICE SUPPL & POST     150. :   I
22. PENS'N/PROFIT SHARE           :   J
23. RENT ON BUS. PROP..           :   K
24. REPAIRS...........      125. :   L
25. SUPPLIES(NOT C-1)..   1,000. :   M
26. TAXES(NOT WINDFALL)           :   N
27. TRAVEL & ENTERTAIN.     200. :   O
28. UTIL. & PHONE......     300. :   P
*********************************************************************
32. TOTAL DEDUCTIONS (6 TO 31).......................... 32.     3,888.
33. NET PROFIT/LOSS(5 LESS 32).......................... 33.     3,112.
34. SOME OF LOSS NOT 'AT RISK'.........? NO
```

SCHED C CONTINUED ON PAGE 2

Exhibit 8-3 (*continued*)

```
SCHED C  (CONT'D)    PAGE 2                              1981
(FORM 1040)
PETER & EMILY MOSS                          SSN 765-34-1234
************************************************************
***** SCHEDULE C-1.....COST OF GOODS SOLD AND/OR OPERATIONS ***********
1.   INVENTORY AT FIRST OF YEAR............................ 1.
2A.  PURCHASES......................................... 2A.
2B.  COST OF ITEMS WITHDRAWN.............................. 2B.
2C.  BALANCE (LINE 2A LESS 2B)........................... 2C.
3.   COST OF LABOR(EXCL'G SELF)........................... 3.
4.   MATERIALS AND SUPPLIES.............................. 4.
5.   OTHER COSTS (ITEMIZED)............................. 5.
6.   SUM OF LN 1:2C; & 3 THRU 5......................... 6.
7.   INVENTORY AT END OF YEAR........................... 7.
8.   COST OF GOODS/OPERATIONS............................ 8.
***** SCHEDULE C-2.....DEPRECIATION   **************************************
1.   DEPRECIATION(FORM 4562)............................ 1.    1,463.
2.   TOTAL FROM FORM 4562............................... 2.    1,463.
3.   DEPRECIATION IN C-1................................ 3.
4.   BALANCE(FOR PART II:LN 13)......................... 4.    1,463.
***** SCHEDULE C-3.....EXPENSE ACCOUNT INFORMATION *********************
EXPENSE ACCOUNT FOR OWNER...............................
...1A. EMPLOYEE'S NAME.................:
...1B. EXPENSE ACCOUNT.................................
...1C. SALARIES & WAGES................................
...2A. EMPLOYEE'S NAME.................:
...2B. EXPENSE ACCOUNT.................................
...2C. SALARIES & WAGES................................
...3A. EMPLOYEE'S NAME.................:
...3B. EXPENSE ACCOUNT.................................
...3C. SALARIES & WAGES................................
...4A. EMPLOYEE'S NAME.................:
...4B. EXPENSE ACCOUNT.................................
...4C. SALARIES & WAGES................................
...5A. EMPLOYEE'S NAME.................:
...5B. EXPENSE ACCOUNT.................................
...5C. SALARIES & WAGES................................
***** DID YOU CLAIM EXPENSES FOR... **********************************
A.   ENTERTAINMENT FACILITY.............? NO
B.   LIVING ACCOMMODATIONS..............? NO
C.   CONVEN'S/MTGS NOT IN U.S...........? NO
D.   FAMILIES AT CONVENTION/MTG.........? NO
....            OUTSIDE U.S.A...........? NO
E.   PAID VACATIONS NOT ON W-2..........? NO
```

what-if cases you expect to run. Some of the less expensive programs don't print any IRS forms, but can still be useful.

One important limit to the usefulness of computers in preparing actual tax forms is the strict set of IRS rules on how tax returns can be prepared by computer. The 1040, for instance, must be submitted on a preprinted IRS form. Other forms must follow strict formats when printed on the computer. If you print a facsimile of a form or schedule other than a 1040, you are required to use lined or green bar paper for easy reading. Pin-feed paper is acceptable, but it must be cut to 8½ × 11 inches, and the format must be precise. Otherwise advance approval for a new form must be obtained from the IRS. If you prepare returns for clients or friends, you may want to order pin-fed 1040s, which are sold as 4-ply forms and are available from several sources.

In tax planning and preparation, as in other areas we have discussed, satisfactory results ultimately hinge not on the program or the computer but on the ability and judgment of the person using the equipment. Basi-

Exhibit 8–3 (*continued*)

```
SCHEDULE D              CAPITAL GAINS AND LOSSES            1981 * 14
(FORM 1040)                               OMB NO. 1545-0074
PETER & EMILY MOSS                             SSN 765-34-1234
**********************************************************************

***** PART I - SHORT-TERM CAPITAL GAINS/LOSSES(HELD 1YR OR LESS)  ******

         (A)        (B)      (C)      (D)       (E)       (F)        (G)
    KIND  OF      DATE     DATE     GROSS    COST OR     LOSS       GAIN
    PROPERTY      ACQD     SOLD  SALE PRICE   BASIS   (E LESS D)  (D LESS E)

1.  SHORT-TERM .......(SEE STATEMENT 405)..  1.                  2,131.

2A. S/T PRINC RES SALE.....................  2A.
2B. S/T SALE(FORM6252).....................  2B.
3.  S/T PARTNERSHIP........................  3.
4.  SUM OF LINES 1 & 3.....................  4.                  2,131.
5.  NET GAIN/LOSS FROM 4F & 4G.........................  5.      2,131.
6.  S/T LOSS CARRYOVER-POST 69.........................  6.      7,200.
7.  NET SHORT TERM GAIN/LOSS...........................  7.     -5,069.

***** PART II-LONG-TERM CAPITAL GAINS/LOSSES(HELD MORE THAN 1 YR) *****

         (A)        (B)      (C)      (D)       (E)       (F)        (G)
    KIND  OF      DATE     DATE     GROSS    COST OR     LOSS       GAIN
    PROPERTY      ACQD     SOLD  SALE PRICE   BASIS   (E LESS D)  (D LESS E)

8.  LONG-TERM.........(SEE STATEMENT 416)..  8.     2,736.

9A. L/T PRINC RES SALE.....................  9A.                 3,500.
9B. L/T SALE(FORM6252).....................  9B.
10. L/T PARTNERSHIP........................  10.
11. SUM OF LINES 8&10......................  11.     2,736.      3,500.
12. NET GAIN/LOSS FROM 11F&11G.........................  12.       764.
13. CAPITAL GAIN DISTRIBUTIONS.........................  13.
14. GAIN FROM FORM4797/LINE5A1.........................  14.
15. SHARE GAIN FROM SUB-S CORP.........................  15.
16. SUM OF LINES 12 THROUGH 15.........................  16.       764.
17. L/T LOSS CARRYOVER-POST 69.........................  17.     1,400.
18. NET LONG TERM GAIN/LOSS............................  18.      -636.
```

cally, tax programs are computational and sorting tools, not automated accountants. If you put bad data into your computer, you will not only get bad data out but you may also be slapped with a penalty from the IRS.

One definite plus to using your computer for tax preparation is that it may allow you to deduct the cost of the system on your personal return. Normally, a computer system can be depreciated over a five-year period. The depreciation for the first year is 15 percent, the second year 22 percent, and 21 percent in each of the last three years. In addition, you may also take a 10 percent investment tax credit.

The Acclerated Cost Recovery System of ERTA provides for the deduction of the first $5,000 of the computer's cost. Thus it's possible that your computer system could be fully expensed in the same year that you purchase it. If the cost of your equipment is greater than the deduction allowed, the excess cost is depreciated by the above annual percentages. Under this provision, however, no investment tax credit is granted on your purchases. In any case you would be well advised to check with your tax advisor before depreciating your computer. Depreciation is a rather complex business, since you must first determine the type and extent of your computer usage. That takes some interpretation of the tax laws,

Exhibit 8–3 (*concluded*)

```
SCHED D  (CONT'D)    PAGE 2                              1981
(FORM 1040)
PETER & EMILY MOSS                          SSN 765-34-1234
***********************************************************
***** PART III - SUMMARY OF PARTS I & II ******************
19. NET GAIN (OR LOSS)................................. 19.     -5,705.
20. LESSER OF LINES 18 OR 19.......................... 20.
21. 60% OF LINE 20.................................... 21.
22. TOTAL CAPITAL GAINS............................... 22.
23. NET REPORTABLE LOSS............................... 23.      5,387.
24. LOSS DEDUCTIBLE THIS YEAR......................... 24.      3,000.
***** PART IV COMPUTATION OF ALTERNATIVE TAX **************
25. S/T GAIN AFTER 6/9/81............................. 25.
26. L/T GAIN AFTER 6/9/81............................. 26.
27. NET GAIN AFTER 6/9/81............................. 27.
28. SMALLER OF #26 OR #27............................. 28.
29. SMALLER OF #20 OR #28............................. 29.
30. TAXABLE INC.(1040 LINE 34)........................ 30.     46,150.
31. 40% OF LINE 29.................................... 31.
32. LINE 30 MINUS LINE 31............................. 32.
33. TAX ON AMT. ON LINE 32............................ 33.
......FROM SCHEDULE X; Y OR Z..........?  NO
......FROM SCHEDULE G...................?  NO
34. 20% OF LINE 29.................................... 34.
35. TAX THIS YEAR..................................... 35.
***** PART V - LOSS CARRYOVER POST '69 ********************
***** ...SEC. A. SHORT-TERM CARRYOVER *********************
36. LOSS FROM LINE 7.................................. 36.      5,069.
37. GAIN FROM LINE 18................................. 37.
38. NET LOSS (36 LESS 37)............................. 38.      5,069.
39. LOSS FROM LINE 24................................. 39.      3,000.
40. LESSER OF LINE 38 OR 39........................... 40.      3,000.
41. S/T LOSS CARRYOVER................................ 41.      2,069.
***** ...SEC B. LONG-TERM CARRYOVER ***********************
42. LINE #39-#40;(OR #24)............................. 42.
43. LOSS FROM LINE 18................................. 43.        636.
44. GAIN FROM LINE 7.................................. 44.
45. NET LOSS (43 LESS 44)............................. 45.        636.
46. TWO TIMES LINE 46................................. 46.
47. L/T LOSS CARRYOVER................................ 47.        636.
***** PART VI - ELECTION OF INSTALLMENT METHOD. ***********
ELECT OUT OF THE INSTL METHOD..........?  NO
FACE VALUE OF NOTE/OTHER OBLIG..........................
% OF VALUAT'N OF NOTE/OBLIG.............................
```

Courtesy of Howard Software Services

Exhibit 8–4. Tax Preparation Sequence

| Title | *Form 1040* | |
	Lines	Schedules and Forms
Filing status	1 to 6	None
Exemptions	6	None
Income	7 to 31	Schedules B to F
		Forms 4797 & 2106
Tax computation	32b to 34	Schedule A
Tax computation	35 to 37	Schedule G & D,
		Part IV
		Form 4726
Credits	38 to 47	Schedule R & RP
		Forms 3468 & 5695
Other taxes and	48 to 66	Schedule SE
payments		Form 4625
		6251
Balance due	66	Form 2210

Source: The "Tax Preparer" by Howard Software Services.

which is best left to the professionals. We must have a basic knowledge of how tax law affects our investing decisions but must be cautious not to assume we know everything about taxes, even though the computer is our ally. Some investors' returns are simply too complicated to file without professional help. The IRS watches out for complex returns and may return them if they have not been worked out by a qualified tax preparer. Although you may use your computer to keep an ongoing record of your year's deductions, and finally to complete the forms at the year's end, you should still consider sending them to an accountant for a review before mailing it to the IRS.

There are certain basic programs that every investor should have in his or her computer library. These include an electronic worksheet, a personal finance manager program, a program for communicating with an information service, and a tax-preparation program. With these four programs one can work out an investment plan, establish a financial database, locate and retrieve timely financial information, assess tax effects, and prepare annual returns. Other programs, such as portfolio managers, technical analyzers, and data management systems, support the basic investor programs and should be considered optional.

APPENDIX

Bibliography

Arenson, Karen W. *Guide to Making the New Tax Law Work for You*. New York: Times Books, 1981.

Bettner, Jill. "Computers Can Make Tax Time Less Taxing, but Can't Substitute for Knowing the Law." *The Wall Street Journal*, February 22, 1982.

"How to Pick a Tax Accountant." *Business Week*, November 9, 1981, pp. 142–146.

"How to Shelter Your Money from the Tax Man." Toronto: Northington Limited, 1980.

Neiburger, E. J., and Cecilia Wessner. "Voice of the IRS: Can Computers Be Deducted." *Personal Computing*, December 1981, pp. 55–56.

Perry, Robert. "Tax Preparation Software: How to Ease the IRS Blues." *Personal Computing*, December 1981, pp. 47–53, 76–80.

Resource List

Product	Resource	Computer
Individual Tax Plan and Personal Tax Plan	Aardvark Software 783 North Walter St. Milwaukee, WI 53202	Apple II+ Western Digital Microengine
Professional Tax System and Tax Plan	Contract Service Assoc. 706 Euclid Anaheim, CA 92802	TRS-80, I,II,III

Product	Resource	Computer
Taxman-82	Atsuko Computing Intl. 303 Williams Ave. Huntsville, AL 35801	Apple II+/III TRS-80 II IBM Personal Computer CP/M Computers
Master Tax Program	CPAids 1640 Franklin Ave. Kent, OH 44240	CP/M Computers
"Tax Preparer"	Howard Software Services 8008 Girard Ave. La Jolla, CA 92037	Apple II+
Tax-Saver	Micromatic Programming Company P.O. Box 158 Georgetown, CT 06892	Apple II+/III
State Returns	E-Z Tax Computer Systems 5 Eagle View Ct. Monsey, NY 10952	CP/M Computers
Tax Model	Professional Software Technology Inc. 180 Franklin St. Cambridge, MA 02139	n/a
Tax Mini-Miser	Sunrise Software Inc. 1056 Chestnut St. San Francisco, CA 94109	n/a
Shortax	Syntax Corp. P.O. Box 8137-W Prairie Village, KS 66208	n/a
Micro-Tax	Micro-Computer Taxsystems INC. 22713 Ventura Blvd. Suite F Woodland Hills, CA 91364	Apple II+ CP/M Computers

Insurance, Pension, and Estate Planning

All of your investing activities should have one common goal—to build up your estate. This is a long-term goal that requires coordination of your investment objectives with your life insurance and retirement plans. Of course you may have short-term and intermediate-term objectives with more immediate and specific purposes, such as raising money for your children's education or buying a home or a vacation retreat. But it is the long-range component of your investment plan that builds your estate.

Building an adequate retirement fund is important to meet your estate plan's objectives. This may entail no more than a coordination of the benefits from your company pension plan and your IRA (individual retirement account). For example, you may decide to structure your retirement plan to pay you varying income amounts at different ages, or you may also choose to build an annuity fund designed to begin paying out at some other age so you will have cash flows appropriate to your needs.

Life insurance should be a key element in estate planning but all too often it is overlooked. Your insurance agent can help you set up a life insurance program to meet your needs. What you should also consider is its impact on your total investment program. Obviously your insurance needs are much greater when your children are growing than when the nest is empty. This declining need for life insurance is heightened in later years by the accumulation of wealth in your investment and retirement programs.

The question you should be asking is, "How should my insurance program be structured to offer me the best protection for my family at all stages of life, taking into account both my investment and my retirement programs?"

The coordination of all three elements—life insurance, retirement, and estate—with your investment plan requires many different judgments and assumptions about your future circumstances. These are often difficult to assess. Your best shot at forecasting your needs is to set up a series of checkpoints at specific intervals in the future. Having done that you can construct a computer model of your future cash flows.

COMPUTER-AIDED LIFE INSURANCE PLANNING

The primary purpose of life insurance is to ensure that your survivors are provided for in the event of your death. If you die when people are financially dependent upon you, those dependents would suffer a serious financial loss. This loss can be either partially or totally eliminated with life insurance. If you choose to use life insurance to provide only partial protection, a properly structured investment program could meet your remaining needs with investment income.

Exhibit 9–1 illustrates the following points: the decreasing need for life insurance over time; that this decreasing net amount of insurance is offset by either your investment or retirement program; and typical post-retirement cash requirements. The vertical distance between the decreasing insurance line and the increasing investment or earned income line is the net difference in the insurance coverage you require at different ages. When you retire, your insurance needs level off. The protection you require at this stage of life is only that needed to cover burial and last illness expenses, repayments of any debts, various taxes related to your estate, a cash emergency fund for your spouse, and any gifts you may want to make.

Several alternatives exist for purchasing the right kind of insurance coverage for your particular situation. You may choose among decreasing or level term, whole life, limited payment life, endowment, or universal life policies, or a combination of these. The benefits and costs of these insurance plans are significantly different and you should, therefore, keep in mind your current investment program and the way its returns may supplement your expected insurance requirements. Your computer can aid you in assessing your life insurance needs and in coordinating them with both your long-term investment program and your retirement plan.

Murnane and Associates offers a computer program, Personal Savings

Exhibit 9-1. Life Insurance Needs

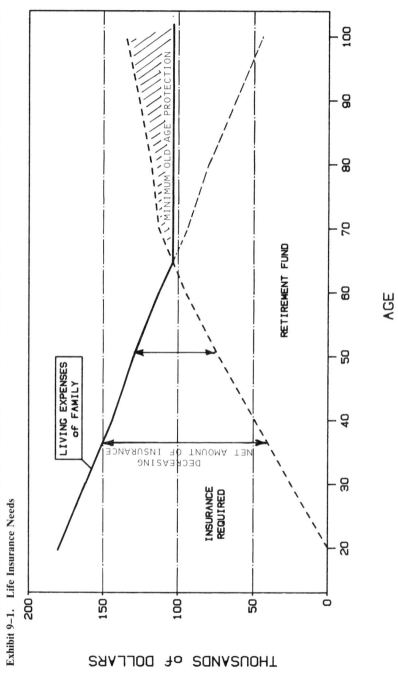

Courtesy of Northington Limited

Plan II (PSP II), which can provide a brief explanation of different policies to compute how much insurance you need and to determine the amount of savings you can accumulate in your insurance policy by retirement age. Generally, insurance simply provides financial protection for your dependents in the event of your death. If your employer does not have a suitable retirement plan, then perhaps the savings aspect of certain types of life insurance will be attractive. It is a decision you have to make, based on your own situation, and PSP II can help you make it.

Besides the differences in the design and purposes of competing types of insurance policies there is often a considerable difference in their cost. Should you take the least expensive policy that meets your minimum requirements, for instance, or should you depend more heavily on insurance? The PSP II program can help you answer these kinds of questions if you feed it the following information:

1. Your spouse's current age.
2. The monthly income desired.
3. Immediate cash needs.
4. Anticipated college costs (assuming you have children approaching college age).
5. Your spouse's income (if he or she works).
6. Other income available, such as social security benefits and investment incomes.
7. The current return on your investments (per annum).

From these inputs, PSP II can help you determine if your current insurance and investment plan provides the financial protection you need. If your current plan falls short, you will see by how much and by what point in time. Thus you can assess the changes needed in both your insurance and investment programs. The computations needed for the assessment are not part of PSP II, but they can be easily handled with an electronic spreadsheet model.

You should also take into consideration the loan value of your existing insurance policies. If you borrow from your policies, the interest charged by the insurance company is very low. Undoubtedly you can find savings plans that would pay you a return at least twice your interest cost. At the very least you should be able to use this loan value, in effect, to reduce monthly premiums on these policies. By reducing the premiums, you can invest your savings in better-paying long-term instruments to build a supplemental life insurance program.

One great advantage of the PSP II program is that it gives you the ability to run multiple "what-if" cases to determine alternate strategies. If you have special factors to be considered—factors which PSP II does not take into account—then perhaps you should write your own program.

Either way it's a great advantage to have a means of quickly evaluating alternative insurance plans with an eye toward providing maximum insurance protection while keeping costs to a minimum.

PENSION PLANNING

A principal goal of your investment program should be retirement income. Your retirement fund investing and your long-term investment objectives should be fully compatible. How you plug your pension plans into your investment strategy depends on the type of plan you choose. Individual, or "self-directed," plans like IRAs or Keoghs let you set the parameters of your investments. A corporate plan, though, offers no such flexibility. In this case, you must separately structure your personal investment portfolio to complement your corporate retirement program.

Integrating these programs means that you must know what to expect upon retirement. The interpretation of such diverse retirement plans as defined benefit or contribution, flat-dollar, and career average or final-pay formulas can be complex, but it is important that you understand what financial benefits these plans will give you at retirement. You should discuss these plans with your personnel manager or someone else familiar with your company plan.

It is particularly important to understand your "vesting" rights. Vesting is a provision of defined benefit plans that lets a participant know when (after a certain amount of time on the job) he has earned the right to claim benefits. If a participant is vested and quits the job, he retains the right to receive benefits from the pension plan at some future date. If he loses his job and has vested rights in a pension plan, he is still eligible to receive some amount of pension at a future date. If he switches jobs and is vested he may choose—in many cases—either a lump-sum payment, which he can put in an IRA, or keep the vested rights for later use.

Whether you lose your job or choose to leave it, it is necessary to keep your pension plans up to date. If you are not vested, you are, in essence, starting over again in the accumulation of a pension fund through a new company or self-directed plan.

Thanks to recent changes in the tax code you can participate in a self-directed plan at the same time that you are accumulating corporate credit toward retirement. These self-directed plans allow you to so hedge your bets that if for some reason you leave your company in the future you won't lose your pension fund. The self-directed account gives you an excellent tax-sheltered opportunity to protect yourself against such changes. The financial benefit resulting from 20 to 30 years of tax-privileged savings in an IRA is a real eye-opener compared to the aftertax profits in other investments. Exhibit 9–2 shows the compound growth of

Exhibit 9–2. Investment Comparisons

A. Comparison ($2,000 per year for 30 years; assume 15 percent return):
IRA = $870,000.
Non-IRA = $103,000.

B. **Typical IRA investment growth:**

	10th Year		20th Year		30th Year	
Annual Investment	*8%*	*12%*	*8%*	*12%*	*8%*	*12%*
$2,000 (individual taxpayer)	$32,183	$41,174	$104,346	$181,460	$266,942	$ 653,941
$2,250 (married couple, one wage earner)	36,113	46,658	117,389	204,142	300,309	735,683
$4,000 (married couple, two wage earners)	64,201	82,949	208,693	362,920	533,883	1,307,882

C. Typical return on a Keogh plan ($1,500, 10 percent return):

Years	Keogh	On Your Own (40% tax bracket)
5	$ 9,200	$ 5,100
10	23,900	11,900
15	47,700	20,900
20	85,900	33,100
25	147,500	49,400
30	246,700	71,200
35	406,500	100,300

Courtesy of Research Institute of America

both an IRA and Keogh plan over different periods compared to a high-yielding corporate bond over the same periods.

Another potential pitfall within a company sponsored program is the "defined contribution" plan, such as a profit-sharing system. Usually companies agree only to match and invest a portion of your savings, or to set aside a percentage of the corporation's profits that is pegged to your salary. If the company invests unwisely or performs poorly, you could find yourself without much of a pension. Therefore careful monitoring is important.

As you can see, few pension plans are foolproof. You need to cover every angle to ensure that you aren't without a pension when it's time to retire. To make sure your retirement income is safe, hire a good financial planner, open a self-directed account with your broker, or get suggestions from your accountant or attorney. Depending on their knowledge of your retirement objectives, they will make suggestions—some good and some perhaps not so good. To choose among them you will need a basic knowledge of the acceptable pension plan alternatives; a solid plan to fund your retirement program, and a personal computer.

The problems you face are how to determine an acceptable retirement income at age 65 and how to equal or exceed this amount with either lump sums of cash or other income. The arithmetic is fairly simple, and a desktop business calculator can help you with the computations. I recommend, however, that you use your personal computer to quickly calculate a variety of alternatives and store the results for reevaluation at some later date should your situation change.

Optimizing your retirement strategy requires that you analyze the impact of some 10 to 15 variables on your retirement objectives. Table 9–1

Table 9–1. Personal Savings Plan I

Summary of Inputs:
  A. Base data:
      1. Current age.
      2. Anticipated retirement age.
      3. Cash objective.
      4. Monthly income objective.
      5. Expected average inflation rate.
  B. Supplemental income:
      1. Expected monthly disability payment amount.
      2. Expected monthly pension payments.
      3. Social security benefits.
      4. IRA/Keogh.
      5. Other income (rentals, dividends, and interest).
      6. Part-time employment.
      7. Spouse's monthly income.
      8. Amount of cash on hand at retirement.

Summary of outputs:
  1. Summarized input.
  2. Monthly income desired.
  3. Monthly income forecast.
  4. Net deficit.
  5. Additional cash required for cash.
  6. Additional cash required for income.
  7. Additional cash required in total.
  8. Monthly savings required to meet objectives.

Courtesy of Murnane and Associates 1056 Metro Circle,
Palo Alto, CA 94303.

---

lists the typical input data you need to compute your required monthly savings until retirement. Murnane and Associates' Personal Savings Plan I uses this data to compute the net deficit or surplus between your forecasted needs and your expected sources of retirement funds. PSP I also tells you what additional income and lump-sum payments will be required to make up any deficit.

A central element in your retirement program will be Social Security. You have probably paid into the Social Security program for many working years and you should get your full entitlement. For example, at any time from age 62 on, you can retire and receive benefits of $650 monthly for life. On a monthly basis this amount may not seem like much, but if your life expectancy is 14 additional years at age 65 the total annuity amounts to $109,200. That is an amount that can hardly be ignored and it should be included in your planning.

The ravages of inflation should also be taken into account when planning for retirement. A recent survey of American managers' attitudes toward retirement, published by the American Management Associations, found that the largest single factor that enters into a retirement decision is concern about inflation. Dollars that you earn and invest today may be worth far less by the time you actually retire. Your personal computer can help counter inflation by suggesting alternate strategies to minimize inflation's effect.

Personal Savings Plan I lets you choose an expected average inflation rate so your forecasted needs in today's dollars can be adjusted for inflation. To be consistent, you should also consider the aftertax returns on the investments you include in your retirement plans. Although PSP I doesn't allow for such tax calculations, you have probably computed these returns previously. It is these aftertax profits that should be used as input to PSP I.

ESTATE PLANNING

We have reached the bottom line: your estate plan. The results of all your investing, insurance, and retirement planning are reflected in your estate plan, but there is nothing particularly complicated about the planning process. The simplest way to think about it is as a continuation of the portfolio management process since you need to know where your assets and liabilities lie to draw up an effective plan. Deciding where you want to go from there is the next step. Finally, by tying this knowledge to an understanding of relevant legal devices (such as trusts, gifts, and bequests), personal and financial constraints, and some idea of your objectives, you can begin the estate-planning process.

Understanding your current financial status means knowing your net worth. And to this the value of your insurance policies and retirement funds and you will have the total value of your estate should you die tomorrow.

In assessing your estate's worth you need to project your personal balance sheet of assets and liabilities over time. One good method is to grow your assets using conservative compound rates of 8 to 10 percent per year minus your assumed rate of inflation over the period. By factoring in the inflation rate, your calculations will yield a good estimate of the real future value of your estate. Your computer can help you make these calculations.

ESTATE TAX PLAN

There is an excellent computer program available to take the tedium out of the many time consuming computations associated with estate planning, the Estate Tax Plan (ETP) from Aardvark Software.

In using the Estate Tax Plan program your first task is data entry. You can enter up to 89 data items (the complete list is shown in Exhibit 9–3).

Exhibit 9–3. Estate Tax Plan by Aardvark Software, Inc.

Input Reference Guide

---

1. Is client married? (Y/N)
2. Anticipated date of death (month-year)

Asset Inventory:
3. Cash, checking and savings
4. Personal residence and effects
5. Value of sole proprietorship (Business #1)
6. Value of sole proprietorship (Business #2)
7. Value of sold proprietorship (Business #3)
8. Value of partnership interest (Business #4)
9. Partnership capital interest percent (Business #4)
10. Number of partners in partnership (Business #4)
11. Value of partnership interest (Business #5)
12. Partnership capital interest percent (Business #5)
13. Number of partners in partnership (Business #5)
14. Value of partnership interest (Business #6)
15. Partnership capital interest percent (Business #6)
16. Number of partners in partnership (Business #6)
17. Value of closely held stock (Business #7)
18. Voting power percentage (Business #7)
19. Number of shareholders (Business #7)
20. Value of closely held stock (Business #8)
21. Voting power percentage (Business #8)
22. Number of shareholders (Business #8)
23. Value of closely held stock (Business #9)
24. Voting power percentage (Business #9)
25. Number of shareholders (Business #9)
26. Other securities and investments
27. Real estate holdings
28. Life insurance on the decedent
29. Other personal property
30. Retirement benefits
31. All other property rights

Special use valuation:
32. Value of farm/business real property
33. Debts against farm/business real property
34. Value of farm/business personal property
35. Debts against farm/business personal property
36. Special use valuation reduction

Deductions from gross estate:
37. Funeral and administrative expense
38. Debts/mortgages/liabilities
39. Net losses

Marital deduction:
40. Marital deduction code
41. Assets passing to surviving spouse
42. Asset growth rate for marital deduction property

Charitable bequests:
43. Outright dollar bequests
44. Variable dollar bequests—percentage of gross estate
45. Variable dollar bequests—percentage of adjusted gross estate

Split bequests: Income interest for a fixed number of years
46. Gross amount of split bequest (Charity #1)
47. Fixed term of income interest (Charity #1)
48. Gross amount of split bequest (Charity #2)
49. Fixed term of income interest (Charity #2)
50. Gross amount of split bequest (Charity #3)
51. Fixed term of income interest (Charity #3)

Split bequests: Income interest for life
52. Gross amount of split bequest (Charity #4)
53. Age of subject whose life measures term (Charity #4)
54. Sex of subject whose life measures term (Charity #4) [1 = male/2 = female]
55. Gross amount of split bequest (Charity #5)
56. Age of subject whose life measures term (Charity #5)
57. Sex of subject whose life measures term (Charity #5) [1 = male/2 = female]
58. Gross amount of split bequest (Charity #6)
59. Age of subject whose life measures term (Charity #6)
60. Sex of subject whose life measures term (Charity #6) [1 = male/2 = female]

Exhibit 9–3 (*concluded*)

Split bequests: Remainder interest via trust:

61. Gross amount of split bequest (Charity #7)
62. Type of trust (Charity #7) [1 = annuity/2 = unitrust]
63. If annuity trust, amount fixed dollar annual payment (Charity #7)
64. If unitrust, percent adjusted payout rate (Charity #7) [5% minimum]
65. If payment is for life, subject age (Charity #7)
66. If payment is for life, subject sex (Charity #7) [1 = male/2 = female]
67. If payment is for a certain term, number of years (Charity #7)
68. Gross amount of split bequest (Charity #8)
69. Type of trust (Charity #8) [1 = annuity/2 = unitrust]
70. If annuity trust, amount fixed dollar annual payment (Charity #8)
71. If unitrust, % adjusted payout rate (Charity #8) [5% minimum]
72. If payment is for life, subject age (Charity #8)
73. If payment is for life, subject sex (Charity #8) [1 = male/2 = female]
74. If payment is for a certain term, number of years (Charity #8)

75. Gross amount of split bequest (Charity #9)
76. Type of trust (Charity #9) [1 = annuity/2 = unitrust]
77. If annuity trust, amount fixed dollar annual payment (Charity #9)
78. If unitrust, % adjusted payout rate (Charity #9) [5% minimum]
79. If payment is for life, subject age (Charity #9)
80. If payment is for life, subject sex (Charity #9) [1 = male/2 = female]
81. If payment is for a certain term, number of years (Charity #9)

Gift tax data:

82. Gross gifts within 3 years of death included in gross estate
83. Gift tax payable on gifts included in gross estate
84. Adjusted taxable gifts after 12/31/76 not in gross estate
85. Tax on gifts after 12/31/76
86. Specific exemption used (9/76–12/76)

Other options:

87. Additional liquid assets
88. Additional cash needs
89. Present value analysis rate

Courtesy of Aardvark Software, Inc.

The asset inventory section lets you enter detailed asset data. Along with investment and personal assets, you need to enter information on any closely held business you or your spouse might own that may be eligible for deferred payment of your estate tax or for stock redemption treatment. The Estate Tax Plan assumes that the value of the assets entered for both you and your spouse is their value at your assumed dates of death. This means that you must project the value of your assets from the time of analysis until these assumed dates.

The special use valuation section of the ETP program reflects the value of real property used by closely held, land-intensive farms and business. These valuations are shown because the Internal Revenue Code allows a reduction in the gross estate valuation for such property.

Four different marital deductions are included in the Estate Tax Plan that allow considerable flexibility in computing the effects of the specific marital deductions included in your will. Marital deductions are important because an allowance is made for certain property that is transferred to your surviving spouse. This property may be transferred to your spouse via survivorship rights in jointly held property, beneficiary status in life insurance policies, or specific bequests contained in your will. In the ETP program it is assumed that the volume of the marital deduction property will increase in the hands of the surviving spouse. Input 42 of the program lets you specify this growth rate. Usually, this property must be included in your spouse's gross estate when he or she dies.

The ETP program also deals extensively with bequests, an important yet potentially complex part of any will. There are four basic types: outright dollar bequests, percentage of your gross estate bequests, income interests (via a trust agreement) for a specified time, and bequests of remainder interests (also by trust agreement).

Item 82 lets you enter the value of gifts given within three years of your death. Gifts such as your life insurance policies or property over which you have control at your death are typical examples. The Estate Tax Plan includes them at their fair market value.

A cash needs analysis can also be generated by the Estate Tax Plan for both you and your spouse by comparing the liquid assets of your estate with its liquidity needs. Liquid assets include cash, retirement benefits, securities, and other assets.

The final item in the ETP program is the present value analysis rate used to compute the present value of the estate tax liabilities of both you and your spouse. The present value of your death tax liability is an amount of money which, if invested now at the rate assumed in Item 89, will grow to equal your tax liability at your death.

To give you an idea of how estate planning using the ETP works, let us take the hypothetical example of Mr. and Mrs. Brown. Let's assume they are the sole shareholders in a small corporation and that their three objectives are keeping the business within the family, contributing to their favorite charities, and minimizing estate taxes. For the Brown's case, we will use 29 of the input elements from Exhibit 9–3 specifically related to their situation (see Exhibit 9–4). They have requested that their church

Exhibit 9–4.   George and Mary Brown (March 1, 1982)

Input Item	*Alternative*		
	1	*2*	*3*
1. Is client married?	Yes	Yes	Yes
2. Anticipated date of death:			
Client	9/89	9/89	9/89
Spouse	11/93	11/93	11/93
4. Personal residence and effects:			
Client	130000	130000	130000
Spouse	130000	130000	130000
17. B7-value of closely held stock:			
Client	325000	325000	325000
Spouse	175000	175000	175000
18. B7-voting power percentage:			
Client	65	65	65
Spouse	35	35	35

Exhibit 9–4 (*concluded*)

Input Item	Alternative		
	1	*2*	*3*
19. B7-number of shareholders:			
Client	2	2	2
Spouse	2	2	2
26. Other securities and investments:			
Client	400000	400000	400000
Spouse	215000	215000	215000
37. Funeral and administrative expense:			
Client	7500	7500	7500
Spouse	7500	7500	7500
38. Debts/mortgages/liabilities:			
Client	25000	25000	25000
Spouse	25000	25000	25000
40. Marital deduction code:			
Client	1	3	4
Spouse	0	0	0
41. Assets passing to surv. spouse:			
Client	85000		
Spouse			
42. Asset growth rate—marital ded. prop.:			
Client	18	18	18
Spouse			
43. Char. outright dollar bequest:			
Client	0	0	0
Spouse	100000	100000	100000
44. Char. var. $ bequests—gross estate:			
Client	10	10	10
Spouse	0	0	0
46. Char. 1—gross amount of split bequest:			
Client	0	0	0
Spouse	50000	50000	50000
47. Char. 1—fixed term of income interest:			
Client	0	0	0
Spouse	12	12	12
82. Gross gifts within 3 years of death:			
Client	30000	30000	30000
Spouse	0	0	0
84. Adj. taxable gifts after 12/31/76:			
Client	115000	115000	115000
Spouse	0	0	0
86. Specific exemption used (9/76–12/76):			
Client	5000	5000	5000
Spouse	0	0	0
88. Additional cash needs:			
Client	0	0	0
Spouse	45000	45000	45000
89. Present value analysis rate:			
Client	20	20	20
Spouse	20	20	20

Courtesy of Aardvark Software, Inc.

and a neighbor benefit from their estate. These requests are shown in inputs 43–47. The Browns are debating the relative merits of three different types of marital deductions and therefore want to compute the effects of all three to arrive at the best possible choice. Their alternatives are:

1. Outright dollar bequest to spouse.
2. Optimal marital deduction, which calculates the amount of marital deduction necessary to generate a zero estate tax liability in the event of the death of one spouse.
3. The equalization marital deduction, which computes the amount of

---

Exhibit 9–5. The Browns: Gross Estate Calculation (March 1, 1982)

	Alternative		
	1	*2*	*3*
Client:			
Date of death	9/89	9/89	9/89
Cash/check/savings	0	0	0
Personal residence	130,000	130,000	130,000
Interest in business/farm	325,000	325,000	325,000
Securities/investments	400,000	400,000	400,000
Real estate	0	0	0
Life insurance	0	0	0
Other personal property	0	0	0
Retirement benefits	0	0	0
Other property rights	0	0	0
Marital property received	0	0	0
Gift within 3 years of death	30,000	30,000	30,000
Valuation reduction	0	0	0
Gross estate	885,000	885,000	885,000

	Alternative		
	1	*2*	*3*
Spouse:			
Date of death	11/93	11/93	11/93
Cash/check/savings	0	0	0
Personal residence	130,000	130,000	130,000
Interest in business/farm	175,000	175,000	175,000
Securities/investments	215,000	215,000	215,000
Real estate	0	0	0
Life insurance	0	0	0
Other personal property	0	0	0
Retirement benefits	0	0	0
Other property rights	0	0	0
Marital property received	164,795	492,048	340,845
Gift within 3 years of death	0	0	0
Valuation reduction	0	0	0
Gross estate	684,795	1,012,048	860,845

Courtesy of Aardvark Software, Inc.

marital deduction that the spouse who dies first would have to establish to generate two taxable estates that are approximately equal.

In using the ETP program the Browns enter their established data into the computer in a series of carefully phased steps. Once these are entered they simply calculate. The resulting seven output reports for the Brown case are shown in Exhibits 9–5 through 9–11.

Exhibit 9–6.   Estate Tax Liability (March 1, 1982)

	Alternative		
	1	*2*	*3*
Client:			
Date of death	9/89	9/89	9/89
Gross estate	885,000	885,000	885,000
Marital deduction	85,000	253,794	175,805
Funeral/admin. expenses	7,500	7,500	7,500
Debts/liabilities	25,000	25,000	25,000
Net losses	0	0	0
Charitable bequests	88,500	88,500	88,500
Taxable estate	679,000	510,206	588,195
Adjusted taxable gifts	115,000	115,000	115,000
Taxable transfers	794,000	625,206	703,195
Transfer tax	265,460	202,126	230,982
Unified credit	191,800	191,800	191,800
Tax paid lifetime gift	0	0	0
State death tax credit	17,160	10,326	13,527
Federal estate tax liab.	56,500	0	25,655

	Alternative		
	1	*2*	*3*
Spouse:			
Date of death	11/93	11/93	11/93
Gross estate	684,795	1,012,048	860,845
Marital deduction	0	0	0
Funeral/admin. expenses	7,500	7,500	7,500
Debts/liabilities	25,000	25,000	25,000
Net losses	0	0	0
Charitable bequests	125,151	125,151	125,151
Taxable estate	527,144	854,397	703,194
Adjusted taxable gifts	0	0	0
Taxable transfers	527,144	854,397	703,194
Transfer tax	165,843	289,015	230,982
Unified credit	192,800	192,800	192,800
Tax paid lifetime gift	0	0	0
State death tax credit	0	25,411	18,153
Federal estate tax liab.	0	70,804	20,029
Total family estate tax	56,500	70,804	45,684

Courtesy of Aardvark Software, Inc.

Exhibit 9-7. Present Value Analysis of Death Taxes (March 1, 1982)

	Alternative		
	1	*2*	*3*
Client:			
Date of death	9/89	9/89	9/89
Interest rate	20	20	20
Death taxes	73,660	10,326	39,182
PV of tax—1 payment	20,557	2,881	10,934
Number of payments—(N)	7	7	7
PV of tax—(N) payments	4,752	666	2,528

	Alternative		
	1	*2*	*3*
Spouse:			
Date of death	11/93	11/93	11/93
Interest rate	20	20	20
Death taxes	0	96,215	38,182
PV of tax—1 payment	0	10,791	4,282
Number of payments—(N)	12	12	12
PV of tax—(N) payments	0	2,025	803

Courtesy of Aardvark Software, Inc.

Exhibit 9-8. Deferred Payment of Estate Taxes (March 1, 1982)

	Alternative		
	1	*2*	*3*
Client:			
Date of death	9/89	9/89	9/89
Type of business:			
Sole proprietorships	0	0	0
Partnerships	0	0	0
Corporations	325,000	325,000	325,000
Valuation reduction	0	0	0
Total business amount	325,000	325,000	325,000
Sec. 6166 available?	Yes	Yes	Yes
Amount of tax deferred	21,539	0	9,780

	Alternative		
	1	*2*	*3*
Spouse:			
Date of death	11/93	11/93	11/93
Type of business:			
Sole proprietorships	0	0	0
Partnerships	0	0	0
Corporations	175,000	175,000	175,000
Valuation reduction	0	0	0
Total business amount	175,000	175,000	175,000
Sec. 6166 available?	No	No	No
Amount of tax deferred	0	0	0

Courtesy of Aardvark Software, Inc.

Exhibit 9–9. Payment Schedule for Estate Tax: Section 6166—Alternative #3 (March 1, 1982)

Client—Date of death: 9/89

Payment Number	Tax Due	Interest Due	Total Payment
1	15,875*	0	15,875
2	0	391	391
3	0	391	391
4	0	391	391
5	0	391	391
6	978	391	1,369
7	978	352	1,330
8	978	313	1,291
9	978	274	1,252
10	978	235	1,213
11	978	196	1,174
12	978	156	1,134
13	978	117	1,095
14	978	78	1,056
15	978	39	1,017

Payment Schedule for Estate Tax: Section 6166—Alternative #1

Client—Date of death: 9/89

Payment Number	Tax Due	Interest Due	Total Payment
1	34,961*	0	34,961
2	0	862	862
3	0	862	862
4	0	862	862
5	0	862	862
6	2,153	862	3,015
7	2,153	776	2,929
8	2,153	690	2,843
9	2,153	603	2,756
10	2,153	517	2,670
11	2,153	431	2,584
12	2,153	345	2,498
13	2,153	259	2,412
14	2,153	172	2,325
15	2,153	86	2,239

Courtesy of Aardvark Software, Inc.

* Amount not deferred.

Several points should be noted about this output. In alternative 1, Mr. Brown's estate tax computations reflect some taxable gifts made within three years of his death and their adjusted status. His estate qualifies for the deferred payment of federal estate taxes and the redemption of closely held shares at the capital gains rates. Finally, Mrs. Brown's gross estate includes the property received from her husband via the marital deduction, compounded at 18 percent for the four years they are assuming separates his death from hers.

Exhibit 9-10. Liquidity Analysis (March 1, 1982)

	Alternative		
	1	*2*	*3*
Client:			
Date of death	9/89	9/89	9/89
Cash/check/savings	0	0	0
Securities/investments	400,000	400,000	400,000
Life insurance proceeds	0	0	0
Retirement benefits	0	0	0
Other liquid assets	0	0	0
Liquid assets available	400,000	400,000	400,000
Death taxes	73,660	10,326	39,182
Funeral/admin. expense	7,500	7,500	7,500
Charitable bequests	88,500	88,500	88,500
Other cash needs	0	0	0
Cash requirements	169,660	106,326	135,182
Estate liquidity	230,340	293,674	264,818

	Alternative		
	1	*2*	*3*
Spouse:			
Date of death	11/93	11/93	11/93
Cash/check/savings	0	0	0
Securities/investments	215,000	215,000	215,000
Life insurance proceeds	0	0	0
Retirement benefits	0	0	0
Other liquid assets	0	0	0
Liquid assets available	215,000	215,000	215,000
Death taxes	0	96,215	38,182
Funeral/admin. expense	7,500	7,500	7,500
Charitable bequests	125,151	125,151	125,151
Other cash needs	45,000	45,000	45,000
Cash requirements	177,651	273,866	215,833
Estate liquidity	37,349	−58,866	−833

Courtesy of Aardvark Software, Inc.

Alternative 2 shows a decidedly different picture. The selection of the optimal marital deduction resulted in a deduction that was precisely large enough to produce a zero tax on his estate. Because of this, however, Mrs. Brown now has a larger death tax liability at her death. The present value analysis indicates that this deferral of taxes actually benefits the family's tax standing but creates a cash flow problem, as indicated by the liquidity analysis.

Alternative 3 results in the lowest possible family estate tax liability by generating the marital deduction necessary to make the transfer of taxes between the two spouses approximately equal. That way, the two remain

---

Exhibit 9–11.   Capital Gain Treatment under Sec. 303 Stock Redemption (March 1, 1982)

	Alternative		
	1	*2*	*3*
Client:			
Date of death	9/89	9/89	9/89
Sec. 303 available?	Yes	Yes	Yes
Redeem at cap. gain rate	81,160	17,826	46,682
	Alternative		
	1	*2*	*3*
Spouse:			
Date of death	11/93	11/93	11/93
Sec. 303 available?	No	No	No
Redeem at cap. gain rate	0	0	0

Courtesy of Aardvark Software, Inc.

---

in the lowest possible estate tax bracket. This is exactly what Mr. and Mrs. Brown are attempting to achieve with their estate plan.

As significant as the goal of minimizing your taxes is, even larger benefits are to be derived from getting your affairs in order and preserving your accumulated wealth through careful estate planning. As you can see from the Browns' case, your personal computer is a very powerful tool in estate planning. The tedious, time-consuming computations are reduced to only a few minutes of computer time. Neatly printed reports let you quickly analyze the results. If you are not satisfied with these results, you can modify your input data, recalculate it, and print out additional what if cases to optimize your personal estate plan.

APPENDIX

Bibliography

"The Bedrock of Executive Wealth," New York: Research Institute of America, 1981.

Carter, Malcolm N. "How Safe Is Your Pension," *Money,* July 1982, pp. 65–70.

Jud, Robert. *The Retirement Decision: How American Managers View Their Prospects.* New York: AMACOM, a division of the American Management Associations, 1980.

"Putting Together a Portable Pension." *Business Week,* May 11, 1981, pp. 142–43.

Randle, Paul A., and Philip R. Swensen. *Personal Financial Planning for Executives.* Belmont, Calif.: Lifetime Learning Publications, a division of Wadsworth, Inc., 1981.

Runde, Robert. "Planning Now for Your Longer Life." *Money,* March 1981, pp. 52–63.

Sloan, Allen. "Charting Your Own IRA Course." *Money,* May 1982, pp. 105–10.

"Successful Investing and Money Management." chaps. 16, 20, 26, and 27. Toronto: Northington Limited, 1974.

Trunzo, Candice E. "Do-It-Yourself Pensions." *Money,* March 1981, pp. 64–67.

"What You Should Know About IRA/Keogh Now." New York: Research Institute of America, 1982.

Resource List

Product	*Resource*	*Computer*
Personal Savings Programs I/II	Murnane and Associates 1056 Metro Circle Palo Alto, CA 94303	TRS-80
Estate Tax Plan	Aardvark Software 783 North Water Street Milwaukee, WI 53202	Apple II+/III Western Digital Microengine

Portfolio Evaluation

Throughout this book you have been asked to change the way you think about solving investment problems, to use your computer not only to do the hard number crunching but also to help you make the best decisions about what to invest in and when to do so. If I have been successful, your perception of investing and your approach to choosing alternative instruments have been somewhat altered. The personal computer is the mechanism by which this change has taken place.

I have asked you to change established procedures by which you view your financial picture and to replace them with new and different ones spelled out by the computer. Remember, though, your methodology for analyzing individual courses of action should not change. Your methodology is what differentiates your approach to investing from someone else's. The computer procedures you ultimately elect to use should be those with which you feel most comfortable. They should be reflections of your personal investing methodology.

One of the greatest benefits to using a computer is that it requires you to explicitly define your investment objectives in quantitative terms, to be precise in recording details, and to fully define the relationship between the various elements of your portfolio. This disciplines your thinking and reinforces it by catching and holding your reasoning each step of the way.

INTEGRATED INVESTOR SYSTEM

The concept of computer-aided investing should be clearer now. Our final task is to combine the personal computer aids to investing that we have discussed into a single integrated investor system (IIS). To do this it is easiest to think in terms of a building block structure representing this integration (see Exhibit 10–1).

Exhibit 10–1. Integrated Investor System

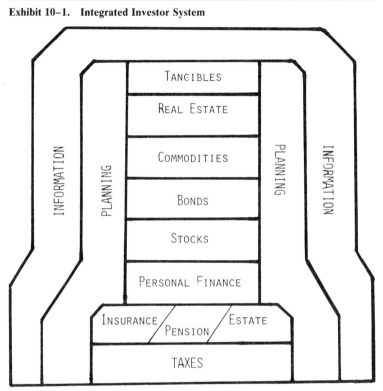

The Integrated Investor System lets the investor think in terms of a building block structure. The traditional investments of stocks, bonds, real estate, et al., build on a base of a personal financial system, a solid program for insurance and retirement, and a careful consideration of tax consequences. A comprehensive investment plan surrounds these programs, and all this is wrapped in an information envelope to help ensure that timely and profitable decisions are made.

Looking at the traditional areas of investing—stocks, bonds, commodities, real estate, stock options, and tangibles—you can see that they are not the central elements in the structure. Instead, the center is taxes. Insurance, pension, and estate-related finances sit one level above taxes. They represent the bottom line of your financial program. Personal finances includes your current assets and liabilities, cash flow, and budgets. It forms the base for traditional investments.

Uniting all the diverse elements of your investment portfolio is your overall investment plan, the central point of which is your set of objectives. Unless you know where you want to go, you will never know if you have arrived. Effective portfolio evaluation is predicated on having specific goals and objectives.

The last element in the integrated investor system is information. It has been said many times that "He who owns the data, owns the business." Getting control of your financial life, selecting an efficient portfolio, and measuring your success depends on having the right information at the right time. You are at an advantage by being able to retrieve by computer all sorts of market and financial data quickly and easily—literally from your armchair. This information is the glue that binds your whole investing structure. Without it you just don't know where you are.

It is these three elements—information, your financial program, and your investing plans and objectives—that are combined to form the integrated investor system. The purpose of the IIS is to let you relate the input and output data from each of your programs into a coherent personal financial system. Implementation of the IIS is done with another computer program called a "database manager," which supplements your individual investment analysis and management, personal finance, and estate-planning programs. It forms the basis for computerized portfolio evaluation.

DATABASE MANAGEMENT SYSTEMS

These may sound like complicated computer programs, but don't let the name fool you. Database management systems is just a fancy way to manage an electronic filing cabinet. Other names commonly used include "file managers," "personal filing systems," and "keyword database programs." The purpose of all these programs is basically the same: to so manage groups of data that the data in related groups can be processed electronically. This allows the user to structure the "filing cabinet" data in such a way it is related by a common format (particularly important to portfolio management) that can control duplicate entries (avoiding the confusion of too much identical data), do some arithmetic on specific data fields (allowing comparison of returns on different investments), and report on the database's contents in a variety of ways (comparing results to objectives and to cost). These reports may be simple searches for specific data records or special summary reports.

The basic, required features in a database management program include a capability for entering data, editing it for accuracy, storing it according to your rules, manipulating it, and preparing reports based on one or more data groupings, such as specific investments. Electronic filing system managers can include a broad range of features. The following list gives you an idea of the kinds of special capabilities that you might want to consider having in your system:

1. A display screen editor that lets you design the forms you need for entering the data.
2. Field labels that give you the ability to enter descriptive labels for the data fields, making the system easier to find and use.
3. Adequate storage capacity so you can know ahead of time the approximate number of records (stocks, real estate, bonds, and so forth) you need to store.
4. Arithmetic capability for computing percentages and ratios between fields in related investment record groups.
5. File maintenance service programs so your investment database will be in constant movement as market prices rise and fall, making it easy to update your valuation data.
6. Reporting flexibility that gives you the ability to search for specific portfolio facts at any time, but especially at tax time.

Making your selection of a database management program is no different from selecting an investor program. You should have a pretty good idea of what you want the database to look like, and you should discuss your needs with your local computer dealer or user group, or call the firm(s) that makes the one(s) in which you are interested.

EVALUATING YOUR PORTFOLIO

The preceding discussions about how personal computers can change your thinking, how to structure an integrated investor system, and how to choose a data management system all lead up to a subject of utmost importance to you: evaluating the performance of your portfolio and taking any necessary corrective action. These two factors will be crucial to your success.

"Where am I?" and "How do I get back on the right road?" are two questions you will ask yourself repeatedly over time. Examinations of your investing status should be done at least annually. The more formal your system, the more frequently you may wish to make this review. The objective is always to get the most mileage out of your investment dollars.

The need to keep good computer records has been underscored many times. Whether it is for tax reasons or to ensure that your investments are headed the right way, each investment requires a separate entry in the database. This aids comparisons among the various data elements. You should use the database system that most closely fits the logical structure of your portfolio records. Similar data fields can be easily computed and summarized using a number of comparisons and ratios. Some of these include:

1. The comparison of returns against the cost of those returns.
2. The annual return on your assets.
3. The percent of income drawn from each investment and the percent of your total capital that each represents.
4. The relative contribution of each type of instrument (stocks, bonds, whatever).
5. A summary of returns by the principal objectives of growth, safety, and income.
6. A comparison to a standard measure like the Dow Jones Industrial Average, Standard & Poor's Composite Average, Salomon Brothers' Bond Index, and so on.

Your database records should contain pertinent data about each investment type. For instance, your securities database may contain stock price, number of shares, dividends paid and their dates, realized and unrealized capital gains and losses, and income returns. Your real estate records may contain purchase price, downpayment, mortgage costs, income descriptions, monthly costs, and so forth. Each set of records should also contain a stated reason for making an investment, based on your overall objectives. This will provide a verbal link to your overall goals.

After making these comparisons you have to examine them in the light of your plans. Are your defensive positions still holding? Is your offense still gaining yardage? If your portfolio's performance isn't up to snuff, then look at alternative investments. The true efficiency of your investments is obtained by minimizing the variances between what you expected to achieve and your actual results. Where necessary, you should weed out your poorly performing instruments, replacing them with ones that you expect will perform better. Set a checkpoint three to six months into the future, and compare the performance of your new instruments to your plan at that time. Annual reviews should include all elements of your program to adjust them for major economic or market shifts, changes in your tax or investor status, the emergence of more attractive alternatives, or risks that have become unacceptable.

The database you create should contain summary data from each investing area. If you are using, for example, a portfolio manager for stocks and bonds, or the Compu Trac account management program, you must extract from these programs the basic data needed for portfolio evaluation. This is then entered into the database that you have created. If you do this with each financial area, and include the numerical objectives from your spreadsheet planning system, you will have all the data you need in one place. Provided that the database management program you choose has the capability, the portfolio data can be electronically handled to provide any set of comparisons you need. You can then fine-tune your investment instruments as often as you wish.

Asking what-if questions may require going back to your generalized spreadsheet model, but that's the beauty of the computer. No matter what questions you need to ask of your entire financial portfolio, there's a way to do it. But remember, it is not magic. You need to use some creativity in structuring your financial database, extracting data from your individual investment portfolio's management programs, and producing comparisons. This is a big challenge. But if you are serious about your investing and are really involved with your computer, meeting this challenge will be rewarding and, often, fun.

APPENDIX

Resource List

Product	Resource	Computer
Datafax	Link Systems 1640 19th Street Santa Monica, CA 90404	Apple II/III
VisiDex	VisiCorp 2896 Zanker Road San Jose, CA 95134	Apple II+
Cardbox	Caxton Software 10–14 Bedford St. Covent Garden London WC2E 9HE England	48K CP/M
DBMaster	Stoneware 50 Belvedere Street San Rafeal, CA 94901	Apple II+
VisiFile	VisiCorp 2895 Zanker Road San Jose, CA 95134	Apple II+
PFS: Personal Filing System	Software Publishing Company 1901 Landings Road Mountain View, CA 94043	Apple II+
T.I.M. III, Rel.5	Innovative Software, Inc. 9300 W. 110th Street Suite 380 Overland Park, KS 66210	IBM Personal Computer

Product	Resource	Computer
Filemanager	Synapse Software 820 Coventry Road Kensington, CA 94707	Atari 800
Versafile	Radio Shack 1800 One Tandy Center Fort Worth, TX 76102	TRS-80, Mod.1
General Manager	Sierra-OnLine Systems, Inc. Mudge Ranch Road Coarsegold, CA 93614	Apple II+/III

Real Estate Opportunity Analysis and Property Management

Most of us probably do not consider our home as simply an investment, even though we could probably sell it for a handy profit. We would have to find a new home to replace it, and chances are the new home would have gone up in value every bit as much as the old one. Thus the profit on the sale may be illusory. There are, however, many types of properties, both residential and nonresidential, where the profit potential is very real indeed. These include apartment houses, condominiums, undeveloped land, office buildings, and shopping centers, to name just a few.

Real estate of all kinds has long been viewed as a classic inflation hedge, an investment whose growth in value may be counted on to outpace the rate of inflation. Recently, however, with inflation coming down to more manageable levels but with interest rates remaining high, real estate has lost a considerable amount of its appeal for the individual investor.

Real estate may not be the unbeatable market play it was 5 or 10 years ago, but it still offers many excellent opportunities for profit, particularly in some sunbelt areas. In the Atlanta suburbs, for example, the construction of shopping centers, office parks, convenience stores, and apartments never seems to end. One should not assume that less dynamic areas, such as the Northeast and Midwest, are without excellent properties. Within an hour's drive of any place in the United States are solid investment properties. The challenge is to find them.

REAL ESTATE RISK

You should be on the lookout for several specific types of investment properties. These include undeveloped land, shopping centers, garden and duplex apartments, office buildings, and high-rise apartments. Like any other investments, various risks are associated with each. The risks associated with each type of property investment—in Exhibit 11–1—are:

Exhibit 11–1. Property Investment Risks

Type	Investment Period (years)	Leverage— Debt to Equity (percent)	Capital Req'd. (k = $1,000)	Potential Return on Investment (ROI in percent)
Undeveloped land	3 to 4	50%	$5k to $10k	300%
Apts., 2–6 units	5 to 10	75 to 80	$8k to $20k	300
Shopping ctr.	5 to 7	75 to 80	$50k	500
Garden apts.	8 to 12	75 to 80	$50k	300
Office bldg.	8 to 12	75 to 80	$100k	500
High-rise apt.	8 to 12	75 to 80	$250k	400

Courtesy of Northington, Ltd.

The emphasis in many books and real estate advisory services is on small income-producing properties. The reasons for this are several. First, the demand for rental property is generally strongest during periods of high interest rates. Squeezed by high mortgage rates and the rapid escalation in home prices it has been estimated that today only about 15 percent of the nation's one-income families can afford the average price of a home. This, along with the fact that many two-income couples are postponing home buying until they have established their careers, has served to keep occupancy rates in rental units unusually high. In addition, government statistics indicate that a record number of new households will be formed in this decade, greatly adding to the demand for housing.

Simply stated, good real estate deals of all kinds will be around for a while—especially income-producing properties. The challenge is to ferret out the best opportunities. It requires considerable market research, an understanding of the industry's vocabulary, and a clear view of the financing alternatives. The first two tasks can be addressed with diligence and study. The latter can be accomplished with pencil and paper or—you guessed it—your computer.

No matter how you approach it, analyzing real estate alternatives requires many calculations and comparisons. You can, of course, do it by hand. Like every other investment we have discussed, however, numerous financial computations have to be worked out. Some fine programs are available for both the buy analysis and for the subsequent management of your income property.

FINANCIAL ELEMENTS OF REAL ESTATE

As real estate investors know well, the three determinants of a good property are location, location, and location. If the train tracks are in the property's backyard, for example, it may be a major deterrent to getting tenants for an apartment building. However, the proximity of the train may mean excellent transportation to a job in the city, making those same tracks a major selling point.

Two other factors to consider are competition for tenants from neighboring apartments and the initial work needed on a property along with its annual upkeep. Competing landlords may be already marketing their apartments in an area, and being the new landlord on the block you may find your apartments slow to fill up. Obviously this could retard your cash flow, and it is a risk that you should weigh before you buy. Furthermore, the cost of initial and ongoing repairs to older properties could bleed you if you aren't prepared.

The following list contains a few key questions you should try to answer:

Do you have several thousand dollars you can afford to tie up for several years?

Do you have adequate credit to qualify for mortgage loans?

What type of financing is available in your area, and at what rates?

What arrangements can be made with the seller, and what offers are you prepared to make? How creative can you be with your deal?

Are operating expenses reasonable, and how stable are both expenses and taxes?

What are the opportunities to increase rents, and can you count on stable occupancy rates?

Is a profit possible after taxes and mortgage payments?

How easy would it be to resell the property if you had to?

When you ask these questions, you should be forming a pattern or model in your mind for evaluating opportunities. Questions related to the property (e.g., neighbors) and market comparison are primarily subjective, but all other questions are quantifiable. This makes it easy to use your computer to, among other things, analyze a cash flow stream. Further, you can ask a variety of what-if questions, such as: When is the optimum time to sell? What is the effect of a balloon mortgage versus a fixed-rate mortgage, or a variable-rate graduated payment mortgage, on your return on investment? What depreciation method should you use to minimize the tax effect?

A property's true value is especially difficult to determine because it involves several subjective and nonsubjective judgments. The three most commonly used methods are:

1. *The market approach,* which compares the price of a property with similar kinds of real estate sold about the same time in the same area.
2. *The cost approach,* which considers the replacement cost of a property.
3. *The income approach,* which attempts to anticipate future income as an indication of a property's income-producing ability.

The computer program you use should focus on income analysis, with backup from the first two methods. Most of the complex mathematics are part of this method, and, once you have estimated the true value of the property and calculated that the property is worth its price, an analysis of the property's cash flow, tax effect, equity buildup, and potential appreciation can be undertaken. The interaction of several variables makes these calculations very complex. That complexity can be heightened by the effects of something like taking on multiple mortgages over varying times. Periodic refinancing may also be desirable to take advantage of dips in interest rates, but don't forget there are costs associated with refinancing that can be prohibitive in many cases. Additionally, you will want your model to tell you when the optimum sell point is reached, and that can be an extremely important calculation since capital appreciation is often the major consideration in real estate deals. The ROIs of 500 percent shown in Exhibit 11–1 are rarely made through cash flow or tax benefits alone. Capital appreciation is the major factor, accounting for as much as 85 percent of the total return.

Another major element in the financing of real estate is leverage. This is similar to buying on margin in the stock and commodities markets. In those markets, however, many buyers are professional traders or, at the very least, very knowledgeable amateurs. In real estate most people buying a home today buy with a mortgage of 50 to 90 percent of the home's cost. This is more than the margin rate allowed by brokerage houses on common stocks. Yet in real estate highly leveraged positions are so common that most of us don't blink twice—that is until we see the cost of this borrowing. But for real estate investors a high degree of leverage is essential to obtaining high appreciation rates. Appreciation with leverage can be 10 times as great as when no leverage is applied. Leverage gives the investor the ability to control a large number of investment dollars with small amounts of money.

A personal computer enables you to estimate the effect of different leverage amounts on your expected ROI. One way to do this is by varying the downpayment. A minimum downpayment usually means you are using maximum leverage by carrying a large mortgage. The level of interest rates will also have a bearing on how much money you will be able to borrow. Certainly, the higher the interest rates the lower your leverage will be.

Your evaluation of income-producing property must, of necessity, take into account many more factors than would be considered if you were simply buying a place to live. A proper analysis of this multiplicity of factors requires complex and highly specialized computer programs. You may want to use the electronic spreadsheet methods, or you may choose one of several property analysis programs. Whichever you choose, the computer will prove to be an indispensable tool for comparing real estate alternatives quickly and more accurately than either pencil and paper or a desk calculator.

COMPARISONS WITH STOCKS AND BONDS

Real estate investments differ significantly from those in stocks, bonds, options, and commodities. The real estate market is essentially local and is not governed by market populations of several thousand stocks or other securities. In the stock market you can make predictions about an individual stock's performance based on an assessment of overall trends in particular groups or industries. That is not the case in real estate, which reacts to local market conditions. Regional influences, such as demographics and economic growth, together with the preferences of residents, have the greatest effect on a property's value. While rises and falls in interest rates will have an impact on the real estate market across the country, local factors determine just how great that impact will be in an area.

Given the importance of local factors it is not too surprising that information utilities aren't terribly useful for real estate analysis. You may be able to retrieve some information on markets in other areas of the country for generalized comparison, but that's about all. If the property isn't within an hour's drive from you, you can't manage it effectively. The management of a property is a significant element, and sometimes that's a problem with real estate—it requires a great deal of attention. Some people find themselves unsuited to real estate investing because they simply don't have enough time to manage it.

Computer techniques offer you several ways to not only evaluate properties but to manage them. The techniques are not new. What is different is the completeness of the results you can achieve with a computer. You punch in your data on the property's mortgage and tax rates, expected income and expenses, and miscellaneous operating costs. Then you push the computer's return button and soon the statistical results are printed out, leaving you free to sit back and compare your prospective purchases. Your computer functions as a calculator, storer of records, and report writer for your analysis and decision making. A number of programs are now making it easy for real estate investors to increase their profits. Let's take a look at some of them.

AUTOMATED REAL ESTATE SELECTION

The Property Analysis System (PAS) from Realty Automation, Inc., is a software package that provides investment analysis for all types of income properties. Like many such programs, PAS is easy to use and requires no previous computer training. Your basic data is entered through the display terminal and can be modified at any time. The effects of changing information can immediately be seen, thus allowing the evaluation of multiple alternatives. For instance, you can run the program assuming a 10-, 20-, or 30-year mortgage. Or you can assume you will get the special tax break you have applied for and see what happens to equity build-up, cash flow, taxes, and other financial factors (see Exhibit 11-2).

The first page of the PAS printout provides a description of the property; its estimated rate of appreciation; financial data, such as mortgage amounts, interest rates, monthly principal and interest, and periodic payments; an income schedule; operating expenses; depreciation schedules; other capital information. Also computed is the cost per square foot, gross multiplier (a ratio of price to income, which indicates the relative value of the property as an income generator), depreciation information, cost per unit, and some prorated purchase costs.

The second and third pages provide analysis of the first 10 years' financial information (done on a prorated basis if owned less than a full calendar year). These projections include estimated market value, selling costs, owner equity, amortization of loans, operating income before and after taxes, tax benefits, cash flow, rate of return before and after taxes, owner net proceeds if sold after capital gains tax, and other ancillary data.

PAS stores data and information about 20 different properties on a single diskette. Multiple diskettes can store a virtually unlimited amount of property information.

Exhibit 11–2. Property Analysis System—Investment Opportunity Factors

```
000                    **** INVESTMENT OPPORTUNITY ****                    6/23/8
==============================================================================
    6 UNIT APT.BLDG.    1234 MAPLE AVE., BIG CITY        SALES PRICE:   $300000

  ESTIMATED AGE:  17    LOT SIZE: 80x150   SQ.FT.: 6000   COST/UNIT:     $50000

  ANNUAL INCOME:   $37800  GROSS MULTIPLIER:   7.94   COST/SQ.FT.:    $   50

                    ++++ CONDITIONS AND ASSUMPTIONS ++++
  1) ESCROW CLOSING DATE:  7 / 82      5) PROPERTY APPRECIATION RATE/YR: 5 %
  2) SELLING COSTS: 7 % OF SALES PRICE  6) INCOME INFLATION RATE/YEAR:  0 %
  3) TAX BRACKET: 35 %   VAC.FAC.: 3 %  7) CAPITAL GAINS TAX RATE: 25 %
  4) NEEDS NEW ROOF                     8) GOOD CLOSE IN LOCATION

                       ++++ FINANCIAL DATA ++++
==============================================================================
               (%)   INT.      AMT.  LOAN  ------- MONTHLY --------    ANNUAL
ITEM   AMOUNT  S.P.  RATE   PP  PER.  TERM  PRIN  INTEREST   PYMT.      PYMT.
----   ------  ----  ----      ----   ----  ----  --------   -----    -------
DWN.    60000  20.0
1ST.   225000  75.0  12.50      30    30     58    2344      2401      28816
2ND.    15000   5.0  15.00      15    10           188        188       2250
                                           ----  --------   -----    -------
TOT  $300,000 100.0                         $58   $2531     $2589     $31066
```

```
    ++++ INCOME SCHEDULE ++++            ++++ OPERATING EXPENSES ++++
===================================  : ====================================
              PRESENT    POTENTIAL   :  EXPENSE      MONTHLY    ANNUAL
 TYPE OF  # OF -------   ---------   :  -------      -------    ------
  UNIT   UNITS RENT TOTAL RENT TOTAL :  GAS             25        300
 ------  ----- ---- ----- ---- ----- :  ELECTRIC        50        600
 1 BRM    2    400  800   450  900   :  WATER           15        180
 2 BRM    4    450  1800  525  2100  :  TRASH           13        156
 GARAGES  6               25   150   :  GARDENING       35        420
                                     :  MAINTENANCE     40        480
                                     :  ADVERTISING     10        120
                                     :  TAXES          250       3000
                                     :  INSURANCE       35        425
                                     :  MGMT.          138       1650
                                     :
 ----------------------------------  : ----------------------------------
 TOTAL  12 MONTHLY  $2600    $3150   :  TOTAL         $611      $7331
           ANNUAL   $31200   $37800  :
```

```
   ++++ DEPRECIATION SCHEDULE ++++         ++++ CAPITAL INVESTMENT ++++
==================================== : ====================================
DEPRECIABLE  % OF           ANNUAL   :                              REQ'D
  ASSETS    S.P.  COST  D.M. RL DEPREC. : PURCHASE  COSTS           CAPITAL
----------- ----  ----  ---- -- ------ : ---------------           -------
BUILDING (S) 80.0 240000  SL 15 16000 : DOWN PAYMENT                60000
GARAGE (S)                            : 1ST.LOAN FEE @    PTS.
CARPETS/DRAPES                        : 2ND.LOAN FEE @    PTS.
PERSONAL PROP                         : ESCROW COSTS @    % SP
OTHER: NONE                           : TAX IMPS. FOR  6.0 MONS.    1500
OTHER: NONE                           : INSURANCE IMPS.
                                      : DEPOSIT CREDIT   %INC.        -0
                                      : OTHER: NONE      % SP
 --------------------------------     : ----------------------------------
   TOTAL   80.0 $240000     $16000    :          TOTAL             $61500
```

```
+++++++++++++++++++++++++++++++++++++++++++++++++++++++++++++++++++++++++++++
 S.P.= SALES PRICE. P.P.= PERCENTAGE PYMT./MON.. AMT.PER.= AMORTIZATION PERIOD
```

REAL ESTATE ANALYZER

There are many similarities in the computer programs that evaluate real estate alternatives. Basically they all provide reports of comparative statistics to aid you in deciding which property is a better investment. When

Exhibit 11–2 (*continued*)

```
 6/23/8              PROJECTED 9 YEAR R.O.I. YEARS (1-4)
-----------------------------------------------------------------------------
                          7/ 82     1982        1983        1984        1985
                     % @ ESCROW  %  1ST.YR  %  2ND.YR  %  3RD.YR  %  4TH.YR
+++ SALES DATA ++++  --  -------- --  --------  --  --------  --  --------  --  --------
PROPERTY VALUE       5:  300000: 5   307500  5   322875  5   339019  5   355970
 (SELLING COST) @    7:           :   21525       22601       23731       24918
 (BALANCE 1ST.)      :   225000:      224645      223866      222984      221986
 (BALANCE 2ND.)      :    15000:       15000       15000       15000       15000
------------------   :--------:    --------    --------    --------    --------
EQUITY               :    60000:       46330       61407       77303       94066
                     :         :
+++ INCOME DATA +++  : ANNUAL  :
GROSS INCOME         :    31200:21     18900       37800       37800       37800
 (VACANCY)       @  3:      936:         567        1134        1134        1134
 (EXPENSES)      @ 23:     7331:        4441        8882        8882        8882
------------------   :--------:    --------    --------    --------    --------
NET OPER.INCOME      :    22933:       13892       27784       27784       27784
 (LOAN PAYMENTS)     :    31066:       15533       31066       31066       31066
------------------   :--------:    --------    --------    --------    --------
NET CASH FLOW        :    -8133:       -1641       -3282       -3282       -3282
                     :         :
TAX BENEFIT      @ 35:         :        3250        6476        6440        6399
------------------   :--------:    --------    --------    --------    --------
NET SPENDABLE INC.   :   N/A   :        1609        3194        3158        3117
                     :         :
==================   :========:    ========    ========    ========    ========
RETURN BEFORE TAXES  :   N/A   :       47939       64602       80461       97183
                     :         :
 (RECAP.DEPREC.TAX)35:         :
 (CAP. GAINS TAX)  14:         :       -2109        3398        7740       12187
==================   :========:    ========    ========    ========    ========
RETURN AFTER TAXES   :   N/A   :       50048       61203       72721       84996
                     :         :
+++ CAPITAL REQMTS.+++:        :
INIT.INVESTED CAP.   :    61500:       61500       61500       61500       61500
CAP.CONTR.(CUMM.)    :         :
------------------   :--------:    --------    --------    --------    --------
TOTAL INVESTED CAP.  :    61500:       61500       61500       61500       61500

+++ (%) R.O.I. PER YEAR ++++++++++++++++++++++++++++++++++++++++++++++++++++++++
+ BEFORE TAXES                        -22.1         3.4        12.3        16.6 +
+ AFTER TAXES                         -18.6        -0.3         7.3        10.9 +
+++++++++++++++++++++++++++++++++++++++++++++++++++++++++++++++++++++++++++++++++
                           +++ ANCILLARY DATA +++
+++ TAXABLE INCOME +++
NET OPERATING INC.   :         :       13892       27784       27784       27784
 (LOAN INTEREST)     :         :       15178       30287       30184       30067
 (DEPRECIATION)      :         :        8000       16000       16000       16000
 (SPECIAL EXPENSE)   :         :
------------------   :--------:    --------    --------    --------    --------
TAXABLE INCOME       :         :       -9286      -18503      -18400      -18283

+++ TAXABLE INC. AT SALE +++
CAPITAL GAINS        :         :       -6025       24274       55287       87052
RECAPTURED DEPREC.   :         :
++++++++++++++++++++++++++++++++++++++++++++++++++++++++++++++++++++++++++++++++++
1. ALL DATES SHOWN ARE: 31 DEC. 19XX, EXCEPT @ ESCROW - 1ST. DAY OF MONTH.
2. CHANGES FOR PROPERTY VALUE AND INCOME ARE (%) FROM PRIOR YEAR.
3. SELLING COST IS (%) OF SALE PRICE.
4. VACANCY AND EXPENSE ARE (%) OF GROSS INCOME.
5. TAX BENEFIT = TAXABLE INCOME * TAX BRACKET
6. RECAPTURED DEPREC.TAX = RECAP.DEPREC. * TAX BRACKET    ** (C) 19AA BY IAS **
```

deciding which program to use, it is important that you feel comfortable with the package. With this in mind, the Real Estate Analyzer from Howard Software Services has focused on providing a "friendly" interface to its user. This feature makes it easy to prepare complex cash flow reports with which you can project true cash flows and return on investment for any period up to 10 years. The purpose of cash flow analysis is to

Exhibit 11–2 (*concluded*)

```
6/23/8              PROJECTED 9 YEAR R.O.I. YEARS (5-9)
-----------------------------------------------------------------------
                     1986          1987          1988          1989          1990
              %   5TH. YR    %   6TH. YR    %   7TH. YR    %   8TH. YR    %   9TH. YR
+++ SALES DATA ++++  --   --------   --   --------   --   --------   --   --------   --   --------
PROPERTY VALUE      5    373768    5    392457    5    412079    5    432683    5    454318
 (SELLING COST) @   7     26164         27472         28846         30288         31802
 (BALANCE 1ST.)          220854        219574        218123        216481        214620
 (BALANCE 2ND.)           15000         15000         15000         15000         15000
--------------------      --------      --------      --------      --------      --------
EQUITY                   111750        130411        150111        170915        192895

+++ INCOME DATA +++
GROSS INCOME              37800         37800         37800         37800         37800
 (VACANCY)      @   3      1134          1134          1134          1134          1134
 (EXPENSES)     @  23      8882          8882          8882          8882          8882
--------------------      --------      --------      --------      --------      --------
NET OPER. INCOME          27784         27784         27784         27784         27784
 (LOAN PAYMENTS)          31066         31066         31066         31066         31066
--------------------      --------      --------      --------      --------      --------
NET CASH FLOW             -3282         -3282         -3282         -3282         -3282

TAX BENEFIT     @  35      6353          6300          6241          6174          6098
--------------------      --------      --------      --------      --------      --------
NET SPENDABLE INC.         3071          3019          2959          2892          2816

==================      ========      ========      ========      ========      ========
RETURN BEFORE TAXES      114821        133430        153070        173807        195711

 (RECAP.DEPREC.TAX)35
 (CAP. GAINS TAX)  14     16745         21418         26213         31135         36192
==================      ========      ========      ========      ========      ========
RETURN AFTER TAXES        98076        112012        126857        142672        159519

++ CAPITAL REQMTS. +++
INIT.INVESTED CAP.        61500         61500         61500         61500         61500
CAP.CONTR.(CUMM.)
--------------------      --------      --------      --------      --------      --------
OTAL INVESTED CAP.        61500         61500         61500         61500         61500

++ (%) R.O.I. PER YEAR ++++++++++++++++++++++++++++++++++++++++++++++++++++++++++++
 BEFORE TAXES             19.3          21.3          22.9          24.3          25.7 +
 AFTER TAXES              13.2          14.9          16.3          17.6          18.8 +
+++++++++++++++++++++++++++++++++++++++++++++++++++++++++++++++++++++++++++++++++++
                      +++ ANCILLARY DATA +++
++ TAXABLE INCOME +++
NET OPERATING INC.        27784         27784         27784         27784         27784
 (LOAN INTEREST)          29935         29785         29615         29423         29206
 (DEPRECIATION)           16000         16000         16000         16000         16000
 (SPECIAL EXPENSE)
--------------------      --------      --------      --------      --------      --------
TAXABLE INCOME           -18151        -18001        -17831        -17639        -17422

++ TAXABLE INC. AT SALE +++
CAPITAL GAINS            119604        152985        187234        222396        258515
RECAPTURED DEPREC.
++++++++++++++++++++++++++++++++++++++++++++++++++++++++++++++++++++++++++++++++++
. CAPITAL GAINS TAX = CAPITAL GAINS * 25% * TAX BRACKET
. CAPITAL CONTRIBUTIONS = THE CUMULATIVE SUM OF NEGATIVE NET SPENDABLE INCOME
. (%) R.O.I.= THE ANNUAL PERCENTAGE BASED ON THE NUMBER OF MONTHS FROM ESCROW.
+++++++++++++++++++++++++++++++++++++++++++++++++++++++++++++++++++++++++++++++++

    Realty Automation Inc., 221 N Lois, La Habra, CA 90631 - 213/947-2762
```

Courtesy of Realty Automation, Inc.

predict the net cash received or paid from holding the investment for a year. A negative cash flow from one property analysis may be offset by income from some other source. Conversely, a positive cash flow may be used to offset a negative cash flow from another investment.

Buy decisions can be based on internal rate of return calculations, and sell decisions on a year's return on equity (ROE). ROE is the equity increase for a year plus the cash flow for that year as a percentage of the net equity for the previous year. It is simply a measure of a property's performance. It is a useful comparison with other investments and can help you to decide if and when it would be worthwhile to sell the property.

Return on equity is just one of several analyses of return on investment possible with the Real Estate Analyzer. Others include: *total ROI* (the total cumulative return on the capital investment); *total internal rate of return* (the annualized version of the total ROI, which can be compared directly with the aftertax interest rate on a savings account); *equity ROI* (the total increase in equity as a percentage of the adjusted investment); *equity IRR* (the annualized version of the equity ROI); *conventional IRR* (the ratio for the money rate that makes the total IRR equal to the equity IRR); and the *financial management IRR* (the best overall measure of an investment's profitability because it reveals the optimum holding period as well as relative investment value).

In summary, the Real Estate Analyzer provides three useful capabilities:

1. It allows the comparison of dissimilar properties on a profitability basis as measured by return on investment (ROI) and internal rate of return (IRR).
2. It helps investors assess risk by determining the impact of adverse economic and market conditions on profits.
3. It determines the optimum holding period on the basis of a maximum ROI or IRR.

Exhibit 11-3 shows the basic property information and assumptions used in two alternate cases (the difference between the two being changes in monthly income). Exhibit 11-4 shows the results of the two analyses, while Exhibit 11-5 graphically illustrates the results.

These measures of real estate investment performance are complex, and have previously been difficult to compute manually. The personal computer has been a boon to real estate analysis because it helps the investor with these calculations without the tedium that used to be involved. Because IRR computations are now easier to do they have become quite popular. If you are not already familiar with these terms, you should be. Their complexity and their subsequent analysis can be made easier with programs like the Real Estate Analyzer. If you spend a few hours getting familiar with the program's mechanics, you can spend the rest of your time mastering the performance measurements that can point the way to better profits.

Exhibit 11–3. Real Estate Analyzer

ANALYSIS OF DEHART PROPERTY (PREPARED BY DON WOODWELL)...PAGE 1

************* BACKGROUND INFORMATION *************

GENERAL INFORMATION
```
PROPERTY  DESCRIPTION...................DEHART PROPERTY
DISK-FILING NAME........................DEHART
DATE OF ANALYSIS........................JUNE,1983
YEAR OF PURCHASE........................       1983
PURCHASE PRICE..........................    174,000
ADDED-ON CHARGES   (%)..................        .5%
YEARS SINCE  PURCHASE...................          0
PAST  LOAN  REDUCTION...................          0
PAST CASH FLOW..........................          0
CURRENT MARKET  VALUE...................    174,000
```

LOAN INFORMATION
```
NUMBER OF LOANS.........................          1

STARTING  YEAR   FOR  LOAN #1...........       1983
REMAINING BALANCE FOR LOAN #1...........     90,000
INTEREST  RATE   FOR  LOAN #1...........      16.8%
REMAINING  LIFE   FOR  LOAN #1..........         30
TYPE(1=AMORT;2=INT ONLY;3=MA)#1.........          1
..REMAINING LIFE FOR AMORT'N #1.........         30
```

DEPRECIATION INFO
```
NO. OF DEPR'N ITEMS.....................          1

STARTING YEAR  FOR  DEPR'N #1...........       1983
TOTAL DEPRECIABLE LIFE FOR #1...........         15
RECAPTURE RULE(1=A;2=E;3=N)#1...........          1
TOTAL  DEPRECIABLE  AMOUNT #1...........    100,000
REMAINING  DEPR'BLE AMOUNT #1...........    100,000
TYPE(1=SL;2=SD;3=DB;4=MA;5=AC)#1........          5
..PROPERTY TYPE(1=PU;2=LI;3=R)#1........          3
```

RENTAL INCOME INFO
```
NUMBER OF LEASES........................          2

STARTING YEAR FOR  LEASE #1.............       1983
ENDING  YEAR  FOR  LEASE #1.............       1983
SCHEDULED MONTHLY INCOME #1.............        550
VACANCY/COLLECTION LOSS(%)#1............       5.0%

STARTING YEAR FOR  LEASE #2.............       1983
ENDING  YEAR  FOR  LEASE #2.............       1983
SCHEDULED MONTHLY INCOME #2.............        500
VACANCY/COLLECTION LOSS(%)#2............       5.0%
```

Exhibit 11–3 (*continued*)

ANALYSIS OF DEHART PROPERTY (PREPARED BY DON WOODWELL)...PAGE 2

```
ANNUAL EXPENSES ($ OR % OF PRICE)
    STARTING YEAR FOR EXPENSES..............    1983
    PROPERTY TAX............................    2,880  (1.7%)
    INSURANCE...............................      480  (.3%)
    UTILITIES...............................    2,700  (1.6%)
    ADVERTISING.............................       17  (0%)
    SUPPLIES................................      500  (.3%)
    INTERIOR REPAIRS........................    1,000  (.6%)
    EXTERIOR REPAIRS........................    2,000  (1.1%)
    POOL SERVICE............................        0  (0%)
    GARDENER................................        0  (0%)
    GARBAGE COLLECTION......................      100  (.1%)
    WORKMEN'S COMP..........................      300  (.2%)
    REPLACEMENTS............................      500  (.3%)
    LICENSES................................      100  (.1%)
    MANAGEMENT FEES.........................      250  (.1%)
    OTHER EXPENSES..........................    1,000  (.6%)
   *TOTAL EXPENSES..........................   11,827  (6.8%)
```

Exhibit 11–3 (*concluded*)

ANALYSIS OF DEHART PROPERTY (PREPARED BY DON WOODWELL)...PAGE 3

```
*************  ASSUMPTIONS FOR ANALYSIS  *************

ANTICIPATED % ANNUAL INFLATION
    PROPERTY VALUE..........................    10.0%
    OPERATING EXPENSES......................     7.0%
    RENTAL INCOME...........................     7.0%
    MONEY RATE(AFTER-TAX)...................     5.0%
    PROPERTY TAXES..........................     1.0%

ANTICIPATED % TAX RATES
    ORDINARY INCOME TAX.....................    35.0%
    CAPITAL GAINS TAX.......................    20.0%

SELLING COST AS % OF PRICE
    BROKER'S COMMISSION.....................     6.0%
    ESCROW CHARGES..........................     1.0%
    OTHER CLOSING COSTS.....................     3.5%
```

Courtesy of Howard Software Services, Inc.

MANAGING YOUR INCOME PROPERTY

Next let's look at ways to manage the property you have bought. The Institute of Real Estate Management (IREM) of the National Association of Realtors established a set of standards in 1978 for computerizing property management accounting functions. These standards are for the operation of a property management office but the principles are universal since they are of equal usefulness to a property management business and

Exhibit 11-4.   Analyses: Cash Flow and ROI

ANALYSIS OF DEHART PROPERTY (PREPARED BY DON WOODWELL)...PAGE 1

************* CASH FLOW ANALYSIS *************

	%	1983	1984	1985	1986	1987
GROSS INCOME-						
ANNUAL RENTS	7	15,390	16,467	17,620	18,853	20,173
OPERATING EXPENSES-						
TAXES	1	2,880	2,909	2,938	2,967	2,997
OTHER EXPENSES	7	8,947	9,573	10,243	10,960	11,728
*TOTAL OP'G EXPENSES	6.8	11,827	12,482	13,181	13,928	14,725
DEBT SERVICE-						
INTEREST	13	12,135	12,101	12,063	12,020	11,970
PRINCIPAL	.26	231	264	302	346	396
*TOTAL DEBT SERVICE	7.1	12,365	12,365	12,365	12,365	12,365
*PRE-TAX CASH FLOW	-5.1	-8,802	-8,380	-7,927	-7,440	-6,917
TAX CREDIT(OR LIAB) DUE TO-						
NET INCOME(LOSS)	35	3,000	2,841	2,669	2,483	2,282
DEPRECIATION	35	2,333	2,333	2,333	2,333	2,333
*TOTAL CREDITS(LIAB'S)	35	5,333	5,174	5,002	4,816	4,616
*AFTER-TAX CASH FLOW	-2	-3,469	-3,206	-2,925	-2,624	-2,301

ANALYSIS OF DEHART PROPERTY (PREPARED BY DON WOODWELL)...PAGE 2

************* R-O-I ANALYSIS *************

	%	1983	1984	1985	1986	1987
*GROSS SALES PRICE	10	191,400	210,540	231,594	254,753	280,229
SALE EXPENSES-						
COMMISSION	6	11,484	12,632	13,896	15,285	16,814
ESCROW	1	1,914	2,105	2,316	2,548	2,802
OTHER SELLING COSTS	3.5	6,699	7,369	8,106	8,916	9,808
LOAN BALANCE		89,769	89,505	89,203	88,857	88,462
TAXES ON GAINS	20	1,085	7,379	13,481	19,960	26,854
*TOTAL SALE EXPENSES		110,951	118,991	127,002	135,567	144,739
CASH RETURN-						
NET EQUITY RETURN		80,449	91,549	104,592	119,187	135,490
CUM CASH FLOW (FV)	5	-3,469	-6,849	-10,116	-13,245	-16,209
*TOTAL RETURN		76,980	84,700	94,476	105,942	119,281
CASH INVESTMENT-						
DOWN PAYMENT		84,870	84,870	84,870	84,870	84,870
CUM CASH FLOW (PV)	5	3,304	6,212	8,738	10,897	12,700
*TOTAL INVESTMENT		88,174	91,082	93,608	95,767	97,570
RETURN ON INVESTMENT (AFTER TAX)-						
TOTAL R-O-I (%)		-9.3%	-.2%	11.3%	24.8%	40.5%
TOTAL I-R-R (%)		-9.3%	-.1%	3.6%	5.7%	7.0%
EQUITY R-O-I (%)		-8.8%	.5%	11.7%	24.5%	38.9%
EQUITY I-R-R (%)		-8.8%	.3%	3.8%	5.6%	6.8%
RETURN ON EQUITY (%)		6.3%	9.8%	11.1%	11.4%	11.7%
CONVENTIONAL IRR (%)		-9.3%	.0%	3.7%	5.7%	6.9%
F-M-R-R (%)		-8.8%	.3%	3.8%	5.6%	6.8%

to an individual investor. In the case of both the business and the investor the objective is the same—to manage properties efficiently. A computer can help in several ways, but the most important is in record-keeping and reporting. The computer organizes tenant files, posts checks to bank accounts, prepares checks for vendors, and keeps track of such important cash flow items as income, expenses, and operating costs.

Exhibit 11–4 (*concluded*)

```
        ANALYSIS OF DEHART PROPERTY (PREPARED BY DON WOODWELL)...PAGE 4

************* CASH FLOW ANALYSIS *************
                          %     1983      1984      1985      1986      1987
                         ---   ------    ------    ------    ------    ------
GROSS INCOME-
    ANNUAL RENTS          7    11,970    12,808    13,704    14,664    15,690

OPERATING EXPENSES-
    TAXES                 1     2,880     2,909     2,938     2,967     2,997
    OTHER EXPENSES        7     8,947     9,573    10,243    10,960    11,728
*TOTAL OP'G EXPENSES     6.8   11,827    12,482    13,181    13,928    14,725

DEBT SERVICE-
    INTEREST             13    12,135    12,101    12,063    12,020    11,970
    PRINCIPAL           .26       231       264       302       346       396
*TOTAL DEBT SERVICE     7.1    12,365    12,365    12,365    12,365    12,365

*PRE-TAX CASH FLOW       -7   -12,222   -12,040   -11,842   -11,629   -11,400

TAX CREDIT(OR LIAB) DUE TO-
    NET INCOME(LOSS)     35     4,197     4,121     4,039     3,949     3,851
    DEPRECIATION         35     2,333     2,333     2,333     2,333     2,333
*TOTAL CREDITS(LIAB'S)   35     6,530     6,455     6,372     6,283     6,185

*AFTER-TAX CASH FLOW   -3.3    -5,692    -5,585    -5,470    -5,347    -5,215


        ANALYSIS OF DEHART PROPERTY (PREPARED BY DON WOODWELL)...PAGE 5

************* R-O-I ANALYSIS *************
                          %     1983      1984      1985      1986      1987
                         ---   ------    ------    ------    ------    ------
*GROSS SALES PRICE       10   191,400   210,540   231,594   254,753   280,229

SALE EXPENSES-
    COMMISSION            6    11,484    12,632    13,896    15,285    16,814
    ESCROW                1     1,914     2,105     2,316     2,548     2,802
    OTHER SELLING COSTS  3.5    6,699     7,369     8,106     8,916     9,808
    LOAN BALANCE              89,769    89,505    89,203    88,857    88,462
    TAXES ON GAINS       20     1,085     7,379    13,481    19,960    26,854
*TOTAL SALE EXPENSES         110,951   118,991   127,002   135,567   144,739

CASH RETURN-
    NET EQUITY RETURN        80,449    91,549   104,592   119,187   135,490
    CUM CASH FLOW (FV)    5    -5,692   -11,561   -17,609   -23,837   -30,244
*TOTAL RETURN                74,757    79,987    86,983    95,350   105,246

CASH INVESTMENT-
    DOWN PAYMENT             84,870    84,870    84,870    84,870    84,870
    CUM CASH FLOW (PV)    5     5,421    10,487    15,212    19,610    23,697
*TOTAL INVESTMENT            90,291    95,357   100,082   104,480   108,567

RETURN ON INVESTMENT (AFTER TAX)-
    TOTAL R-O-I (%)            -11.9%     -5.8%      2.5%     12.3%     24.0%
    TOTAL I-R-R (%)            -11.9%     -2.9%       .8%      3.0%      4.4%
    EQUITY R-O-I (%)           -10.9%     -4.0%      4.5%     14.1%     24.8%
    EQUITY I-R-R (%)           -10.9%     -2.0%      1.5%      3.3%      4.5%
    RETURN ON EQUITY (%)         3.2%      6.9%      8.3%      8.8%      9.3%
    CONVENTIONAL IRR (%)       -11.9%     -2.7%      1.1%      3.1%      4.5%
    F-M-R-R  (%)               -10.9%     -2.0%      1.5%      3.3%      4.5%
```

Courtesy of Howard Software Services, Inc.

IREM broke its recommendations into three groups: a mandatory, a secondary, and an optional group.

The mandatory items are:

Cash flow statement.

Vacancy and rent loss statement.

Exhibit 11-5. Dehart Property Analysis Results

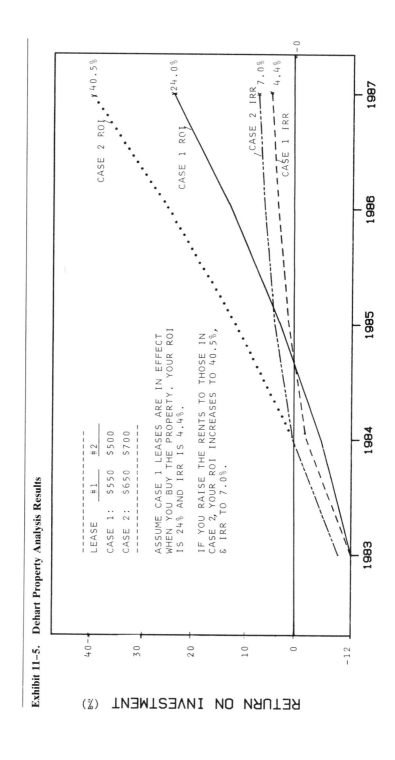

LEASE   #1   #2

CASE 1: $550 $500

CASE 2: $650 $700

ASSUME CASE 1 LEASES ARE IN EFFECT
WHEN YOU BUY THE PROPERTY. YOUR ROI
IS 24% AND IRR IS 4.4%.

IF YOU RAISE THE RENTS TO THOSE IN
CASE 2, YOUR ROI INCREASES TO 40.5%,
& IRR TO 7.0%.

CASE 2 ROI   40.5%

CASE 1 ROI   24.0%

CASE 2 IRR   7.0%

4.4%

CASE 1 IRR

1983   1984   1985   1986   1987

40 — 30 — 20 — 10 — 0 — -12

RETURN ON INVESTMENT (%)

Cash receipt register.

Check register.

Security deposit listing.

Rent roll.

Miscellaneous charge listing.

Tenant transfers.

Bad debt write-off.

File maintenance.

The secondary items are:

Profit and loss statement.

General ledger.

Monthly payroll processing.

Budget subsystem.

Delinquency listing.

Lease expiration report.

Finally, the optional items put icing on the cake. They're probably not necessary but are nice to have. They are:

Check-writing capability.

Calculation of costs per square foot.

Budget comparisons year to year.

Calculations of management fees.

Analysis of vacancies.

Tenant profiles.

Building profiles.

Address label printing.

These criteria are helpful guides as you evaluate the computer programs available for property management.

THE PROPERTY MANAGEMENT SYSTEM

The Property Management System (PMS) from Realty Automation was specifically developed to meet the suggested standards of IREM. It is designed to be a full general ledger system that keeps track of all sources of income and expenses while automatically printing financial statements and management information.

PMS keeps track of all tenant activity through a tenant activity and rent roll, a vacancy report, a rental payment delinquency list, and lost rent and lease expiration reports. A general ledger capability lets you create your own chart of accounts and is the heart of the financial reporting subsystem. Budgeting is covered in monthly and yearly periods and cash receipts and disbursements, including a check-writer, are available. Other features include vendor reports and an audit trail to trace entries through the system. Exhibits 11–6 through 11–11 are samples of the output from the Property Management System.

Realty Automation also offers four programs that use the Property Management System as a base and are specifically directed at unique

---

Exhibit 11–6.

```
            T E N A N T    A C T I V I T Y    R E P O R T
                         R E N T    R O L L

                       DEMONSTRATION PROPERTY
                            221 N. LOIS
                          LA HABRA, CA  90631

                REALTY AUTOMATION, INC. - 213/947-2762              PAGE   1
==============================================================================
LINE# - UNIT#     NAME                     LEASE/RENT   DUE DATE
                  PHONE              CODE                  RENT      AMT-PAID
       COMMENT#1                  COMMENT#2              COMMENT#3
==============================================================================


    1 - 101       ADAMS, BILL             03/01/79   07/01/81
                  (213) 999-3455  LATE RENT: 0            $250.00      $0.00
2BRM/1BTH, UNFURN., 650' - RENT RAISED $25 ON 2/80 - NEW PAINT, CARPETS 10/78


    2 - 102       BAKER, BOOBY            02/01/79   07/01/81
                  (213) 999-2234  LATE RENT: 1            $250.00      $0.00
2BRM/1BTH, FURN., 650' - RENT RAISED $50 ON 2/79 - NEEDS PAINT


    3 - 103       CHARLES, RAY            03/01/79   07/01/81
                  (213) 999-7650  LATE RENT: 0            $250.00      $0.00
2BRM/1BTH, UNFURN., 635' - RENT RAISED $25 ON 10/79- NEW CARPETS, DRAPES 3/79


    4 - 104       DAVIS, BILL             03/15/79   07/01/81
                  (213) 999-4565  LATE RENT: 0            $225.00      $0.00
1BRM/1BTH, UNFURN., 500' - RENT RAISED $35 ON 10/79- PAINTED, NEW DRAPES 3/77


    6 - 106       WADE, FRANK             11/10/79   07/01/81
                  (213) 698-9638  LATE RENT: 0            $195.00      $0.00
1BRM/1BTH, UNFURN., 475' - RENT RAISED $25 ON 10/79- PET - TWO CATS


    7 - 107       FERMA, TERA             03/01/79   07/01/81
                  (213) 695-4678  LATE RENT: 2            $225.00      $0.00
2BRM/1BTH, UNFURN., 500' - RENT RAISED $40 ON 4/80 - PAINTED, CARPETED 4/80


    8 - 108       BROWN, ROBERT           11/01/79   07/01/81
                  (213) 696-1534  LATE RENT: 0            $300.00      $0.00
2BRM/2BTH, UNFURN., 625' - RENT RAISED $50 ON 6/80 - PAINT,DRAPES,CARPETS 6/80


==============================================================================
TOTALS:  BALANCE DUE = 1695     100.00 %               $1,695.00      $0.00
==============================================================================
VACANT =    3    VACANCY LOSS =    $725.00    REVENUE PER/SQ.FT. =     $0.00
==============================================================================
```

Courtesy of Realty Automation, Inc.

Exhibit 11–7.

```
              T E N A N T    A C T I V I T Y    R E P O R T
                          R E N T    R O L L
                           VACANCY LIST
                       DEMONSTRATION PROPERTY
                            221 N. LOIS
                          LA HABRA, CA  90631

              REALTY AUTOMATION, INC. - 213/947-2762              PAGE    1
==================================================================================
LINE# - UNIT#     NAME          RENT
==================================================================================


   5 - 105        VACANT        $250.00

   9 - 109        VACANT        $275.00

  10 - 110        VACANT        $200.00
==================================================================================
NO TENANTS FALL WITHIN PARAMETERS SELECTED
==================================================================================
VACANT =    3    VACANCY LOSS =      $725.00    REVENUE PER/SQ.FT. =       $0.00
==================================================================================
```

Courtesy of Realty Automation, Inc.

Exhibit 11–8.

```
              T E N A N T    A C T I V I T Y    R E P O R T
                          R E N T    R O L L
                *** OVERDUE ACCOUNTS *** 5 DAYS ***
                       DEMONSTRATION PROPERTY
                            221 N. LOIS
                          LA HABRA, CA  90631

              REALTY AUTOMATION, INC. - 213/947-2762              PAGE    1
==================================================================================
LINE# - UNIT#     NAME                    LEASE/RENT  DUE DATE
                  PHONE              CODE                  RENT    AMT-PAID
       COMMENT#1                     COMMENT#2          COMMENT#3
==================================================================================

   1 - 101        ADAMS, BILL             03/01/79    07/01/81
                  (213) 999-3455 LATE RENT: 2                $250.00       $0.00
2BRM/1BTH, UNFURN., 650' - RENT RAISED $25 ON 2/80 - NEW PAINT, CARPETS 10/78

   2 - 102        BAKER, BOOBY            02/01/79    07/01/81
                  (213) 999-2234 LATE RENT: 1                $250.00       $0.00
2BRM/1BTH, FURN.. 650'   - RENT RAISED $50 ON 2/79 - NEEDS PAINT

   4 - 104        DAVIS, BILL             03/15/78    07/01/81
                  (213) 999-4565 LATE RENT: 0                $225.00       $0.00
1BRM/1BTH, UNFURN.. 500' - RENT RAISED $35 ON 10/79- PAINTED, NEW DRAPES 3/77

----------------------------------------------------------------------------------
 OTALS:  BALANCE DUE = 725     100.00 %                      $725.00       $0.00
==================================================================================
VACANT =    2    VACANCY LOSS =      $525.00    REVENUE PER/SQ.FT. =       $0.00
==================================================================================
```

Courtesy of Realty Automation, Inc.

Exhibit 11–9.

```
===========================================================================
               V E N D O R   A C C O U N T S   R E P O R T
                        DEMONSTRATION PROPERTY
                            221 N. LOIS
                         LA HABRA, CA  90631
               REALTY AUTOMATION, INC. - 213/947-2762           PAGE   1
===========================================================================
LINE# - NAME                      ACCOUNT#    PHONE#             YTD-PAYMENTS
        ADDRESS
===========================================================================
   1 - ACE MORTGAGE COMPANY          1ST       (213) 999-0876      $7,000.00
       2345 MAIN STREET   YOUR CITY, ST 99999

   2 - BIG CITY UTILITIES            BIG       (213) 999-7650        $763.21
       450 MAIN AVE.  BIG CITY, ST 99999

   3 - DAVIS POOL SERVICE            POOL      (213) 999-0789        $385.00
       3400 MAPLE  BIG CITY, ST 99999

   4 - GEORGE'S HARDWARE             GH        (213) 999-0799         $89.56
       990 WESTERN AVE.  BIY CITY, ST 99999

   5 - GEORGE SMITH                  GS        (213) 999-7689        $135.90
       234 WILLOW AVE.  BIG CITY, ST  99999

   6 - IMCO CLEANING SERVICE         IMCO      (213) 999-1234        $135.90
       879 1ST STREET  BIG CITY, ST 99999

   7 - NATIONAL MORTGAGE CO.         2ND       (213) 999-3456      $1,400.00
       3550 S. E. ADAMS  BIG CITY, ST  99999

   8 - PROPERTY MANAGEMENT           PMS       (213) 947-2762        $800.00
       221 LOIS STREET  LA HABRA, CA 90631
===========================================================================
TOTAL:                                                           $10,709.57
===========================================================================
```

Courtesy of Realty Automation, Inc.

types of properties—namely, single units like condominiums and townhouses, condominium association management, mini-warehouses, and commercial property.

The capabilities of the PMS are quite comprehensive. The amazing thing is that they are all available on a personal computer. Just a few years ago you would have needed a system worth $100,000 to $150,000 to support this type of real property management system. In addition, you no longer need multiple special purpose computers to run these different programs. PMS can be run on the same computer as your stock tracking or tax-planning programs.

THE LANDLORD®[1]

If you want to invest only in apartment buildings, you should review the Landlord® offered by MIN Microcomputer Systems, Inc. The Landlord®

---

[1] The Landlord is a registered trademark of MIN Microcomputer Software, Inc.

Exhibit 11-10.

```
      Y T D    E X P E N S E    B U D G E T    A N A L Y S I S

                    DEMONSTRATION PROPERTY
                         221 N. LOIS
                      LA HABRA, CA 90631
                                                      PAGE    1
-----------------------------------------------------------------------
   DESCRIPTION          ACTUAL    BUDGETED   DIFFERENCE   PERCENTAGE
-----------------------------------------------------------------------
4100 RENTAL INCOME    15,595.00  16,800.00   -1,205.00    92.83 %
4200 ADVANCE RENTALS     200.00      70.00      130.00   285.71 %
4300 SEC. DEP. INCOME     87.25     350.00     -262.75    24.93 %
4400 OTHER INCOME        125.77     175.00      -49.23    71.87 %

TOTALS                16,008.02  17,395.00   -1,386.98    92.03 %
-----------------------------------------------------------------------

5100 ADVERTISING           0.00     105.00     -105.00     0.00 %
5110 AUTO & TRAVEL         0.00      70.00      -70.00     0.00 %
5120 CLEANING            135.90     175.00      -39.10    77.66 %
5130 ELECTRICITY         265.35     245.00       20.35   108.31 %
5140 GARDENING           290.26     280.00       10.26   103.66 %
5150 GAS/OIL             332.86     350.00      -17.14    95.10 %
5160 INSURANCE           250.00     291.67      -41.67    85.71 %
5170 LEGAL & ACCOUNTING   50.00     350.00     -300.00    14.29 %
5180 MAINTENANCE         342.50     350.00       -7.50    97.86 %
5190 MANAGEMENT          800.00     816.67      -16.67    97.96 %
5200 MISCELLANEOUS        45.90     140.00      -94.10    32.79 %
5210 PLUMBING             67.43     210.00     -142.57    32.11 %
5220 POOL SERVICES       385.00     350.00       35.00   110.00 %
5240 SERVICES - OUTSIDE   70.00     105.00      -35.00    66.67 %
5250 SUPPLIES            110.00      70.00       40.00   157.14 %
5260 TAXES               500.00     583.33      -83.33    85.71 %
5270 TELEPHONE            75.00      87.50      -12.50    85.71 %
5280 WATER                95.00     175.00      -80.00    54.29 %
5510 MORTGAGE 1ST      7,000.00   7,000.00        0.00   100.00 %
5520 MORTGAGE 2ND      1,400.00   1,400.00        0.00   100.00 %

-----------------------------------------------------------------------
TOTALS                12,215.20  13,154.17     -938.97    92.86 %
-----------------------------------------------------------------------

End Of Report
-----------------------------------------------------------------------
```

Courtesy of Realty Automation, Inc.

is an apartment management system, which contains two major subsystems: the Resident Manager and the Financial Manager.

The Resident Manager automates all paperwork and record-keeping, such as apartment availabilities, rent payments, security deposits, leases, and other administration functions normally done by a resident manager.

The Financial Manager takes over the work normally done by a bookkeeper or accountant. It is a simple system for apartment managers who keep their books on a cash basis. For example, the Financial Manager shows rent as income in the period when it was collected, not necessarily when it was charged. It contains 26 resident accounts to record payments in as many categories. Forty-five expense accounts are provided, along with five revenue accounts to record nonresident income. Accounts are also provided for the following: appreciation, depreciation, capitalized expenses, note payment—interest, note payment—principal, deposit refunds, and transfer payments. All of these are organized into a chart of

Exhibit 11–11.

OPERATING STATEMENT

DEMONSTRATION PROPERTY
221 N. LOIS
LA HABRA, CA 90631

PAGE 1

	CURRENT ACTUAL	CURRENT BUDGET	VARIANCE DOLLARS	PERCENT OF REVENUE	Y-T-D ACTUAL	Y-T-D BUDGET	VARIANCE DOLLARS	PERCENT OF REVENUE
# INCOME #								
RENTAL INCOME	$200.00	$2,400.00	-2,200.00	100.00 %	$15,595.00	$16,800.00	-1,205.00	97.42 %
ADVANCE RENTALS	$0.00	$10.00	-10.00	0.00 %	$200.00	$70.00	$130.00	1.25 %
SEC. DEP. INCOME	$0.00	$50.00	-50.00	0.00 %	$87.25	$350.00	-262.75	0.55 %
OTHER INCOME	$0.00	$25.00	-25.00	0.00 %	$125.77	$175.00	-49.23	0.79 %
TOTAL INCOME	$200.00	$2,485.00	-2,285.00	100.00 %	$16,008.02	$17,395.00	-1,386.98	100.00 %
# EXPENSES #								
ADVERTISING	$0.00	$15.00	-15.00	0.00 %	$0.00	$105.00	-105.00	0.00 %
AUTO & TRAVEL	$0.00	$10.00	-10.00	0.00 %	$0.00	$70.00	-70.00	0.00 %
CLEANING	$0.00	$25.00	-25.00	0.00 %	$135.90	$175.00	-39.10	0.85 %
ELECTRICITY	$0.00	$35.00	-35.00	0.00 %	$265.35	$245.00	$20.35	1.66 %
GARDENING	$70.00	$40.00	$30.00	35.00 %	$290.26	$280.00	$10.26	1.81 %
GAS/OIL	$95.00	$50.00	$45.00	47.50 %	$332.86	$350.00	-17.14	2.08 %
INSURANCE	$0.00	$0.00	$0.00	0.00 %	$250.00	$291.67	-41.67	1.56 %
INTEREST	$0.00	$0.00	$0.00	0.00 %	$0.00	$0.00	$0.00	0.00 %
LEGAL & ACCOUNTING	$0.00	$50.00	-50.00	0.00 %	$50.00	$350.00	-300.00	0.31 %
MAINTENANCE	$0.00	$125.90	-125.90	0.00 %	$342.50	$350.00	-7.50	2.14 %
MANAGEMENT	$115.00	$120.00	-5.00	57.50 %	$800.00	$816.67	-16.67	5.00 %
MISCELLANEOUS	$0.00	$20.00	-20.00	0.00 %	$45.90	$140.00	-94.10	0.29 %
PLUMBING	$0.00	$30.00	-30.00	0.00 %	$67.43	$210.00	-142.57	0.42 %
POOL SERVICES	$35.00	$50.00	-15.00	17.50 %	$385.00	$350.00	$35.00	2.41 %
SEC. DEP. RETURNED	$0.00	$0.00	$0.00	0.00 %	$256.25	$0.00	$256.25	1.60 %
SERVICES - OUTSIDE	$20.00	$15.00	$5.00	10.00 %	$70.00	$105.00	-35.00	0.44 %
SUPPLIES	$10.00	$10.00	$0.00	5.00 %	$110.00	$70.00	$40.00	0.69 %
TAXES	$0.00	$0.00	$0.00	0.00 %	$500.00	$583.33	-83.33	3.12 %
TELEPHONE	$0.00	$12.50	-12.50	0.00 %	$75.00	$87.50	-12.50	0.47 %
WATER	$45.00	$25.00	$20.00	22.50 %	$95.00	$175.00	-80.00	0.59 %
OPERATING COSTS	$390.00	$633.40	-243.40	195.00 %	$4,071.45	$4,754.17	-682.72	25.43 %
MORTGAGE 1ST	$0.00	$1,000.00	-1,000.00	0.00 %	$7,000.00	$7,000.00	$0.00	43.73 %
MORTGAGE 2ND	$0.00	$200.00	-200.00	0.00 %	$1,400.00	$1,400.00	$0.00	8.75 %
MORTGAGES - OTHER	$0.00	$0.00	$0.00	0.00 %	$0.00	$0.00	$0.00	0.00 %
TOTAL MORTGAGE EXP.	$0.00	$1,200.00	-1,200.00	0.00 %	$8,400.00	$8,400.00	$0.00	52.47 %
TOTAL PROPERTY EXP.	$390.00	$1,833.40	-1,443.40	195.00 %	$12,471.45	$13,154.17	-682.72	77.91 %
# NET CASH FLOW #	-190.00	$651.60	$1,443.40	-95.00 %	$3,536.57	$4,240.83	-704.26	22.09 %

End Of Report

Courtesy of Realty Automation, Inc.

accounts, whose names can be customized to suit your needs. Two hundred checks per month may be kept in computer storage, and each check may be distributed into one of six different accounts; you may make up to 100 journal entries each month.

You can use the Landlord® software to manage multiple properties of up to 400 units each as long as the combined number of units does not

Exhibit 11-12.   The Landlord®: Tenant Listing

```
                              TENANT LISTING
                          MGT COMPANY NAME INC.
PAGE 01                       FOR JUNE 1982                            06/01/82

BEAUMONT SQUARE              002                  SIMPSON & SIMPSON INC.    002

                                  PRP#/   UNIT
TEN#    TENANT NAME / ADDRESS     STATUS   CODE    RENT    COMMENTS / TEL#
----    ---------------------     ------  ------   -------  ---------------------

030    THOMPSON AND ASSOCIATES    002     STE120   900.00  MANAGEMENT CONSULTNG
       5500 PEACHFORD ROAD                                 FIRM
       STE120                                              850 SQ FT.
       ATLANTA   GA 30309         PRESENT                  404-428-7622

031    DOBER INDUSTRIES           002     STE123   900.00  ENGINEERING FIRM
       5500 PEACHFORD ROAD                                 GEORGE DOBER-PRES.
       STE123                                              900 SQ FT.
       ATLANTA   GA 30309         PRESENT                  404-898-1300

032    DR. GEORGE LUCAS           002     STE126   900.00  DENTIST
       5500 PEACHFORD ROAD                                 CLOSED WEDNESDAYS
       STE126                                              910 SQ FT.
       ATLANTA   GA 30309         PRESENT                  404-981-3098

033    NANCY'S GIFTS AND THINGS   002     STE129   900.00  HOURS 8AM TO 9PM M-F
       5500 PEACHFORD ROAD                                 SAT HOURS 8AM 6PM
       STE129                                              780 SQ FT.
       ATLANTA   GA 30309         PRESENT                  404-981-7632

034    JOB SEARCHERS              002     STE203   800.00  PERSONNEL SERVICE
       MR. SAM MAYNARD                                     NEW COMPANY
       156 PARKWAY BLVD.                                   2000 SQ FT.
       ATLANTA   GA 30318         FUTURE                   404-876-1234

035    DUNN AND MOORE LTD.        002     STE300   700.00  ACCOUNTING FIRM
       5500 PEACHFORD ROAD
       STE300                                              1000 SQ FT.
       ATLANTA   GA 30309         PRESENT                  404-981-7624

036    GENERAL BUSINESS SYSTEMS   002     STE301   700.00  CONSULTANTS
       5500 PEACHFORD ROAD                                 MOVING BUS.TO NSIDE
       STE301                                              910 SQ FT.
       ATLANTA   GA 30309         PRESENT                  404-981-7000

037    HUEY AND COMPANY   INC.    002     STE310   700.00  DISTRIBUTORS OF
       5500 PEACHFORD ROAD                                 WOMENS CLOTHING
       STE310                                              703 SQ FT.
       ATLANTA   GA 30309         PRESENT                  404-981-7612

038    THE BEST PICTURE           002     STE310   700.00  OUT OF BUSINESS
       NONE
                                                           703 SQ FT.
                                  PAST                     404-898-1234
```

Courtesy of MIN Microcomputer Systems, Inc.

exceed 1,000. Exhibits 11–12 through 11–15 show the kinds of reports produced by the Landlord®.

The purpose of the foregoing descriptions of property and apartment management systems was to provide a comparison of the two with a sample of their output reports. These kinds of comparisons will be important to your selection of the right software for your particular style of property management. Although the Property Management System is comprehensive and meets all the IREM standards, it may not be the right program for some investors in income properties. The Landlord®, Apartment Manager, or other simpler and less expensive systems may be better choices. A careful comparison of a program's methodology, its ease of use, and report formats with your requirements will help you pinpoint the one for you; just as the programs available for real estate opportunity

Exhibit 11–13. The Landlord®: Lease Expiration Report

```
                              LEASE EXPIRATION REPORT
                               MGT COMPANY NAME INC.
                                   FOR JUNE 1982                        06/25/82
```

TERRACE GARDENS   001   JOHN J. MORRIS   001

DATE LEASE EXPIRES	PROP#	UNIT CODE	UNIT TYPE	TN#	TENANT NAME	NOTICE TO VACATE
06/19/82	001	101-B	2BR GARDEN	005	TOM AND LINDA DOLE	YES
07/11/82	001	100-B	1BR GARDEN	002	JEFFREY ELLINGTON	YES
07/18/82	001	101-C	2BR GARDEN	007	JESSI SMITH & MARGE WELLS	NO
08/19/82	001	300-C	3BR GARDEN	019	SOPHIE TURNER	YES
09/04/82	001	200-A	1BR GARDEN	009	PAUL & CONNIE VICKERS	NO
09/18/82	001	400-B	2 BR TWNHS	024	VICKIE AND FRED THOMAS	NO
10/09/82	001	400-C	2 BR TWNHS	025	DENNIS C. SCHAAR	YES
10/10/82	001	200-D	2BR GARDEN	013	MARK V. HAMMOND	YES
11/14/82	001	100-A	1BR GARDEN	001	ROGER MOORE	NO
12/09/82	001	101-D	3BR GARDEN	008	MARVIN HAMBY	NO
12/12/82	001	401-C	2 BR TWNHS	028	TOM AND TRUDY STUDMAN	NO
12/14/82	001	301-A	3 BR TWNHS	020	HOWARD B. JOHNSON	YES
02/02/83	001	301-B	2 BR TWNHS	021	AMANDA JONES & SALLY GIBB	NO
02/12/83	001	101-A	1BR GARDEN	004	CYNTHIA SOUTHARD	NO
03/15/83	001	201-B	2BR GARDEN	014	MICHAEL E. BECK	NO
03/18/83	001	400-D	3BR GARDEN	026	BUCK AND JANETTE CROSBY	NO
04/04/83	001	401-A	3 BR TWNHS	027	DOT V. DECKER	NO
04/15/83	001	300-B	2 BR TWNHS	018	JIM AND SYLVIA PATTERSON	NO
04/15/83	001	201-D	1BR GARDEN	016	SAMMY AND JANIS THOMPSON	NO
05/04/83	001	100-C	2BR GARDEN	003	ANDREW GIBSON	NO
05/09/83	001	200-B	3BR GARDEN	010	DORIS J. DOBBS	NO
06/14/83	001	201-C	3BR GARDEN	015	KATHY PARKER	NO
06/28/83	001	101-B	2BR GARDEN	006	HARVEY KOHN	NO
07/01/83	001	300-A	2 BR TWNHS	017	ELIZABETH THOMPKINS	NO
07/01/83	001	301-C	3BR GARDEN	022	JERAHME STINSON	NO
07/05/83	001	401-D	3BR GARDEN	029	SUSAN P. WALKER	NO
12/08/83	001	200-C	2BR GARDEN	012	TAMMY SMITH	NO

Courtesy of MIN Microcomputer Systems, Inc.

Exhibit 11–14. The Landlord®: Disbursement Report

```
                              DISBURSEMENT REPORT
                               MGT COMPANY NAME INC.
                                   FOR JUNE 1982                        06/25/82
```

TERRACE GARDENS   001   JOHN J. MORRIS   001

PROP/ ENTRY	CHECK DATE	CHECK NO.	PAYEE/MEMO	ACCOUNT CODE	PROP CODE	AMOUNT
1 001	06/06/82	100	ACE HARDWARE LOCKS	127	001	256.13
1 002	06/08/82	101	SOUTHERN BELL TELEPHONE EXPENSE	141	001	157.18
1 003	06/08/82	102	EVERGREEN LANDSCAPERS GROUNDS MAINTENANCE	108	001	160.00
				125	001	85.00
				134	001	20.00
						————
						265.00
1 004	06/15/82	103	TOM AND LINDA DOLE SECURITY DEPOSIT REFUND	157	001	100.00
1 005	06/15/82	104	SOUTHERN VENDING COMPANY SNACK MACHINE IN CLUBHSE	128	001	75.90
1 006	06/15/82	105	ATLANTA GAS LIGHT SERV THRU 5/29/82	129	001	489.36
1 007	06/20/82	106	SAMS JANITORIAL SERVICE INVOICE 3479	106	001	260.00
				124	001	107.00
						————
						367.00
1 008	06/20/82	107	ACME GENERAL CONTRACTORS INV. 678 MAY SERVICES	111	001	568.90
				127	001	450.00
				106	001	150.00
				114	001	200.00
						————
						1368.90
1 009	06/22/82	108	THE ATLANTA JOURNAL JUNE-NOV SUBSCRIPTION	112	001	155.80
						==========
						3235.27

Courtesy of MIN Microcomputer Systems, Inc.

Exhibit 11–15. The Landlord®: Property and Tax Analysis

TERRACE GARDENS   001   JOHN J. MORRIS   001

	CURRENT MONTH	%	YEAR TO DATE	%
GROSS INCOME:				
RENT	81021.76	93.8	1060219.02	96.1
APPLICATION FEE	380.00	0.4	3300.00	0.3
LATE FEE	380.00	0.4	4100.00	0.4
SECURITY DEPOSIT FORFEIT	4600.00	5.3	35200.00	3.2
GROSS OPERATING INCOME	86381.76	100.0	1102819.02	100.0
OPERATING EXPENSES:				
ANSWERING SERV & PAGING	185.24	0.2	1257.56	0.1
CARPET CLEANING & REPAIR	988.50	1.1	8463.40	0.8
CONTRACT MAINTENANCE	213.75	0.3	8071.65	0.7
ELECTRIC POWER	786.54	0.9	12570.60	1.1
FICA	1000.00	1.2	14354.02	1.3
INSURANCE	1425.71	1.7	23931.71	2.2
LANDSCAPING	650.25	0.8	20466.25	1.9
MAINTENANCE SUPPLIES	1421.76	1.7	15119.76	1.4
PROPERTY TAXES	5120.00	5.9	65480.00	5.9
REFURBISHING	3439.66	4.0	24811.66	2.3
SALARIES	6270.30	7.3	71350.30	6.5
TELEPHONE	281.99	0.3	4511.99	0.4
UNIFORM RENTAL	0.00	0.0	8762.00	0.8
WATER SERVICE	559.88	0.7	10379.88	0.9
TOTAL OPERATING EXPENSES	22343.58	25.9	289530.78	26.3
NET OPERATING INCOME	64038.18	74.1	813288.24	73.8
LESS:				
NOTE PAYMENT – INTEREST	43750.00	50.7	611616.00	55.5
NOTE PAYMENT – PRINCIPAL	536.72	0.6	13882.72	1.3
CAPITALIZED EXPENSES	536.31	0.6	2108.31	0.2
TOTAL NOTE PAYMENTS & CAPITALIZED EXPENSES	44823.03	51.9	627607.03	56.9
GROSS SPENDABLE INCOME	19215.15	22.2	185681.21	16.8
PLUS: PRINCIPAL PAYMENTS	536.72	0.6	13882.72	1.3
CAPITALIZED EXPENSES	536.31	0.6	2108.31	0.2
GROSS EQUITY INCOME	20288.18	23.5	201672.24	18.3
LESS: DEPRECIATION	22500.00	26.1	292502.00	26.5
TAXABLE INCOME	-2211.82	-2.5	-90829.76	-8.1

Exhibit 11–15 (concluded)

TERRACE GARDENS   001   JOHN J. MORRIS   001

	CURRENT MONTH	%	YEAR TO DATE	%
TAXABLE INCOME	-2211.82	-2.5	-90829.76	-8.1
GROSS EQUITY INCOME	20288.18	23.5	201672.24	18.3
LESS TAX CONSEQUENCES @ 50%	-1105.91	-1.2	-45414.88	-4.0
AFTER TAX INCOME	21394.09	24.8	247087.12	22.4
PLUS: APPRECIATION	20000.00	23.2	20000.00	1.8
NET EQUITY INCOME	41394.09	47.9	267087.12	24.2
GROSS SPENDABLE INCOME	19215.15	22.2	185681.21	16.8
LESS TAX CONSEQUENCES @ 50%	-1105.91	-1.2	-45414.88	-4.0
NET SPENDABLE INCOME	20321.06	23.5	231096.09	21.0

Courtesy of MIN Microcomputer Systems, Inc.

analysis need to be compared on a function basis in relation to your specific needs. A wise step is to see them demonstrated either at a local dealer or at the vendor's showroom. Find out what kind of programming advice they will give you, what kind of ongoing service you can expect, and what kind of commitment they have to improving their software over time. Each real estate program must be evaluated according to how well it fits your needs and how well it stacks up against competing software.

APPENDIX

Bibliography

"The Coming Boom in Housing." *Changing Times,* May 1980, pp. 21–22.

"Computer Applications in Property Management Accounting," Institute of Real Estate Management, 1982.

"Computerized Accounting: Recommended System Capabilities." *Journal of Property Management,* January/February 1978.

Downing-Faircloth, Margo. "Personal Computing Pays Off for Property Managers." *Personal Computing,* June 1982, pp. 55–58.

"Real Estate I & II." *Successful Investing & Money Management.* Toronto: Northington Limited, 1974.

Runde, Robert. "The Durable Case for Real Estate." *Money,* June 1980, pp. 50–54.

Resource List

Product	Resource	Computer
1. Property Analysis:		
Real Estate Analyzer	Howard Software Services 8008 Girard Avenue La Jolla, CA 92037	Apple II+/III IBM Personal Computer
Property Analysis System	Realty Automation Inc. 221 N. Lois La Habra, CA 90631	Apple II+ TRS-80, Xerox 820, IBM Personal Computer
Real Estate Analysis	Powersoft, Inc. P.O. Box 157 Pitman, NJ 08071	Apple II/II+
VisiCalc Real Estate Templates	Apple Computer Inc. 10260 Bandley Drive Cupertino, CA 95014	Apple II+
Incoprop	E-Z SOFTWARE P.O. Box 591 Novato, CA 94948	TRS-80

Product	Resource	Computer
VisiCalc Real	Sofstar 13935 U.S. 1 Juno Square Juno Beach, FL 33408	IBM Personal Computer
Quickcalc Real Estate Investor	Simple Soft, Inc. 480 Eagle Drive Suite 101 Elk Grove, IL 60007	IBM Personal Computer Apple II+ Osbourne Xerox 820
Cashflow	RealData, Inc. P.O. Box 691 Southport, CT 06490	CP/M-based
Real Estate Cash Flow Analysis	Atari Program Exchange Atari, Inc. P.O. Box 3705 Santa Clara, CA 95055	Atari 800

2. Property Management:

The Landlord® 2.0	MIN Microcomputer Software, Inc. 1501 Johnson Ferry Road Suite 220 Marrieta, GA 30062	Apple II+
Property Management System	Realty Automation Inc. 221 N. Lois La Habra, CA 90631	Apple II+ TRS-80 Xerox 820 IBM Personal Computer
Apartment Manager	Software Technology for Computers P.O. Box 428 Belmont, MA 02178	Apple II+
Property Management	Peachtree Software, Inc. 3445 Peachtree Road, N.E. Atlanta, GA 30326	CP/M-Systems
Apartment Management	Emeritus Software Library 5110 E Clinton Way Suite 202 Fresno, CA 93727	CP/M-Systems
Real Focus	Centennial Software 410 17th Street Suite 1375 Denver, CO 80202	Apple II+ IBM Personal Computer TRS-80

Commodities and Stock Options Trading

As trading in commodities and options has gained in popularity with the investing public there has been an explosion in the number of excellent computer programs designed to simplify and speed the normally laborious task of analyzing the commodities and options markets. For example, there are the Stock Tracker and Market Tracker programs, discussed in Chapter 6, which can be used for commodities and options trading as well as for stock trading. Also excellent is the Compu Trac series from the Personal Computer Technical Analysis Group, which contains a vast array of programs, many of which are specifically tailored to the needs of persons investing in commodities and options. If options are your primary interest perhaps you should try SOAP, the Stock Option Analysis Program offered by H&H Scientific. All of these programs provide technical analysis tools for speculating in both the commodities and options markets.

If you are new to investing in these two markets, it is a good idea to read some of the publications available on how to trade commodities and options. They are perhaps more volatile and leveraged than any other investment vehicles, reacting quickly, at times violently, to news developments and to changes in speculative psychology.

If you are seeking to protect your capital in tried-and-true investments, then commodities and options are probably not for you. If, however, you are inclined to take a flyer with at least some of your money these markets are certainly worth looking into.

Once you take the plunge, you will quickly discover that your personal computer is the best moneymaking tool you have. It should help you tame the risks and reap the rewards.

The personal computer helps trades by preparing technical analyses of both current and historical commodity data in much the same way that it performs stock analysis. Many of the methods are actually identical, though others are totally unique. Brokers and personal investors alike have praised their personal computers for the machine's ability to improve investor productivity by automating much of the complicated commodity and options analysis. They also speak highly of the computer's capacity for upgrading their trading program by allowing the investor to analyze more commodities, make better trading decisions, and be in the market more often. Before discussing specific program aids, however, it's important to get a grip on the unique properties of both the commodities and options markets.

WHAT ARE COMMODITIES?

When trading in the stock market, you are faced with thousands of choices. In the commodities market a relatively smaller number of investment instruments are traded. Actively traded commodities include:

Meats: cattle, pork bellies (bacon), hogs.

Foods: coffee, sugar, orange juice, cocoa.

Grains: wheat, corn, oats, soybeans.

Metals: gold, silver, copper, platinum.

Currencies: Swiss franc, German mark, English pound, Japanese yen.

Financial futures: Treasury bills and bonds, Government National Mortgage Association (Ginnie Mae) securities, commercial paper, Eurobonds.

Commodities are traded as "futures" contracts, which are agreements that a specific commodity will be delivered at a fixed date some 8 to 18 months in the future at a predetermined price. Between the time a contract for a particular commodity is purchased and the time it is to be delivered, many speculators guess at what the price will be when the contract closes. Traders may buy and sell a futures contract many thousands of times in its 8 to 18 month lifespan, taking profits and losses and hoping to be on the winning side when the contract closes. In short, commodities futures trading is speculating on the price movements of futures contracts and of the underlying commodities involved (see Exhibit 12–1).

Exhibit 12–1.   Sample Commodity Trade and the Effect of Leverage

Depending on the commodity involved, the volatility of the market when you enter it, and your broker's requirements, you can put up just 10% to 15% of the contract's value.

Let's assume that you purchase a July wheat contract (5,000 bushels) at $3.80 per bushel (contract value $19,000), and put up $2,500 margin. Each one cent change in the wheat price represents $50. If the price goes up 50 cents, you're out $2,500. Furthermore, as the price declines, you must pay in additional capital (margin call) or your position is sold out at a loss.

Reprinted with permission. Copyright © by The Research Institute of America, Inc.

The position you establish on a given commodity may be either "long" or "short." A long position is the purchase of a commodity in the hope that its price will rise and that, when the contract falls due, its market value will be above what one paid for it. A short position is basically an agreement to sell a commodity at a predetermined price. Thus the short position counts on declining prices to generate a profit.

The lure of the commodities markets is the opportunity to realize fantastic profits of 2, 10, or 500 times your original investment in less than a year. But as common sense would suggest, the opportunities for losing money are every bit as great as those for making it. Take, for instance, the huge run-up in prices of precious metals in 1979–80. Vast fortunes were made in that market, but equally vast fortunes were lost in the subsequent slide in the value of those metals. One nice feature of the commodities markets, however, is that the investor, by taking short positions, can make as much money in declining markets as he or she can by taking long positions in booming markets. Regardless of the economic climate there is always money to be made in the commodities markets.

An astute trader times his moves precisely. He cuts his losses short and runs his profits and stands to earn more in a few short months than he ever could in years of everyday work. But don't be fooled into thinking that this happens all the time. There are no sure things. The rewards are great and so are the risks, but you can use a number of trading tricks to hedge your bets in an especially volatile market. One hedge is a "straddle," a trade in which you simultaneously execute counterbalancing long and short positions. The purpose is to have the difference between the prices of your original positions move in your favor, and for that reason you are more concerned with changes in price difference than in absolute price change (see Exhibit 12–2).

For many traders—both individuals and large commodity trading firms—computers have become indispensable in managing their trading program. Computers don't take the place of market knowledge, nor can they guarantee instant success in the commodities market. What they can do is help you become more productive in your interpretation of market indicators and make you better able to set up profitable trading programs.

Exhibit 12–2. Sample Commodity Spread

You buy a June live cattle contract and simultaneously sell an October live cattle contract based on a projected change in supply and demand. Instead of paying about $3,000 margin for one contract, the two-contract spread requires only about $500 up front. Since each contract is for 40,000 pounds, each one cent change equals $400.

Thus, if your June contract moves up one cent you make $400 on each, or $800 on your $500 investment. If both contracts fall in price, the profit from the October contract would balance out the loss on the June contract.

Reprinted with permission. Copyright © by The Research Institute of America, Inc.

RULES OF THE GAME

It has been said that playing the commodities market is like playing an all-night poker game. You have to be able to cover all conceivable financial contingencies. In commodities you must set limits for yourself on the "margin" you are prepared to lose. Once that limit is set you can guarantee that it will not be exceeded by establishing "stop orders," under which your broker will automatically close out your position in the market once the price of your contract falls to the level that would produce what you regard as the maximum tolerable loss. If the commodities markets are going against you, you have to be prepared to cut your losses short.

The "stop loss" is a device to enable you to get out of the market at a predetermined time. Your pretrade analysis should suggest the probable extent of price moves both positive and negative. Your sensitivity to adverse movements should be high, but on the profit side "market feel" must be equally high to recognize when it is time to either let profits run or cash in your chips. Although your profit objectives can be set more loosely than your stop losses, you need to detail in advance exactly what amount of price movement will cause you to drop out of the trade. By deciding in advance you can protect yourself against the bad decisions you might make in the highly charged atmosphere of a sharp move in prices.

What you need is a carefully prepared trading program that allows you to trade in an orderly and logical manner. This plan provides the discipline you need to avoid following the herd. Only a long-term and disciplined plan to cut losses or let profits run will return profits consistently over time. The typical investor can expect 40 percent losses and 40 percent profits. The remainder of your trades will net you a zero return. You should be content with staying ahead of or at least equal to the game in 60 percent of your trades.

Sound management of your trading position requires that you know when and where to enter and exit the market, as well as where to look for ways to manage your position in a manner that cuts losses and lets profits accumulate. As in any management task, you must first organize your thinking.

Several tools are needed to set up your trading program, and basically they are the same tools used in all investing programs. First and foremost you need information about commodities and their prices. This you can get from a commodity yearbook, technical charts, specialty publications, and fundamental data provided by government agencies. Your personal computer can give you access to several commodity databases for current prices on futures contracts.

Once you get into the market you will find there is another very important flow of information to keep track of—the account control forms provided by your broker in the form of confirmation slips and monthly statements. These are important because they give you written confirmation on the status of your equity position. Since money management is the key to the health of a commodity account, your personal account record is a singularly important aid to knowing how many chips you have left to bet on the next deal.

You will also need to keep close track of your cash transactions, and trading results, including the commissions you've paid. This data should provide a firm foundation from which to execute future trades by allowing you to study your previous decisions and their results. By looking back before you move forward into the market again you can learn from your mistakes and capitalize on your successes. You might also want to keep good notes on the opening, high, low, and closing prices on the commodities that interest you, as well as a record of their volume and open interest. You may wish to keep notes on fundamental news items, charts, newsletters, and so forth, that apply to your program.

All this data should help you position yourself for the next big breakout and a run for the profits. The time you spend waiting on the market sidelines studying market trends is just as important as actually making your trades. Knowing the right time and place in the commodities markets and preparing yourself for your next trade is the key to success.

FUNDAMENTAL ANALYSIS

The laws of supply and demand are the principal determinants of commodity performance. Affecting both of these is a variety of other short-term and long-term factors. In agricultural commodities, for instance, such short-term elements as current stocks on hand, the volume of the commodity reaching the market daily, and weather conditions are important to track. Long-term fundamentals include the factors that affect agricultural products or their markets, such as yield per acre, the number of acres used, and new uses for raw commodities. Metals, especially precious metals, are particularly sensitive to politics and to such broad economic trends as the changing value of the dollar, interest rates, and inflation.

Fundamental price movements can be predicted over a reasonable time period, but you must be aware of the inherent cycles in the commodities you favor. There are seasonal cycles and cycles affected by business conditions. There is also a considerable amount of "noise" caused by random market occurrences that must be sorted out. From all these factors you can establish a trend. The standard method is a "linear regression" analysis. An example of price movement and its trend line is shown in Exhibit 12–3. The confidence you have in this projection is expressed as percentages above and below the trend line (Exhibit 12–4).

Exhibit 12–3.   Price and Trend Line

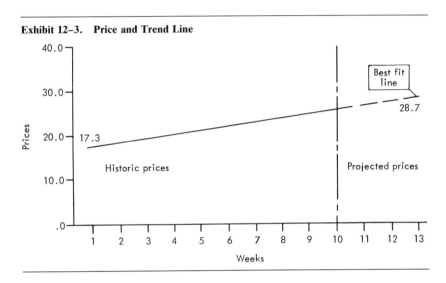

Exhibit 12–4.   Projection Confidence

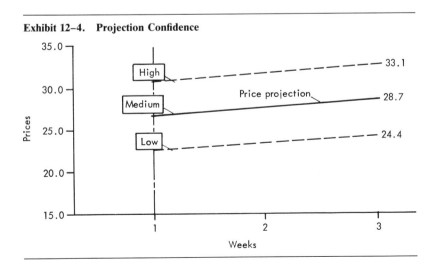

The question you need to ask now is: "Do I believe the projected trend, and can I set up my trading program based on it?"

TECHNICAL ANALYSIS

Frankly, the answer to the above question is no. A trend line does not give you the essential information you need to enter the market. You must know if a trend has actually started and, if so, the direction in which the market is moving. The strength of the trend must also be known. The problem with most trend forecasts is that it is very difficult to determine entry and exit points because you are only dealing with price ranges and not with specific prices. To understand what specific prices are doing now, you need a system of technical analysis—how you can discover patterns of market behavior by using charts that plot the amount of open interest and volume alongside historic price patterns. Technical analysis has its limitations, too, the most glaring being that, unlike fundamental analysis, it does not lend itself to specific forecasts. A blending of both fundamental and technical analysis is the best tool for understanding the fundamental factors and the market's reaction to them. Knowing these things will provide you with a solid position on which to establish your trading program.

COMPUTER-AIDED ANALYSIS

Your personal computer can help you with the work involved in both fundamental forecasting and technical analysis. For example, if you need information on the supply of certain agricultural products and current levels of worldwide demand, you can call up an information service and scan commodity history reports. You can also retrieve the latest news stories from the wire services.

Specialty databases serve the commodity markets and provide data that are uniquely important to traders in these markets. Historic and current price data for technical analysis are as near as our computer. Compu Trac uses the database of Commodity Systems, Inc., though, other information services are also available (see the resource list at the end of Chapter 5). You should evaluate each database according to the data it provides and the services it offers.

Computer-aided analysis is one of the keys to productive trading. The work associated with constructing charts, graphs, and indicators has been automated by a number of fine computer programs, all but eliminating the two to three hours of daily homework required to gather price data and construct the charts. Your computer allows you to escape the mechanical drudgery and to concentrate on analyzing and interpreting data while fine-tuning your investment program.

BASICS OF CHARTING

Just as it is necessary to understand the mechanics of commodity trading, so too is it important to become familiar with the primary tool of the technician—charts. The purpose of charts is to show price behavior in a graphic form. The technician is not concerned with why the prices act the way they do. His or her interest lies in what is happening and what it means in terms of the trading program.

Technical analysis is a study of market behavior, which is best represented by patterns and trends. The problem you must solve is one of knowing when a trend is about to begin or end so you can benefit from it no matter which direction it takes. Your primary goal should be to discover price trends quickly and profit from them. For instance, a potential breakout from a sideways-moving market through a support or resistance level may be indicated by a fundamental forecast, but the actual timing of the breakout will be indicated on your technical analysis chart. This may kick off your specific trading program. Following the current trend daily with your computer should give you an edge in your overall program.

The simplest and most familiar type of chart is the vertical bar. The length of the bar represents the daily price range of the commodity. The small horizontal bar intersecting the vertical is the closing price (see Exhibit 12–5). This chart is easy to construct and maintain, but its interpretation requires skill and a knowledge of the markets. Several variations and mathematical supplements to the vertical bar can aid your interpretation. A few of the simplest are:

1.   Channels.   These delineate trends, whether up, down, or sideways.

2.   Support/Resistance Levels.   Within a channel the lower boundary is the supporting price level while the upper is the resistance price. Price breakouts are indicated whenever the current price breaks through either the support or the resistance line. When these lines are broken it is likely that a new trend could start in the direction of the broken line. Exhibit 12–6 shows a channel and breakout occurring.

3.   Moving Averages/Oscillators.   One of the problems in reading the simple vertical bar chart is the number of often rapid changes that can take place in commodity prices. In turbulent markets, the charts can become difficult to interpret. To overcome that constraint, analysts generally use moving averages by which they average closing prices for the previous 4, 8, 15, or 20 days and plot that average as representing that

Exhibit 12–5.   Sample Vertical Bar Chart

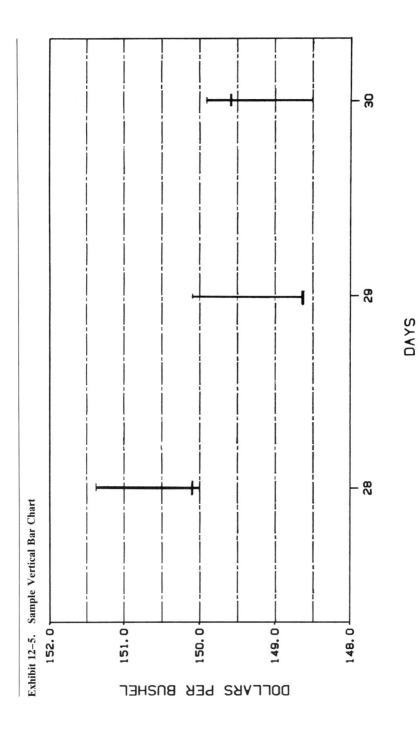

Source: Commodity Research Bureau, Inc.

Exhibit 12–6. Soybeans, January 1976 (breakout example)

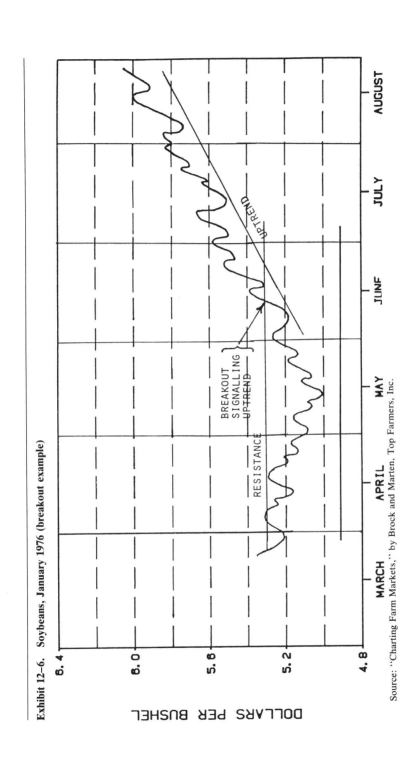

Source: "Charting Farm Markets," by Brock and Marten, Top Farmers, Inc.

Exhibit 12–7. Cotton No. 2, July 1980 (N.Y.): Sample Moving Average Chart

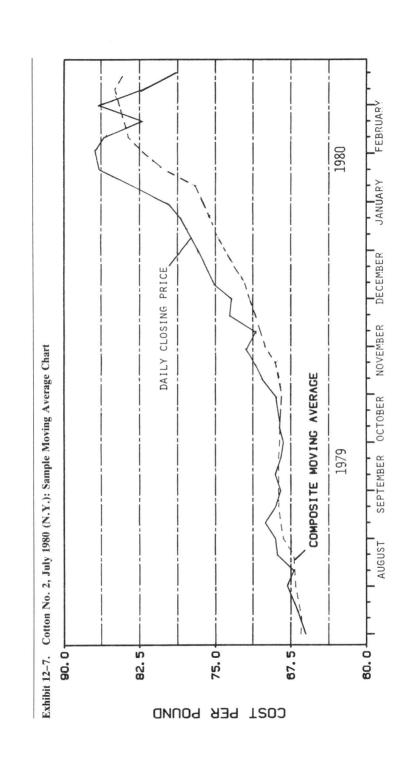

day's price. Each day they "move" the average by dropping the first day's data and adding the last day's to it. Since plots of the moving average points form a curve over time, you can get a clear picture of how prices are actually performing (see Exhibit 12–7). The fewer the number of days in the average the "faster" it moves. Conversely, a 20-day moving average is said to be "slow." The risk of missing a market breakout is greater with a slow average than with a fast one, particularly in a volatile market. The slow-moving average, however, is a better indicator of a trend. Consequently, moving averages are often developed that combine averages of different speeds to minimize risk and still give a good feel for trends. Any of these moving averages can provide indicators of when a breakout or trend has begun if one measures the difference between the average and current prices. A mathematical measure of these price differences is an "oscillator," which measures price changes rather than price levels. It calculates the "momentum" and "velocity" of price changes and is most useful in a volatile market.

4. Volume and Open Interest. Both of these reflect a day's trading activity. Since commodity volume is a function of the interest in a contract it gives some indication of the "quality" of the current market. For example, if on the one hand volume and open interest are up and prices are down, the market is weak, probably as a result of shorts being in control of the market and driving prices down. On the other hand, if prices are up and volume is up, prices are strong.

The potential direction of the market can be predicted by other technical tools and possibly verified by a fundamental forecast. Thus a combination of techniques is necessary to adequately determine the market's direction, strength, and duration. Your personal computer can prepare these analyses and should help you to profit from your trading program. Remember, though, the computer doesn't spit out magic answers or provide a sure-fire cookbook approach to your trading program. As in all other investment areas it simply mechanizes the boring and repetitive tasks. It is up to you to interpret the results of its work in light of the current market.

COMPUTER-AIDED COMMODITY TRADING

There is an old adage in the business world that goes: "Plan your work and work your plan." That goes for commodities trading, too. Without a workable plan you can't hope to establish a successful trading program. In executing your plan you will quickly find that your computer is no less important than your pencil. In fact, you don't even need a pencil if you have a computer since all your record-keeping, charting, and note-taking can be done on your machine.

Your computer can aid you in creating your plan, gathering data for both fundamental and technical analysis, constructing charts and indicators, and maintaining a running tally of your open contracts and net equity.

One outstanding advantage of today's computer programs is their ability to customize the system to your trading style, enabling you to pick and choose the technical charts and methodologies with which you feel most comfortable from a lengthy menu provided by a system like Compu Trac. Perhaps you have a trading method of your own that you have used for years, but you want to automate it to save time. You can either program your system yourself or hire a programmer to do it. Compu Trac has a feature for writing your own programs in support of your tried and true indicators.

Compu Trac provides not only the software for technical analysis but a host of special services designed to make computer-aided commodity trading easier. These services include comprehensive system documentation, operating instruction tapes, telephone support, and simple display screen prompting messages since Compu Trac programs assume that you have no computer experience. There is even a mode of operation in which you can instruct the computer to complete certain studies automatically— even while the computer is unattended.

Commodities, however, are not the only investment vehicle that Compu Trac supports. Stocks can also be analyzed with the same studies used for commodities, except of course where a study is unique to a commodity. Stock options and mutual fund portfolios can be updated through an interface with Interactive Data Corporation. The studies currently available in Compu Trac are shown in Table 12–1.

Compu Trac also provides an account management system for commodity accounts that can help an individual who has one or several accounts at one or more brokers, as well as brokers with multiple accounts. The system can attack a variety of data. For example, you can categorize a trade as regular, spread, hedge, or spot; or you can follow margin, maintenance, or equity requirements; or automatically post current equity and open profits and losses whenever the latest closing data are received. You may print out a number of account management reports, too. Support of these capabilities is accomplished with two user-specified displays—namely, the account display that reflects current account information and a commodity table containing information pertaining to each commodity being followed.

The Compu Trac programs are among the best available for commodity trading, but they are not for beginners. They may be easy to use but you must remember that the concepts behind their statistical measurements and pattern recognition techniques are complex and require an understanding of their mathematical roots. In addition, the indicators they gen-

Table 12–1. Compu Trac Programs and Studies

Program/Study	Commodity	Stock	Stock Option	Mutual Fund
1. Jim Sibbet's Demand Index:[1] this is volume and price data combined into a leading indicator. The lead time is based on the fact that volume tends to peak before prices.	X	X		
2. Welles Wilder's Relative Strength Index, Directional Movement System, Swing Index, Commodity Selection Index, and Parabolic Time/Price Systems.[2]	X	X		
3. Walt Bressert's Cyclical Detrending.[3]	X	X		
4. Overbought/Oversold Index: it was first designed by Larry Williams and modified by Walt Bressert to key on the underlying operative cycles.	X	X		
5. Momentum Index I: this is a Bressert-designed index program that is keyed to underlying cycle movement.	X			
6. Momentum Index II: this is defined as the continuous difference between prices at a fixed interval. This rate of change index may be smoothed by a moving average.	X	X		
7. Spread: two commodities, commodity months, or contracts may be spread against cash and graphically displayed or printed. Two stocks may also be spread to point out relative performance.	X	X		
8. On-Balance Volume™:[4] this program charts all days of On-Balance Volume and prints a numerical report.	X	X		
9. Regression Analysis: these programs calculate the trend lines which approximate the best fit of a series of price data.	X	X		
10. Gann Cardinal Squares: this program generates a chart of the GCSs. Numbers which fall into the "Cardinal Cross" and numbers which end cycles are natural support/resistance numbers.	X	X		
11. Trendline Slope: the computer gives the extrapolated points of any trendline which extends off the display past the last day posted.	X	X		
12. Moving Averages: a series of programs that calculate simple and linearly weighted moving averages, compute the popular 4-9-18-day three-crossover moving averages, and calculate exponentially smoothed moving averages.	X	X		
13. Oscillator: this indicates the differences between any two moving averages, and is in the form of a histogram revolving around a zero line.	X	X		

Table 12–1 (*concluded*)

Program/Study	Commodity	Stock	Stock Option	Mutual Fund
14. Percent Retracement: by using the live cursor (unique to Compu Trac) and a control key, the user can pick a high, low, and retracement. The computer will give the difference between two specified points and the percent retracement of a third point.	X	X		
15. Volume Display: this display is in the form of a histogram, starting at a base line = 0 and extending up to their relative volume level. A volume moving average may also be calculated.	X	X		
16. Relative Strength Index: this offers a variable choice of days in the moving average, and uses the same formula as Welles Wilder and the Commodity Perspective Charts.	X	X		
17. Commodity Channel Index: this is a timing study which works best with seasonal or cyclical contracts.	X	X		
18. Fourier Analysis: this analysis assists in finding the underlying cycles in a commodity and projecting them into the future.	X	X		
19. Demand Aggregate: this study combines price, volume, and open interest movement to show the relative effect of one on another.	X	X		
20. Ratio: this study may be used to track the relationship between two distinct but related commodities and securities.	X	X		
21. IDC Interface:[5] allows the user to automatically collect price data (high, low, close, bid and asked) for 12,000 North American equities, fixed-income securities, and interest rate futures.			X	X
22. Programming Subsystem: this allows the user to program a special analysis not presently in the Compu Trac collection. A series of productivity aids lets you easily program with only a few lines of Basic programming code.	X	X		

Credits:

[1] Jim Sibbert is publisher of "Let's Talk Silver and Gold," 380 East Green Street, Suite 200, Pasadena, CA 91101.

[2] Welles Wilder's studies are contained in his book: *New Concepts in Technical Trading Systems*, Consensus Bookshelf, 30 W. Pershing Road, Kansas City, MO 64108.

[3] Walter Bressert is president of HAL Commodity Cycles, P.O. Box 40070, Tucson, Arizona 85717.

[4] On-Balance Volume is a registered trademark of the Joseph Granville organization and is described in the book, *New Strategy of Daily Stock Market Timing for Maximum Profit*, Joseph Granville, published by Prentice Hall, NY.

[5] Interactive Data Corporation (IDC), 4896 Totten Pond Road, Waltham, MA 02154

Exhibit 12–8. Compu Trac: Apple II+ Equipment

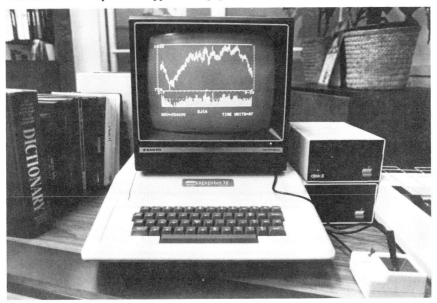

erate must be interpreted in light of market experience. If you have a desire to improve your speculating ability in commodities consider joining the Technical Analysis Group. For an initiation fee of $1,800 and an annual maintenance fee of $200 members are provided with all the programs and services I have described. In addition to these fees, you also need an Apple II+ computer system (Exhibit 12–8) and the peripheral equipment specified by TAG. Exhibits 12–9 through 12–18 illustrate just a few of the many different charts available from Compu Trac.

If you are a part-time trader in commodities and in the market infrequently, you may wish to consider less expensive programs for both account management and charting. Alternatively, you might want to consider developing a set of your own programs to do your charting for you. The actual preparation of the charts may not be as automatic as in Compu Trac, but you could build your own database of historic prices and use it to construct charts on your computer. You can do this by writing your own graphics program to construct moving averages, oscillators, trends, and the like, or you can modify one of the graphics packages currently on the market.

There are other possible solutions to creating your own charting programs. The biggest task is collecting the historic and current price data.

Exhibit 12–9. Compu Trac: Four Varied Examples of Chart Density, Composites, Split Screens, Demand Index

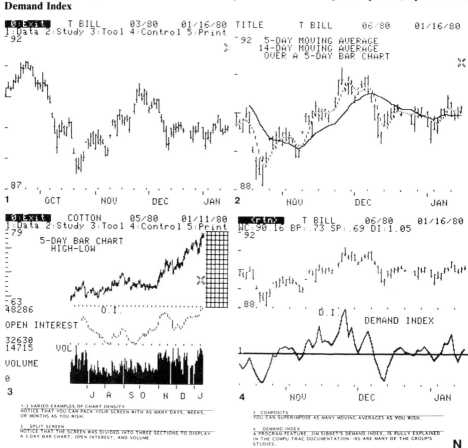

Courtesy of Compu Trac, Inc.

Since you can easily obtain this data through a number of information services, it's relatively easy to build your own database. Your charting program could be an interesting project, and may give you the opportunity to customize your favorite system.

In summary, commodities trading can be an extremely rewarding form of investing—financially and psychologically. It is, however, filled with pitfalls that can cause you to lose hundreds or thousands of dollars faster than if you set fire to them. Your personal computer can aid you in the collection of important price, volume, and open interest data, as well as in charting the trends and generating market timing indicators. It can give

Exhibit 12–10. Compu Trac: Trend Line, Bar Chart, Commodity Channel Index

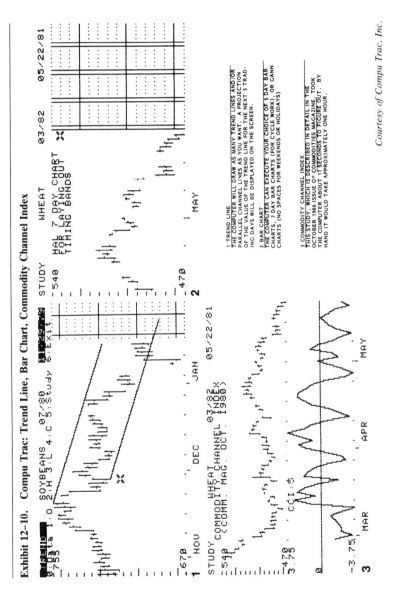

1 TREND LINE
THE COMPUTER WILL DRAW AS MANY TREND LINES AND/OR
PARALLEL CHANNEL LINES AS YOU WANT. A PROJECTION
OF THE VALUE OF THE TREND LINE FOR THE NEXT 5 TRAD-
ING DAYS WILL BE DISPLAYED ON THE SCREEN.

2 BAR CHART
THE COMPUTER CAN EXECUTE YOUR CHOICE OF 5 DAY BAR
CHARTS, 7 DAY BAR CHARTS (FOR CYCLE WORK), OR GANN
CHARTS (NO SPACES FOR WEEKENDS OR HOLIDAYS)

3 COMMODITY CHANNEL INDEX
THIS STUDY, WHICH IS DESCRIBED IN DETAIL IN THE
OCTOBER 1980 ISSUE OF COMMODITIES MAGAZINE, TOOK
THE COMPUTER ABOUT 1.5 SECONDS TO FIGURE OUT. BY
HAND IT WOULD TAKE APPROXIMATELY ONE HOUR.

Courtesy of Compu Trac, Inc.

Exhibit 12–11. Compu Trac: Granville's On-Balance Volume™, Linear Regression, Stochastic K%D

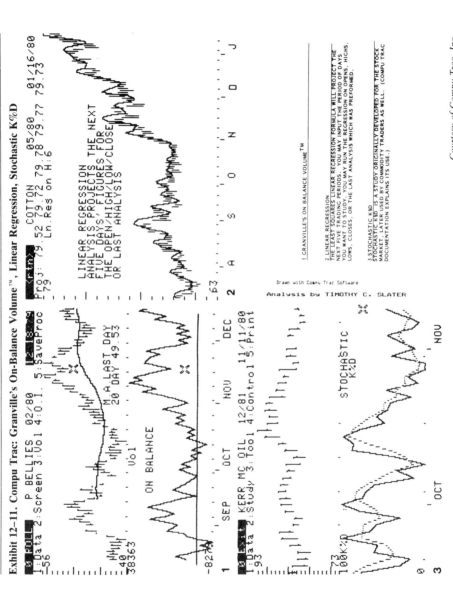

Drawn with Compu Trac Software

Analysis by TIMOTHY C. SLATER

Exhibit 12–12. Compu Trac: Vertical Bar Chart, Moving Average, 10-Day Detrend

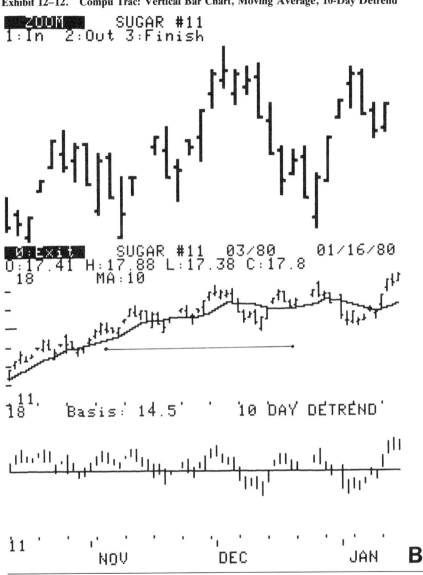

Courtesy of Compu Trac, Inc.

you more time to analyze the market and your particular commodities before committing capital. Money management is also improved because your record-keeping is made easier with a computer. You can exercise more control and discipline in any trading program if you have the proper tools, but your computer is the most important.

Exhibit 12–13. Compu Trac: Point and Figure Chart, Spread, On-Balance Volume™, Relative Strength Index

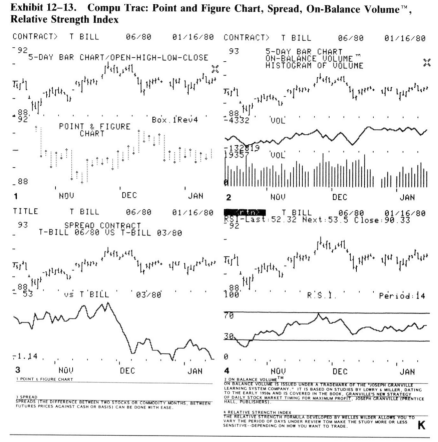

Courtesy of Compu Trac, Inc.

OPTIONS TRADING

Options trading is similar to commodities trading in that considerable leverage is involved. Although options may be traded on equities as well as commodities, for our purposes we will only cover stock options.

A single stock option contract covers 100 shares of an individual stock. The option sets a specified price (the striking or exercise price), which may be exercised at any time until the third Saturday of a stipulated month as far as one year into the future (Exhibit 12–19). There are four kinds of options trading actions, two bullish and two bearish. Exhibit 12–20 outlines these. Within these boundaries there are many different combinations of trades, but the big magnet for investors is leverage. For a

Exhibit 12–14. Compu Trac: Gann Square, 3-Year Bar Chart, Hal Momentum Index and Hal Overbought/Oversold Index

IMM GOLD 3/80

GANN SQUARE

Of Size 11 Starting At 500

With Step Size 1

F1					C2					F2
590	591	592	593	594	595	596	597	598	599	600
589	556	557	558	559	560	561	562	563	564	601
588	555	530	531	532	533	534	535	536	565	602
587	554	529	512	513	514	515	516	537	566	603
586	553	528	511	502	503	504	517	538	567	604
C1 585	552	527	510	501	500	505	518	539	568	605 C3
584	551	526	509	508	507	506	519	540	569	606
583	550	525	524	523	522	521	520	541	570	607
582	549	548	547	546	545	544	543	542	571	608
581	580	579	578	577	576	575	574	573	572	609
620	619	618	617	616	615	614	613	612	611	610

| F4 | | | | | C4 | | | | | F3 |

Commodity Analysis Group   (504) 895-1474

1

1   GANN SQUARE
A GANN SQUARE CAN BE PRINTED TO ANY SIZE, INCREMENT, AND CAN BE EITHER POSITIVE (BULL MARKET) OR NEGATIVE (BEAR MARKET). EXPLANATIONS OF THE SIGNIFICANCE OF THIS GANN TECHNIQUE ARE GIVEN IN THE COMPU TRAC DOCUMENTATION.

2   THREE YEAR MONTHLY BAR CHART
AS MANY AS EIGHT YEARS CAN BE PRINTED OUT IN MONTHLY INCREMENTS (OPEN, HIGH, LOW, CLOSE).

3   HAL MOMENTUM INDEX & HAL OVERBOUGHT/OVERSOLD INDEX
DEVELOPED BY WALT BRESSERT, THIS PROGRAM USES THE NATURAL CYCLE LENGTH OF A COMMODITY OR SECURITY TO CALCULATE MOMENTUM AND AN OVERBOUGHT/OVERSOLD INDICATOR.

0:Exit   GOLD_CMX   39/81   05/20/81
1:Data 2:Study 3:Tool 4:Control 5:Print
900

-90

2   J   J   J

TITLE   SOYBEANS   07/80   01/16/80

42.25 H.M.I.   □:2TC   ○:TC   A/B   10:20
HAL MOMENTUM INDEX

-67.5
08/05   □:2TC   ○:TC   A/B   10:20
10

HAL
OVERBOUGHT/
OVERSOLD
INDEX

90

3   JAN   **L**

Courtesy of Compu Trac, Inc.

relatively small investment, the investor can realize profits of 20 to 25 percent in only weeks.

Buying an option requires two sets of judgments, one on underlying stock value and the other on time value. Underlying value depends on the market price of the underlying stock and the expectations of its future market value. Obviously this means that you have to know what you're buying because an option's performance is only as good as its underlying security. The computer stock evaluation techniques will help you find the right stock on which to buy options. Particularly important in options is knowing when a stock is going to move in a desired direction. An option is a wasting asset which means that it has a finite life, and when that life

Exhibit 12–15. Compu Trac: 10-Day Moving Average

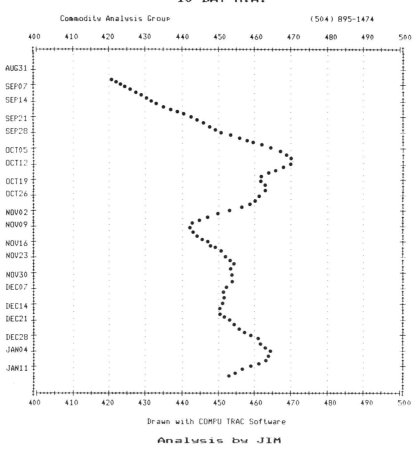

Courtesy of Compu Trac, Inc.

expires the option is worthless. That is the time value of the contract. The longer the time left in the stock option contract, the higher the premium; that is, the more it is worth. This is because speculators believe that the more time there is left in the contract the more time there is for the underlying stock's price to move to the contract level.

What is the theoretical value of an option? It is based on a range of factors. Certain market services, such as William O'Neil & Company's *Daily Graphs/Stock Option Guide* and Valueline's *The Option Strategist* compute options' values.

Exhibit 12–16. Compu Trac: T-Bill High, Low, Close

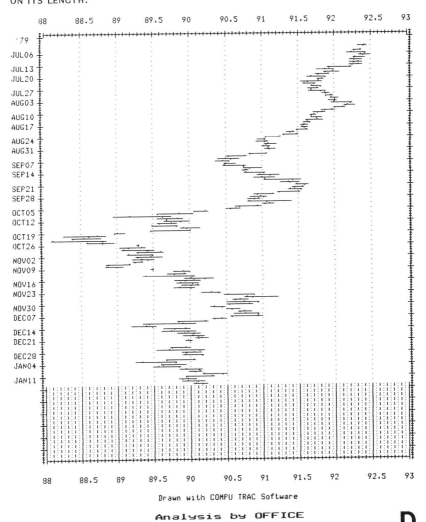

THIS "PRECISION" CHART
IS ACCURATE TO 1/84 OF
AN INCH. IT WILL PRINT
OUT IN APPROXIMATELY
1-1¼ MINUTES DEPENDING
ON ITS LENGTH.

T BILL   06/80

Drawn with COMPU TRAC Software

Analysis by OFFICE

D

Exhibit 12–17. Compu Trac: DJIA Relative Strength Index

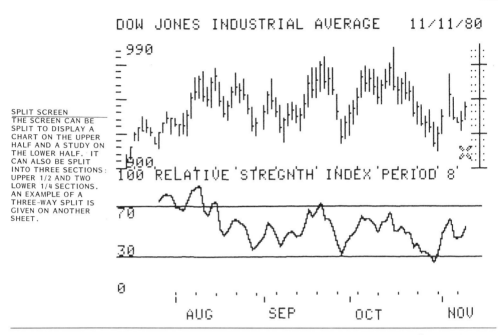

SPLIT SCREEN
THE SCREEN CAN BE
SPLIT TO DISPLAY A
CHART ON THE UPPER
HALF AND A STUDY ON
THE LOWER HALF. IT
CAN ALSO BE SPLIT
INTO THREE SECTIONS:
UPPER 1/2 AND TWO
LOWER 1/4 SECTIONS.
AN EXAMPLE OF A
THREE-WAY SPLIT IS
GIVEN ON ANOTHER
SHEET.

Courtesy of Compu Trac, Inc.

Exhibit 12–18. Compu Trac: Point and Figure Chart (Box and Reversal)

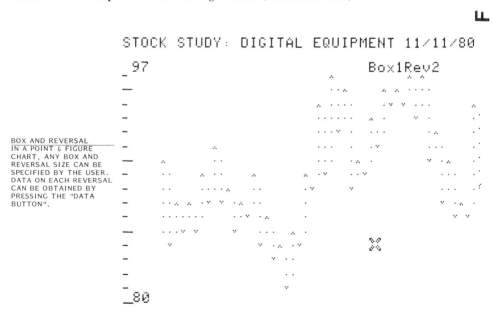

BOX AND REVERSAL
IN A POINT & FIGURE
CHART, ANY BOX AND
REVERSAL SIZE CAN BE
SPECIFIED BY THE USER.
DATA ON EACH REVERSAL
CAN BE OBTAINED BY
PRESSING THE "DATA
BUTTON".

Courtesy of Compu Trac, Inc.

Exhibit 12–19. Sample Option Trades

Stock A is trading at $40 per share, therefore, 100 shares cost $4,000. Assume that (1) the option cost is $300 (three-month option) and (2) the option expires with stock A still at $40. The stockholder still has his original stock position. The optionholder, however, has lost his entire $300 investment because the stock price did not move up to make his purchase profitable.

Stock B is trading at $60, therefore 100 shares cost $6,000. The option cost is $500 (three-month option). Stock B rises to $80 per share. The stockholder's return is $2,000 or 33.3 percent. The return for the optionholder (who can buy this stock at $60) is $1,500 ($8,000—$6,000—$500) or 300 percent return on the original investment.

Summary:

Return	*Stockholder*	*Optionholder*
$	2,000	1,500
%	33.3	300

Note: commissions are ignored in these examples.

Exhibit 12–20. Options Trading Actions

	Bearish (*Expect Stock Price Decline*)	*Bullish* (*Expect Stock Price Increase*)
Action:		
1	—	Buy a "Call"
2	—	Sell (write) a "Put"
3	Sell (write) a "Call"	—
4	Buy a "Put"	—

Action 1 = the privilege of buying 100 shares at a certain price in the hope that the stock's price will rise.

Action 2 = is the obligation to buy 100 shares of stock at a price, and collect the "premium."

Action 3 = an obligation to sell 100 shares.

Action 4 = the privilege of selling 100 shares.

A COMPUTER AID TO OPTIONS PRICING

Another way to establish price is with the Stock Options Analysis Program (SOAP) for your computer. This program calculates the fair price of options, based on the price of the underlying stock, dividends paid, price volatility, current interest rates, and the time remaining on the option. The expected profit or loss on transactions involving up to three classes of options can be calculated and graphed for any time until the options expire (see Exhibit 12–21).

Exhibit 12–21. Evaluating Options

```
          H&H SCIENTIFIC
   STOCK OPTION EVALUATION SYSTEM
=======================================

DO YOU WISH TO RUN:

1) THE STOCK OPTION ANALYSIS PROGRAM
2) THE AUTO PRICE FETCH PROGRAM
   (REQUIRES MODEM)
3) THE VOLATILITY FILE UPDATE PROGRAM
4) EXPIRATION DATES UPDATE PROGRAM
5) COMMISSION SCHEDULE UPDATE PROGRAM
6) FIXED PARAMETER FILE UPDATE PROGRAM
7) OPTION DOWNLOAD FILE UPDATE PROGRAM
8) CONVERT FILE FORMAT
9) QUIT

ENTER A '1' THROUGH A '9': *6
            LOADING

    FIXED PARAMETERS UPDATE PROGRAM
CURRENT PARAMETERS ARE:

1) NUMBER OF DISK DRIVES      1

2) MICROMODEM SLOT #          0

3) DOW JONES LOCAL PHONE #

4) PASSWORD

5) LOG ON TYPE

6) PRINTER SLOT #             0

7) PRINTER TYPE

8) PRINTER CONTROL CHARS
   (80 COL TEXT)
   (40 COL TEXT)
   (PRINT GRAPHICS)
   (GRAPHICS OFF)

ANY CHANGES TO ABOVE? (Y/N) *




ENTER A '1' THROUGH A '9': *1
            LOADING

          STOCK OPTION
        ANALYSIS PROGRAM
        COPYRIGHT 1981
      BY RICHARD G. DONALD
          VERSION 6.7

         30 OCT 1982
         SERIAL NO:
PLEASE INSERT DISK CONTAINING YOUR DATA
FILES INTO DRIVE #1

      [PRESS ANY KEY TO CONTINUE]
INPUT IDENTIFIER FOR COMMISSION SCHEDULE
YOU WISH TO USE FOR THIS RUN --
(PRESS [RETURN] FOR 'OLD' NYSE): 2

INPUT COMMISSION SCHEDULE IS FOR
CHARLES SCHWAB & CO.
CORRECT? *
```

```
DISCOUNT ON COMMISSIONS (%, <RTN> FOR NO
DISCOUNT):

COMMISSIONS WILL BE DISCOUNTED 0%
INPUT STOCK TICKER SYMBOL: BLY

INPUT CURRENT STOCK PRICE: 21 1/2

INPUT VOLATILITIES:
   A) SPECIFY ANY VALUE     => 0.XXX
OR B) MARKET ASSIGNED VALUE => 0
OR C) HISTORICAL VOLATILITY => -1

FOR OPTION PRICE EVALUATION: 0

FOR STOCK PRICE DISTRIBUTION: .4

INPUT INTEREST RATE (%): 16

INPUT PRESENT MONTH: DEC

BUSINESS DAYS REMAINING IN DEC: 4
           OPENING TRANSACTIONS
IS THIS TRANSACTION:
   1) A CALENDAR (HORIZONTAL) SPREAD
   2) A VERTICAL SPREAD
   3) A STRADDLE
   4) WRITE COVERED CALL, OR
   5) OTHER
*1

1) PUTS, OR
2) CALLS
*CALLS

ENTER THE STRIKE PRICE: 25

NUMBER OF CONTRACTS: 10

FOR THE OPTION YOU WISH TO BUY:
ENTER THE EXPIRATION MONTH: MAY

OPTION PRICE (PER SHARE): 2 5/8

FOR THE OPTION YOU WISH TO SELL:
ENTER THE EXPIRATION MONTH: FEB

OPTION PRICE (PER SHARE): 1 3/16

---------------------------------------



         [PRESS ANY KEY TO CONTINUE]
NO       NO.   TYPE   STRK  EXP PRICE
         CONTR         PRICE MON
1  BUY   10    CALL    25    MAY 2.625
2  SELL  10    CALL    25    FEB 1.1875

OK? *
            COST ANALYSIS

NO    COST    COMMISSION    NET

1    2625.00    59.00      2684.00
2   -1187.50    39.38     -1148.12


TOTAL COST: $1535.88
```

Exhibit 12–21 (*concluded*)

```
        [PRESS ANY KEY TO CONTINUE]

    MARKET ASSIGNED VOLATILITY

NO          NO.   TYPE   STRK  DAYS PRICE
            CONTR              PRICE REM
1    BUY    10    CALL    25    102 2.625
2    SELL   10    CALL    25    39  1.1875

DIVIDEND AMOUNT: .025
 DATE PAID: 2/3/XX
CHANGE DIVIDEND AMOUNT? *

            PLEASE`WAIT

VOLATILITY FOR OPTION #1 = .623

VOLATILITY FOR OPTION #2 = .659

       VOLATILITY TO USE = .64
            INPUT SUMMARY
1) STOCK SYM & PRICE: BLY    21.5
2) VOLATILITIES- OPTION:.64, STOCK:.4
3) MONTH, DAYS, INT RATE: DEC, 4, .16
4) OPENING TRANSACTIONS
         NO   TYPE   STRK   EXP  PRICE
         CONTR              MON
BUY      10   CALL   25     MAY  2.625
SELL     10   CALL   25     FEB  1.1875

5) EXECUTE

6) QUIT

(1-4 ABOVE TO CHANGE LISTED VALUES)
ENTER ONE OF ABOVE NUMBERS: *
    PREDICTED PRICE DISTRIBUTION
-------------------------------------
```

```
    NO.   TYPE   STRK  DAYS PRED H.R.
    CONTR              PRICE REM  PRICE
BUY   10   CALL    25   102 2.71 2.02
SELL  10   CALL    25   39  1.12 2.83

WHEN WOULD YOU LIKE A PREDICTION FOR
(INPUT NUMBER OF DAYS FROM START--ENTER
0 TO RETURN TO MENU) ?37

AFTER 37 DAYS THE STANDARD DEVIATION
ON THE STOCK PRICE IS 3.29

THE PRICE RANGE FOR EVALUATION WILL BE
FROM 14.01 TO 32.97

       [PRESS ANY KEY TO CONTINUE]
            [ESC] TO QUIT
    SITUATION AFTER 37 DAYS FOR BLY
-------------------------------------

                    PREDICTED OPTION PRICE
STOCK    PROFIT     CALL    CALL
PRICE               MAY     FEB
                    25      25
-------------------------------------
14.01    -1437      0.12    0.00
15.90    -1260      0.30    0.00
17.80    -926       0.64    0.00
19.69    -415       1.16    0.00
21.59    292        1.88    0.00
23.49    1093       2.81    0.10
25.38    1472       3.91    0.80
27.28    1167       5.19    2.35
29.17    702        6.60    4.20
31.07    308        8.13    6.10
32.96    7          9.74    7.99

EXPECTED PROFIT IS: $244

RETURN ON INVESTMENT: 107.44%
```

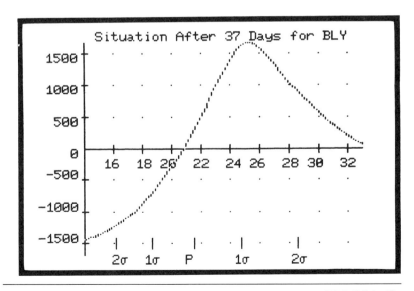

Using statistics on the stock's historic volatility SOAP computes the standard deviation of the stock price. The prices of the stock are then calculated for three standard deviations on either side of the mean. Within this range 51 different prices of the underlying stock will be examined, and the fair price of each option class and the proceeds (including commissions) from closing that transaction will be calculated. The net gain or loss from a trade will be calculated, assuming that the stock closes at that price.

Of the 51 calculated values, only every fifth one is displayed on the screen, for a total of 11 displays. SOAP will then calculate the probability of occurrence for each stock price, and multiply this probability by the expected profit (or loss) at that price. The sum of all 51 calculations is the statistically expected gain (or loss), which is then printed. If there is a gain, the annualized percentage rate of return is also calculated. Finally, the expected profit will be graphed as a function of the stock closing prices. To aid in data collection, an interface program to the Dow Jones News/Retrieval® service is provided.

APPENDIX

Bibliography

Gould, Bruce G. *The Dow Jones-Irwin Guide to Commodities Trading.* Homewood, Ill.: Dow Jones-Irwin, 1981.
"How to Play the Options Game." *Business Week,* December 22, 1980, pp 88–92.
"Is Commodity Trading for You?" *The Research Institute,* May 17, 1982, pp 1–4.
Kaufman, P. J. "Review of Systems." Lecture delivered at the Compu Trac conference, New Orleans, La., 1982.

Resource List

Product	Resource	Computer
Compu Trac	Compu Trac, Inc. P.O. Box 15951 New Orleans, LA 70175	Apple II+
Stock Option Analysis Program	H&H Scientific 13507 Pendleton Street Fort Washington, MD 20744	Apple II+
Option X	Crawford Data Systems P.O. Box 705 Somis, CA 93066	Apple II+
Options-80	Options-80 Box 471 Concord, MA 01742	Apple II+ TRS-80 Models I/III

Tracking Tangibles[1]

Tangible investments have a dual role because they not only appreciate in price but also give you the pleasure of possessing and using them as well.

A tangible asset is often called a "collectible." Many of us collect old things that have a touch of nostalgia to them, such as bottle caps, cigarette lighters, toy trains, and memorabilia. We collect these things because we enjoy doing so, not just to make money. But other items, from jewelry to gemstones, from Persian rugs to Picassos, are tangibles with obviously significant profit potentials.

Tangible items like investment-grade diamonds, rare coins, stamps, colored gemstones, and the old masters' paintings are usually considered investment objects. There are defined markets for these products and they can fit into your investment portfolio as well as stocks or real estate. In fact, many financial planners will recommend tangibles for a client's portfolio to balance the stock or bond holdings. Tangible investments, compared to other standard investments, have histories of long-term appreciation. These investments have lasting and durable qualities that go

---

[1] George Adcock, of 1147 Village Way, Stone Mountain, Ga. 30088, provided an excellent tutorial on the uniqueness of the tangibles market. His expert knowledge in this investment area provided the basis for developing the computer techniques described in the chapter.

beyond their monetary value. Although their inclusion in your portfolio may be as much emotional as logical, they are nevertheless important investments that can be considered as means for rounding out your investment strategy.

Some tangible markets are not as orderly as the stock, bond, or real estate markets. Keeping track of colored gemstone prices, for instance, has been difficult because of wide variations in judgments of their quality. Fine art is another example. The going prices at auctions are the prime indicators of market prices. If you have an old master's painting and want to know its value, you can ask an art gallery for an estimate of its value. Through no fault of the appraiser, however, that estimate may prove to be totally wrong when the painting actually goes on the auction block. A depressed art market may bring auction bids substantially lower than the estimate. You are in effect at the mercy of an unstructured and often irrational market. Diamonds, coins, and stamps, however, have more coherent price structures that are periodically clarified and updated in publications issued by industry sources.

Your personal computer can help you with the record-keeping for your tangible investments. A structured file for each tangible will aid you in keeping your prices up to date and will provide a repository for all important information. This includes place and date of purchase, as well as a detailed description of each item.

TANGIBLES AS INVESTMENTS

Many investors who follow the tangibles markets believe these have the best long-term performance of any investment media. This investment performance has been measured for long periods. The chart in Table 13–1 shows how tangibles have performed in recent years, compared to the popular stock market averages.

Of all investments, hard assets have been the most difficult to understand. Price-tracking has been extremely difficult, and trend-projecting virtually impossible. Until recently there has been no formal pricing mechanism, not to mention indices, available to the investor. This lack of data is largely due to the nature of the tangible and collectible markets themselves. The markets for most tangibles are extremely thin and disjointed. Prices can fluctuate widely between auctions and sales in different areas of the country.

The Bradex, an index of collectible plates published by the Bradford Galleries, tracks 12 of the most popular plate issues. Recently, however, most plate activity has been in new designs not covered by the Bradex. Although prices in this market have been rising, they are not reflected in the Bradex because the newly issued plates are not included. What this shows, for plates anyway, is that collectors probably have more influence

Table 13–1. Compound Annual Rates of Return*

	10 Years	Rank	5 Years	Rank	1 Year	Rank
Oil	30.8%	1	20.9%	5	14.3%	6
Gold	28.0	2	30.7	3	−13.9	14
Oriental carpets	27.3	3	20.9	6	−0.2	11
U.S. coins	27.1	4	29.7	4	−8.0	12
U.S. stamps	23.5	5	32.9	1	18.0	4
Chinese ceramics	22.9	6	30.7	2	36.5	1
Silver	21.5	7	20.1	7	−26.6	16
Rare books	16.8	8	13.8	11	18.0	5
Old masters	15.4	9	16.8	9	22.9	3
Farmland	14.6	10	14.8	10	9.7	8
Diamonds	14.5	11	16.9	8	0.0	10
Housing	10.3	12	11.6	12	8.1	9
CPI	8.3	13	9.7	14	10.0	7
Stocks	5.8	14	9.8	13	25.3	2
Foreign exchange	5.3	15	3.1	15	−17.3	15
Bonds	3.8	16	1.1	16	−9.6	13

* All returns for the period ending June 1,1981, based on latest available data.
Source: Salomon Brothers.

over this market than investors, and thus it cannot be effectively indexed. Some hard assets, such as precious stones, rare coins, and stamps, have reached a maturity, however, that results in a more coherent market. In some cases, fine art has matured in the same way. This maturity produces an internal consistency that yields verifiable results.

Several attempts to quantify and track hard assets have been made with varying degrees of success. Of the dozen or so market indices, only two have truly addressed the problems of inconsistent prices, disjointed activity, and changes in supply and demand. One of these is the Fine Art Index recently created by the Sotheby Galleries of London and published in *Barron's*. Sotheby's has effectively indexed diverse fine art objects into perhaps a dozen categories from Norman Rockwell to the old masters. These are also combined into an overall fine art index, which is weighted according to the dollar volume of business in each individual category.

Another index that appears workable is the Colored Gemstones Index published by Financial Information Systems. Colored stones are a unique problem for investors. Historical price data is of inconsistent or even questionable quality, which makes it almost impossible to forecast future price movements based on history. A problem of equal significance is the lack of a standard unit price, such as price per carat. For example, a one-carat ruby may sell for $11,000 or $1,000 depending on its quality. A five-carat ruby of comparable quality may sell for $20,000 per carat. The reason is that there aren't as many five-carat rubies as there are one-carat ones. The relative rarity dictates the price and consequently complicates the development of an effective index. Financial Information Systems has developed a moving average index, which takes into account such diverse elements as rarity, quality, and the level of market activity of the stones.

There are problems with both these indices. Sotheby's index, for instance, is subjective. It is based solely on art experts' subjective judgments and not on anything quantifiable. The FIS Colored Gemstones Index attempts to overcome the subjectivity hurdle with a computer program that generates the moving average on the basis of trading activity.

Tracking Tangibles with Data

If you have the data, forecasting hard asset price trends with your personal computer is not difficult. The tenuous tangibles markets, however, don't provide consistent prices like the stock, bond, or commodities markets. Without periodic price updates, any index is merely a gross estimate. Your challenge with tangible investments, therefore, is to update your portfolio with reasonably frequent repricing.

A few sources of data in the form of trade publications are available. Three of these publications are:

Linn's Stamp News, a monthly newspaper that publishes United States stamp prices once or twice a year. This data should be sufficient to help you build a historic database of stamp prices.

Coin Prices, one of several monthly magazines for coin prices that should provide you with good price data.

Jeweler's Circular—Keystone, the bible for the precious stone trade. This biweekly publication provides complete diamond price data, plus fairly good data on rubies, sapphires, and emeralds. Prices for semiprecious stones are also published on occasion.

Unlike in their other investments, most investors don't have access to multiple sources for hard asset prices. This presents a problem when managing these types of investments, but it doesn't detract from the value they provide to your portfolio. What you need to do is develop a system for periodically repricing your portfolio.

HOW CAN THE COMPUTER HELP?

There are two ways you can use your computer in tracking your tangibles. You can either use it to structure your tangibles records or to project price trends. Your objective should be to structure your file logically, item by item, so you can update the price information easily and accurately record data on each of the tangibles. The "database management system" approach to portfolio evaluation discussed in Chapter 10 is useful in building a tangibles file structure.

A major benefit of the structured file approach is the ability to project future price data. A price projection requires historical data to put into the mathematical formula that actually does the projection. One of the most common formulas is the "method of least squares" or linear regression.

The longer the historical trail of a tangible's price, the better the projection. If the tangible's history is several time periods in length and contains peaks and valleys, the method of least squares will average these variations (called "smoothing") and produce a straight trend line. If you have, for example, 12 to 20 periods (weeks, months, or years) of data, you can expect a reasonable projection for at least 3 to 5 subsequent periods. Conservatively, a two to three period projection should give you reasonable confidence (plus 15 percent or minus 15 percent) in the projected data. The confidence limits will drop precipitiously beyond 5 periods because there are many variables affecting the tangible market that cannot be factored with certainty, and it is, of course, better to project trends with the most confidence possible.

If you want confidence in your price projections, there are two general rules to follow. First, you should have at least 12 periods of historic price data. And second, you should not use projections that extend out for more than 25 to 30 percent of the total number of your historic periods. For example, if you have 20 months of historic data, you can feel confident in a projection that goes 5 to 6 months beyond the current date. You can measure confidence by setting limits above and below the projection. Thus, a projection with confidence limits of +15 percent or −15 percent is better than confidence limits of +25 percent or −25 percent because there is potentially a smaller divergence in the projection. Less variance means more confidence. Exhibits 13–1 and 13–2 illustrate this concept.

An alternative to a database management system in recording your tangibles or collectibles is the electronic spreadsheet. With VisiCalc, for example, you can record a few pertinent facts about a tangible and use the columns for recording periodic updates to your price data. Two other products from VisiCorp, VisiTrend and VisiPlot, allow you to plot your historical data and make projections from it. Similarly, Personal Software's graphics program also allows you to plot data from its PFS: Filing System as well as from VisiCalc files. The sample projection shown in Exhibit 13–3 was completed using Graphpower from Ferox Microsystems on a Hewlett-Packard 7470A plotter.

There are several other ways to keep your records and graph price data, but they should not be confused with the technical analysis methods used with stocks and commodities. These more complex methods are not really feasible with tangibles because usually there is either insufficient price data or their activity (volume) is too low to develop reliable statistics, particularly over short periods.

In conclusion, tangibles may complement one's investment portfolio while providing the pleasure of owning them. Although there are some unique problems in managing a tangibles portfolio your personal com-

Exhibit 13–1. Sample Confidence Limits (+25% and −25%)

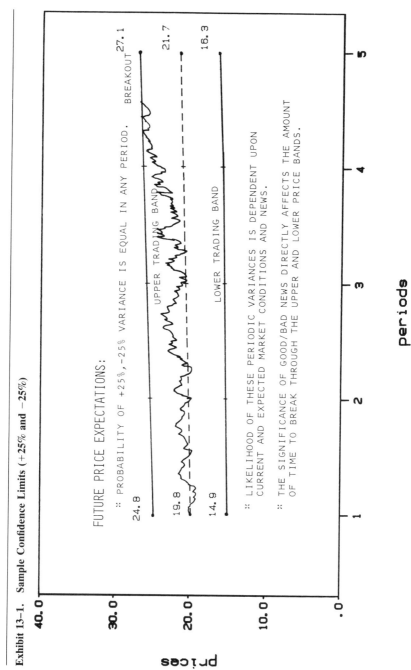

periods

Exhibit 13–2. Sample Confidence Limits (+15% and −15%)

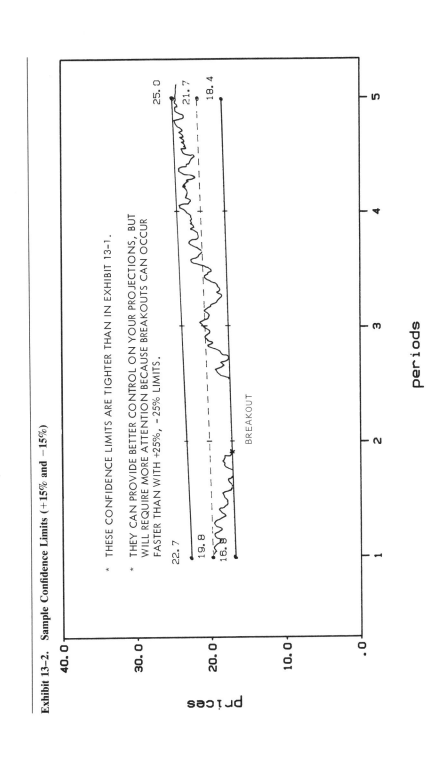

Exhibit 13–3. Tangible Price Projection (least squares method)

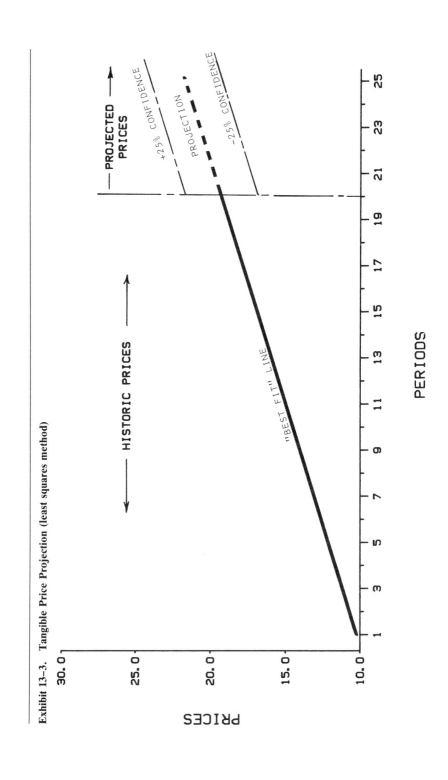

puter can still be of help, particularly for keeping records and projecting price data. Specific software for these applications is not yet available, but existing database management or computer filing systems can be easily tailored to fit your needs. Graphics programs with trending formulas are also adaptable.

Resource List

Product	*Resource*	*Computer*
Graphpower	Ferox Microsystems 1701 N. Ft. Myer Drive Suite 601 Arlington, VA 22209	Apple II+/III IBM Personal Computer
PFS: Graph	Software Publishing Corp. 1901 Landings Drive Mountain View, CA 94043	Apple II+/III
VisiTrend/Plot VisiPlot	VisiCorp 2895 Zanker Road San Jose, CA 95134	Apple II+/III
Fastgraph	Innovative Software 9300 W. 110th St. Suite 380 Overland Park, KS 66210	IBM Personal Computer
BPS Business Graphics	Business and Professional Software, Inc. 143 Binney St. Cambridge, MA 02142	IBM Personal Computer

The Investor, the Computer, and the Future

Nearly four decades have gone by since the great grandfathers of today's personal computers first appeared. The computing power of those old computers wasn't much better than today's desktop calculators. The modern personal computer can outperform many of the intermediate size mainframe computers of just 15 years ago. Not only that, but they are much cheaper, a lot more compact, and easier on the electric bill. The different investor software systems that have been discussed in some detail in this book have been designed to take full advantage of the new, awesome power of microcomputers.

THE FUTURE EFFECT OF PERSONAL COMPUTERS

As we look to future technological advances, computer-based investor software will have a significant impact not only on trading practices but on the way the market operates. Fundamental changes are coming. The reason is that never before has so much computing power been available to so many. In the future, computer-aided investment decisions will be based on logical and well-planned strategies rather than hit-or-miss hunches.

Playing the investment game in volatile markets—markets that can swing violently in the face of unpredictable developments on the far side of the world—is no child's pastime. The linkage between American and overseas markets grows stronger every day because the entire system is growing more interdependent and complex. For the investor that means more information will be needed to trade in these markets. You will need to analyze market data as never before. Tried-and-true methods may still have merit, but you will have to speed up the decision-making process. No longer can you spend days or weeks agonizing over a decision to buy a particular security and then hold it for the long term. Instead, you will have to put your decision-making process into high gear by quickly gathering and analyzing data. Once you have made your buy decision you will need to constantly scrutinize the market with an eye toward quickly selling your old positions and establishing new ones if and when the market moves.

To prepare yourself for investing in tomorrow's markets, you must get started on a computerized investment program of your own. Begin automating your financial portfolio early, and start developing a good planning system supported by the latest in computer aids. Astute money managers and investors are increasingly seeing the need to arm themselves with computer technology to stay ahead of fast-moving markets.

A big change in the markets will also occur if a so-called national market system should develop. Such a development, contemplated by the investing community and the U.S. Congress for years, would permit stocks to be bought and sold merely by pushing a few buttons on a personal computer. Certainly this system could be a major plus for the individual investor. The system could operate similar to the one used to retrieve data from an information service. Data on the current bid and asked prices of securities could be called up on your computer, and the transaction could then be made on the basis of up-to-the-second market information. It would be like bringing the New York Stock Exchange directly into your home via your computer and its electronic linkage with the national market. At this point the technology for such a market revolution already exists. The only hurdles appear to be political and financial ones. At some point in the not too distant future, however, these obstacles will probably be overcome and you and I will be able to trade freely in domestic markets.

NEW TECHNOLOGIES AND INNOVATIONS

Future prospects for computer technology in the home are already apparent. Computers now help control everything from your microwave oven to your thermostat to your automobile. The list of everyday applications of computer technology is growing at a fantastic clip.

Where does the computer belong within this electronic complex? Some believe that the computer will be at its core. Others believe that television will be the focal point, with the computer merely another module within the enclosure. In either case, your computer will undoubtedly be an integral component within the electronic heart of your home. Not only will it support your investor programs, it will control the flow of communications into and out of your home by way of telephones and cable. Information services will be available from several databases. If you use today's information services for gathering financial data, you are aware of consumer information that's available as well. As these technologies converge, the biggest problem you will have will be deciding what data services you really need.

The office of the professional investor, trader, or broker will also benefit from these changes. The professional money managers and brokers will have new sources of data and a direct link to their own advisory services. They can automate their client's records to better plan their recommendations and fine-tune them to individual client's needs. Consequently, broker's services to their clients will improve, client satisfaction will increase, and everyone will make more money.

You will benefit from these emerging technologies in two ways: by buying into the companies participating in this growth and by using the technology to your own investing advantage.

MAKING YOUR FUTURE
COMPUTER COMMITMENT

You should consider the purchase of a personal computer as an investment that will produce a financial return in the form of increased profitability and productivity. Getting started at this time will ensure that you gain the needed familiarity with investor software early on. This can help you better understand the new products as they become available. More important is the chance you will have to get your financial life under control. Your computer will put new meaning into your personal finances while helping you build your estate plan. No matter what your favorite investment may be—stocks, bonds, commodities, real estate, tangibles, or options—the personal computer will give you a different perspective on it. It puts the information you need to make profitable trading decisions at your fingertips.

The merits of personal computers are undeniably great. But as a savvy investor you may be thinking, "Prices are sure to come down significantly. Maybe I should delay my purchase and pick up a computer at a bargain price later on." I think that could be a mistake. It is a virtual certainty that we will see big improvements in the computer price/performance ratio in the next few years. For an active investor, however, today's computers at today's prices are still a buy. Yes, computers will constantly be improved in terms of capabilities as well as affordability. But the improvements in terms of investor productivity and profitability that can be realized right now from buying a computer are simply too great to be ignored or even postponed.

FUTURE DIRECTIONS

In the next several years personal computer performance will continue to be improved and new functions will be added. Competition among suppliers both in the United States and abroad will be the driving force behind these changes. Investors will benefit from smaller yet more powerful computers that will become less expensive and easier to use.

The large pools of software currently available for today's computers represent major investments mostly for the independent software providers. Much of this software has been written for the 8-bit processors that currently dominate the market (8 bits is the amount of data processed at one time by the computer). The software suppliers will influence the hardware manufacturers such that new computers must still be able to run the 8-bit software. Perceived or real incompatibilities would seriously jeopardize the sale of newer computer models, such as the 16- or 32-bit microprocessor-based personal computers. The newest computers will, therefore, need either an "emulator" program to allow the new microprocessors to run the older 8-bit software, or both an 8- and 16-bit microprocessor within the same computer enclosure. At least two computer suppliers have offered the latter, while the former has been a frequent solution to the problem of incompatibility between the two technologies.

Investment software also will continue to undergo changes and improvements. Current offerings described in this book will be constantly updated and become available for a broader range of computer types. Today's offerings are mostly available for Apple computers. Other manufacturers' computers, particularly as they increase their share in the personal computer market, will be candidates for investor programs. The program suppliers—in an effort to broaden their customer base—will convert their investor programs for use on these computers. You gain by having not only better programs due to increased function but also with a broader choice of computers on which to use the newer software.

Investor software will go through several stages in the next few years. Stage 1 has already occurred. It was characterized by the development of the early checkbook balancing programs and the growing awareness that microcomputers could be an aid to investors. The current period of development, Stage 2, is characterized by a plethora of new and improved personal finance programs as well as new versions of portfolio analysis and management packages coming on the market. Tax planning and preparation, real property management, estate planning, and commodities trading are examples of other programs offered for the first time in this period.

Stage 3 will see integrated investor software become a reality. Already several portfolio management and technical analysis programs are combined with communications to an information utility. Further examples of program integration would be insurance, pension and estate planning or portfolio management, fundamental and technical analysis, and tax planning. The biggest advantage would be the use of a common database of information. Passing common data between programs would allow for faster and more coherent selection of an optimum investment strategy.

Some of the best opportunities are yet to come for investors who take the plunge by purchasing a computer. And since the markets are not about to become any easier to predict, you need every advantage you can get.

As an investor you are at an exciting point in history. You have the opportunity to significantly improve your method of investing by applying an expanding computer technology to it. The computer's potential for improving investor profits is just beginning to be recognized. As you gain experience with today's computers and investing software, future computer tools will be even more useful.

Index